KALLIS' iBT TOEFL® PATTERN

Listening 2

TOEFL® is a registered trademark of Educational Testing Services (ETS), Princeton, New Jersey, USA. The content in this text, including the practice questions, Hacking Strategy, and Quick Look, is created and designed exclusively by KALLIS. This publication is not endorsed or approved by ETS.

KALLIS' iBT TOEFL® Pattern Listening 2

KALLIS EDU, INC.
7490 Opportunity Road, Suite 203
San Diego, CA 92111
(858) 277-8600
info@kallisedu.com
www.kallisedu.com

Copyright © 2015 KALLIS EDU, INC.

All rights reserved. No part of this book may be reproduced, stored in a retrieval system, or transmitted in any form or by any means, electronic or mechanical, including photocopying, recording, or otherwise, without the prior written permission of the copyright owner.

ISBN-10: 1-5078-4276-7
ISBN-13: 978-1-5078-4276-8

iBT TOEFL® Pattern - Listening II is the second of our three-level iBT TOEFL® Listening Exam preparation book series.

Our **iBT TOEFL® Pattern Listening** series simplifies each TOEFL Listening question type into a series of simple steps, which ensures that students do not become overwhelmed as they develop their listening skills. Moreover, our commitment to minimizing instruction and maximizing student practice assures that students have many opportunities to strengthen their listening skills.

KALLIS

KALLIS'

TOEFL® iBT
PATTERN
LISTENING
CAPTURE **2**

Getting Started

A study guide should familiarize the reader with the material found on the test, develop methods that can be used to solve various question types, and provide plenty of practice questions. *KALLIS' iBT TOEFL® Pattern Series* aims to accomplish all these tasks by presenting iBT TOEFL® test material in an organized, comprehensive, and easy-to-understand way.

KALLIS' iBT TOEFL® Pattern Listening Series shows students how to identify and solve each question type found on the iBT TOEFL Listening section. Thus, students can identify which types of questions they find most challenging, and then develop strategies for solving them. Additionally, each book in our Pattern Listening Series contains hundreds of practice questions, ensuring that students can develop the skills they need to succeed on the iBT TOEFL.

Putting the Questions into Context

Chapters 1 and 2

- ▶ These chapters provide general information about what you will listen to during the iBT TOEFL Listening section.
- ▶ These chapters explain and provide focused practice for each type of multiple-choice question found on the iBT TOEFL Listening section.
- ▶ Each listening passage in these chapters includes **Key Terms, Vocabulary,** and **Notes** sections to help you organize your thoughts as you listen.
- ▶ These chapters conclude with **Exercises** that allow you to practice the skills in a longer format.

Enhancing Test-Taking Skills through Practice

Chapters 3 and 4

- Located in Chapter 3, **Actual Practices** provide listening passages (conversations and lectures) with multiple question types. In order to complete these, you must combine skills that you developed in Chapters 1 and 2.
- Located in Chapter 4, the **Actual Test** is meant to familiarize you with the format of the official iBT TOEFL Listening test. Thus, you should be familiar with all question types before attempting to complete the **Actual Test**.
- A scaled scoring chart is located at the beginning of the **Actual Test**, so you can grade yourself and get an idea of how you might score on the official iBT TOEFL Listening section.

Checking Your Own Progress

Chapters 5 and 6

- The **Appendix** in Chapter 5 contains transcripts of all the conversations and lectures found throughout this book.
- The **Answer Key** in Chapter 6 contains the correct answers to all multiple-choice questions found throughout this book. It also includes answer explanations and example notes that can help guide your studies.
- If you do not want to repeatedly flip to the back of the book for answers, simply cut out the **Simple Answers** at the very back of the book. **Simple Answers** provides a quick reference so you can confirm that all your answers are correct.

Table of Contents

Chapter 1

Campus-Related Conversations — 1
Type 1: Main Idea — 4
    Main Idea Questions — 6
Type 2: Detail — 10
    Detail Questions — 12
Type 3: Purpose — 16
    Purpose Questions — 18
Type 4: Inference — 22
    Inference Questions — 24

Exercise 1 — 28
Exercise 2 — 30
Exercise 3 — 32
Exercise 4 — 34
Exercise 5 — 36
Exercise 6 — 38

Chapter 2

Academic Lectures — 41
Type 1: Main Idea — 44
    Main Idea Questions — 46
Type 2: Detail — 50
    Detail Questions — 52
Type 3: Purpose — 56
    Purpose Questions — 58
Type 4: Inference — 62
    Inference Questions — 64

Exercise 1 — 68
Exercise 2 — 70
Exercise 3 — 72
Exercise 4 — 74
Exercise 5 — 76
Exercise 6 — 78

LISTENING 2 CAPTURE

Chapter 3

Actual Practices 81
Actual Practice 1 — 82
Actual Practice 2 — 88
Actual Practice 3 — 94
Actual Practice 4 — 100
Actual Practice 5 — 106
Actual Practice 6 — 112
Actual Practice 7 — 118
Actual Practice 8 — 124
Actual Practice 9 — 132
Actual Practice 10 — 138

Chapter 4

Actual Test 143
Listening Passage 1 — 144
Listening Passage 2 — 146
Listening Passage 3 — 148
Listening Passage 4 — 150
Listening Passage 5 — 152
Listening Passage 6 — 154

Appendix

Listening Scripts 157
Chapter 1 — 158
Chapter 2 — 168
Chapter 3 — 179
Chapter 4 — 200

Appendix

Answer Key 207
Chapter 1 — 208
Chapter 2 — 213
Chapter 3 — 219
Chapter 4 — 234

Appendix

Simple Answers 239

Before You Begin...

OVERVIEW

The iBT TOEFL Listening section consists of four to six academic lectures and two to three campus-related conversations. At the end of each lecture, you must answer six multiple-choice questions, and at the end of each conversation, you must answer five multiple-choice questions. The Listening section takes 60 to 90 minutes to complete. Each lecture and conversation is 3 to 6 minutes long.

 Because this is the intermediate-level book in the series, the conversations and lectures in this book are shorter and use simpler language than those you will encounter on the iBT TOEFL.

LISTENING CONTENT

The lecture portions of the Listening section will consist of a professor discussing a topic that you might hear in an introductory-level university course. Because these Listening-section lectures replicate lectures that you might hear at an American university, you should expect the professor to pause, stammer, digress, and repeat himself or herself.

The conversation portions of the Listening section will consist of a dialogue between a student and a professor or some other university employee. If students are speaking to a professor, they will discuss something related to the professor's class, such as a student's project, the contents of a recent lecture, or classroom rules. If students are talking to any other university employee, they will discuss something related to campus life, such as class registration, housing concerns, or financial aid. The speakers in the conversations will use normal speech patterns, including pauses, stammers, and repetition.

LISTENING SECTION QUESTIONS

Once you have finished listening to a lecture/conversation, you will be asked to answer several multiple-choice questions. Some questions will ask you to select one correct answer, some will ask you to select more than one correct answer, and others will ask you to fill out a small table or chart. Each question will fall under one of four broad categories: Main Idea Question, Detail Questions, Purpose Questions, or Inference Questions.

TAKING NOTES

Because you will only hear each lecture and conversation once, taking notes is important. But knowing what to include in your notes can be difficult: trying to write down everything you hear will reduce your comprehension of the lecture or conversation, yet taking few notes might make answering the multiple choice questions difficult or impossible.

Therefore, write down information from the lecture or conversation if it addresses one of the following three questions:

    1) What is the lecture mainly about?
    2) Why is the speaker discussing this topic?
    3) How is the speaker structuring the information?

Addressing question (1) in you notes will help you identify the lecture or conversation's main idea and details; addressing question (2) will help you identify the purpose of the lecture or conversation; and addressing question (3) will help you understand the passage fully.

SYMBOLS AND ABBREVIATIONS

When taking notes, save time by using **symbols** instead of words. In addition to using the symbols in the chart that follows, you can create your own symbols.

Symbol	Meaning	Symbol	Meaning
&	and	=	equals, is
%	percent	>	more than
#	number	<	less than
@	at	→	resulting in
↓	decreasing	↑	increasing

ABBREVIATIONS FOR UNIVERSITY ACTIVITIES

Abbreviation	Meaning	Abbreviation	Meaning
edu.	education	RA	resident assistant
GE	general education	stu.	student
GPA	grade point average	TA	teaching assistant
prof.	professor/professional	univ.	university

ABBREVIATIONS FOR ACADEMIC TOPICS

Abbreviation	Meaning	Abbreviation	Meaning
bio.	biology/biological	exp.	experience/experiment
c.	century	info.	information
chem.	chemistry/chemical	gov.	government
def.	definition	hyp.	hypothesis
dic.	dictionary	psych.	psychology
econ.	economics/economy	theo.	theory
env.	environment	vocab.	vocabulary

OTHER ABBREVIATIONS

Abbreviation	Meaning	Abbreviation	Meaning
abt.	about	min.	minute
b/c	because	pic.	picture
comm.	community/communication	ppl.	people
ex.	example	pref.	preference
fam.	family	pt.	point
fav.	favorite	ques.	question
gen.	general/generation	s/b	somebody
H2O	water	s/o	someone
hr.	hour	sec.	second
impt.	important	w/i	within
loc.	location	w/o	without
lvl.	level	yr.	year

CHAPTER 1

Campus-Related Conversations

Chapter 1

Campus-Related Conversations

EXPLANATION OF TASK

Each iBT TOEFL Listening section will include two or three campus-related conversations. The speakers in these conversations will discuss issues that you may encounter as a student at an American university. The conversations are generally between a university student and a university employee. Some common conversation topics include:

- students asking their professors about project or research-paper requirements
- students asking their professors for clarification regarding confusing class materials
- students asking university employees for advice on academic, financial, or housing matters
- students discussing a campus issue or a class assignment with each other

Each conversation is 3 to 5 minutes long. Because these conversations are supposed to replicate natural-sounding speech in an American university setting, the speakers may use English speech patterns such as repetition, digression from the main topic, false starts, pauses, and fillers (um, uh, eh, well). You will hear each conversation only once, so you are encouraged to take notes as you listen.

After you have listened to the conversation, you must answer five multiple-choice questions that relate to the contents of the conversation. These questions will be related to the main idea, purpose, organization, or implications of the conversation. You may use any notes that you have written down when answering the multiple-choice questions.

 Because this is the intermediate-level book in the series, the conversations in this book are shorter and use simpler language than those you will encounter on the iBT TOEFL.

NECESSARY SKILLS

In order to successfully complete the conversation portions of the Listening section, you must be able to:

- comprehend vocabulary regarding a variety of campus-related issues
- take notes on conversational English
- summarize spoken information
- recognize the main idea and details of a spoken conversation
- determine the purpose of a spoken conversation
- make inferences about the organization and content of a spoken conversation
- make inferences about the tones and attitudes of the speakers

Question Types

The iBT TOEFL Listening section consists of four main types of questions.

1 Main Idea Questions

Main Idea Questions require you to identify the main topic of the conversation. Because the answers to these questions are drawn directly from the conversation content, taking notes may prove helpful when answering these questions.

2 Detail Questions

Detail Questions require you to identify a detail, an example, or an explanation related to the main idea of the conversation. Because the answers to these questions are drawn directly from the conversation content, taking notes may prove helpful when answering these questions.

3 Purpose Questions

Purpose Questions require you to identify *why* a speaker makes a particular statement or asks a particular question Therefore, when listening to the conversation, concentrate on fully comprehending the purpose of the conversation.

4 Inference Questions

Inference Questions require you to make an *inference*, or assumption, based on the contents of the conversation. An inference question might ask you to identify the speaker's tone or the conversation's basic structure.

Conversation Question Type 1: Main Idea

WHAT IS A MAIN IDEA QUESTION?

The *main idea*, or topic, is the overall subject of the conversation. Be careful when answering a **Main Idea Question**: the speakers will not always directly state their main ideas. Therefore, you may have to infer the main idea based on the context of the conversation. Some conversations will not contain any **Main Idea Questions** while others will ask one **Main Idea Question**. If it appears, the **Main Idea Question** will be the first question you are asked.

HOW TO TAKE NOTES

When taking notes on a campus-related conversation, the main idea will likely be one of the first things that you write down. As you listen to the conversation, ask yourself, "**WHAT** is the conversation about?" Asking this question will make identifying and answering the **Main Idea Question** easier.

MAIN IDEA QUESTION FORMATS

Main Idea Questions usually ask you to identify the main idea, issue, or topic presented in the conversation. Common formats for **Main Idea Questions** include:

> *What is the conversation mainly about?*
> *Why does the student visit the professor/advisor/university employee?*
> *What is the main issue being discussed in the conversation?*

> **Note** **Main Idea Questions** that begin with "why" are very similar in structure to **Purpose Questions** (page 16). But **Main Idea Questions** that begin with "why" ask for the main purpose of the conversation, while **Purpose Questions** ask *why* the speaker discusses certain details and examples.

TIPS

Listening Tips: When listening for **Main Idea Questions**, focus on information presented at the beginning of the conversation. This part of the conversation sometimes contains important words, phrases, and sentences that indicate the main idea.

Answer Tips: In questions about the topic, main idea, or main purpose, the correct answer will deal with the overall subject of the conversation. Incorrect answer choices will be:

- broader than the focus of the conversation
- details of the conversation, not the main idea
- inaccurate or untrue according to the speaker
- about a subject not mentioned in the conversation

Main Idea Questions

Listen to **Track 1.01**. Take notes using the template below as you listen to the conversation.

Key Terms
- analysis
- movie reviews
- film critic

Vocabulary
cinematography (n): the techniques and processes involved in filming and developing a movie

Things to Consider

WHAT is the conversation about?

Notes

stu. confused about assignment (analyze fav. movie)

prof. talks about assignment

tells stu. to pretend she's film critic

Answer the following multiple-choice question.

1) Why does the student visit the professor?
   (A) To ask the professor for more time on an assignment
   (B) To ask the professor how to become a film critic
   (C) To ask the professor to clarify an assignment
   (D) To ask the professor about his favorite movie

Answer Explanation

The student states that she is "confused about the assignment" given by the professor. Because the professor spends the rest of the conversation describing the assignment, one can conclude that the main purpose of the conversation is **Choice C**.

Main Idea Questions

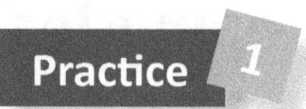
Practice 1

Listen to **Track 1.02**. Take notes using the template below as you listen to the conversation.

Key Terms
- student email
- university website
- "Student Center"

Vocabulary
dumb (adj): describing someone who lacks intelligence/is foolish

Things to Consider

WHAT is the conversation about?

Notes
_____
_____
_____

Answer the following multiple-choice question.

1) Why does the student visit the university employee?
   (A) To ask for the domain name of the university's website
   (B) To learn how to create a student email account
   (C) To see if the university employee can fix her broken computer
   (D) To sign up for a computer programming class

Main Idea Questions

Listen to **Track 1.03**. Take notes using the template below as you listen to the conversation.

Key Terms

nervous
speak up

Vocabulary

insightful (adj): demonstrating a deep understanding of something
articulate (adj): demonstrating the ability to speak clearly and persuasively

Things to Consider

WHAT is the conversation about?

Notes

_____
_____
_____

Answer the following multiple-choice question.

2) Why does the professor ask to speak with the student?

   (A) To congratulate her for writing an excellent paper
   (B) To make sure that she understands the class material
   (C) To encourage her to participate in class discussions more often
   (D) To tell her that she must attend class more often

Main Idea Questions

Listen to **Track 1.04**. Take notes using the template below as you listen to the conversation.

Key Terms
- group project
- library's basement level

Vocabulary
- heads up (idiom): advance notice of a particular problem; a warning

Things to Consider

WHAT is the conversation about?

Notes
_____
_____
_____

Answer the following multiple-choice question.

3) Why does the man talk with the woman?
   (A) To help her complete a project for her business class
   (B) To ask about good locations to work on a group project
   (C) To ask for directions to the basement level of the library
   (D) To ask her to tutor him in one of his classes

Main Idea Questions

Listen to **Track 1.05**. Take notes using the template below as you listen to the conversation.

Key Terms
- introductory classes
- professor interaction
- upper-division classes
- large classes

Vocabulary
- whiny (adj): describing someone who frequently complains
- impersonal (adj): not showing strong emotions; detached

Things to Consider

WHAT is the conversation about?

Notes
_____
_____
_____

Answer the following multiple-choice question.

4) Why does the student visit the advisor?
   (A) To explain that one of her professors is intentionally giving her bad grades
   (B) To complain that she cannot hear her professors speak in the university's large lecture halls
   (C) To claim that she is having trouble making friends with other students
   (D) To remark that class sizes are too large and that her professors are rarely available

Conversation Question Type 2: Detail

WHAT IS A DETAIL QUESTION?

Details are specific pieces of information that relate to a larger topic. These pieces of information can be facts, descriptions, reasons, examples, or opinions. **Detail Questions** will ask you to recall specific information from the conversation. There will be one to three **Detail Questions** in each campus-related conversation.

HOW TO TAKE NOTES

When taking notes on a campus-related conversation, you will notice that the details are distributed throughout the conversation. Focus on writing down only details that relate to the main idea of the conversation. **Before taking notes, try to identify the main topic of the conversation.**

As you listen to the conversation, ask yourself, "**WHAT** details contribute to the main idea?" Answering this question will make identifying and answering the **Detail Questions** easier.

DETAIL QUESTION FORMATS

Detail Questions will ask you to identify specific details, explanations, examples, or opinions that relate to the main topic of the conversation. Common formats for **Detail Questions** include:

> *What does the speaker say about _____ in the conversation?*
> *According to the speaker, what/why/where/when/how _____?*
> *What is the speaker's opinion of _____?*

Whereas **Main Idea Questions** always appear as multiple-choice questions with one correct answer, **Detail Questions** have one, two, or three correct answers.

TIPS

Listening Tips: When listening, notice information that contributes to the main idea of the conversation. This may include numbers, dates, names, definitions, reasons, connections, choices, and processes.

Answer Tips: In questions about details, the correct answer will always restate facts, descriptions, reasons, examples, or opinions from the lecture. When you answer **Detail Questions**, try to recall exactly what was said by the speaker. Look at your notes if you cannot remember exactly what was said. Incorrect answer choices may:

- repeat some of the speaker's words but convey a different meaning
- use words that sound like, but are actually different from, the speaker's words
- be inaccurate or irrelevant based on what you hear in the conversation

Detail Questions

Listen to **Track 1.06**. Take notes using the template below as you listen to the conversation.

Key Terms

meal points

Vocabulary

worth (adj): equal in value to

Things to Consider

WHAT is the conversation about?

WHAT details contribute to the main idea?

Notes

stu. wants to know about meal points

gets 15,000 for semester, use @ dining hall, store, café

1 meal point = 10 cents. 80 meal points = dining hall access

Answer the following multiple-choice questions.

How many meal points does the student have for one semester?
(A) 10 meal points
(B) 80 meal points
(C) 1,500 meal points
(D) 15,000 meal points

At which of the following locations can the student use his meal points?

Choose 2 answers.

(A) The on-campus vending machines
(B) The on-campus grocery store
(C) The on-campus cafes
(D) The on-campus food trucks

Answer Explanation

Early in the conversation, the student states that he has "15,000 meal points for the semester," so the correct answer is **Choice D**.

Answer Explanation

The university employee explains that meal points can be used at the "two main dining halls, one on-campus grocery store, and two on-campus cafes." Thus, the correct answers must be **Choice B** and **Choice C**.

Detail Questions

Listen to **Track 1.07**. Take notes using the template below as you listen to the conversation.

Key Terms
Hildegard of Bingen
Know the Ways of the Lord
Scivias

Vocabulary
monastic (adj): having to do with the lives or residences of religious figures such as nuns and monks

Things to Consider

WHAT is the conversation about?

WHAT details contribute to the main idea?

Notes
_____
_____
_____

Answer the following multiple-choice questions.

1) What is the name of the professor who teaches the class on monastic life in Medieval Europe?
   (A) Jodie Davis
   (B) Jodie Scivias
   (C) Jodie Dayton
   (D) Davis Dayton

2) Why was the student unable to find the book she was looking for?
   (A) The title is written in a language other than English.
   (B) The library does not have the book she is looking for.
   (C) She does not know the name of the book's author.
   (D) She was looking in the wrong section of the library.

Detail Questions

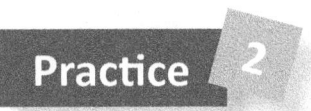

Listen to **Track 1.08**. Take notes using the template below as you listen to the conversation.

Key Terms
- on-campus garden
- landscaping
- volunteer

Vocabulary
- an extra hand (idiom): additional assistance
- look forward to (phrasal verb): wait for eagerly, expect

Things to Consider

WHAT is the conversation about?

WHAT details contribute to the main idea?

Notes

_____
_____
_____

Answer the following multiple-choice questions.

3) Why does the man want to volunteer to work in the on-campus garden?
   (A) He wants to become a professional landscaper after graduating.
   (B) He wants to earn extra credit for a plant biology class.
   (C) He wants to take fruits and vegetables from the garden.
   (D) He enjoyed working on similar projects in the past.

4) Based on the conversation, when do the garden volunteers meet?
   (A) Saturday mornings
   (B) Saturday afternoons
   (C) Sunday mornings
   (D) Sunday afternoons

Detail Questions

Practice 3

Listen to **Track 1.09**. Take notes using the template below as you listen to the conversation.

Key Terms
"Vocal Chords"
a cappella
tryouts

Vocabulary
a cappella (n): a type of choral music that is performed without any instrumental accompaniment
laid back (idiom): relaxed, calm

Things to Consider

WHAT is the conversation about?

WHAT details contribute to the main idea?

Notes
_____
_____
_____

Answer the following multiple-choice questions.

3) Where did the man see the woman perform with "Vocal Chords"?
   (A) In the campus plaza
   (B) In the campus bookstore
   (C) In the auditorium
   (D) In the dining hall

4) According to the woman, when will "Vocal Chords" hold their tryouts?
   (A) Tomorrow
   (B) In one week
   (C) In two weeks
   (D) Next month

Detail Questions

Listen to **Track 1.10**. Take notes using the template below as you listen to the conversation.

Key Terms
study room
reservation
university library website

Vocabulary
first-come, first-served (idiom): a system in which customers are served or helped in the order that they arrived

Things to Consider

WHAT is the conversation about?

WHAT details contribute to the main idea?

Notes
_____
_____
_____

Answer the following multiple-choice questions.

7) According to the conversation, why was the student asked to leave the study room?
(A) She was being too noisy.
(B) The library was closing for the night.
(C) She had not reserved it.
(D) The time slot she reserved had passed.

8) Why does the student like using the study rooms?
(A) They are quiet and tidy places to study.
(B) They can be used for many hours at a time.
(C) They have excellent Internet access.
(D) They are ideal places to study with a group.

CAMPUS-RELATED CONVERSATIONS ♦ CHAPTER 1

Conversation Question Type 3: Purpose

WHAT IS A PURPOSE QUESTION?

The "purpose" of a statement is the speaker's intention; you must infer purpose based on what the speaker says. In some **Purpose Questions**, you will listen to part of the conversation again before answering. There are usually one or two **Purpose Questions** that accompany each campus-related conversation.

HOW TO TAKE NOTES

The speakers usually state their purpose early in the conversation and continue to imply it through what they say and ask. **When taking notes on the purpose of the conversation, try to quickly identify the main idea.**

As you listen to the conversation, ask yourself, "WHY are the speakers having the conversation?" Doing so will make identifying and answering **Purpose Questions** easier.

PURPOSE QUESTION FORMATS

Purpose Questions will usually ask you why a speaker made certain claims. Common formats for **Purpose Questions** include:

Why does the student/professor mention _____?
Why does the student/professor say this?

 For information on questions that ask about the main purpose of a conversation, see page 4.

TIPS

Listening Tips: When listening for the purpose of a statement or a claim, you must rely on your ability to draw logical conclusions as to *why* the conversation is taking place or *why* a statement is being made. Your notes may help you piece together information.

Answer Tips: The correct answers to **Purpose Questions** may be implied. Thus, these questions are slightly more difficult to answer than **Main Idea** or **Detail Questions**. When answering **Purpose Questions**, look at your notes if you cannot remember exactly what the speakers said. Incorrect answer choices may:

- repeat some of the speaker's words but convey a different meaning
- be inaccurate based on what you hear in the conversation
- be irrelevant and not about anything mentioned in the conversation

Purpose Questions

Listen to **Track 1.11**. Take notes using the template below as you listen to the conversation.

Key Terms

off-campus housing
housemate

Vocabulary

silverware (n): cutlery, such as forks, knives, and spoons, made of silver or stainless steel

Things to Consider

WHY are the speakers having the conversation?

Notes

MS moving off-campus, needs moving advice

MS moving in with 2 others   FS tells him to have ea. housemate list what they can bring

Answer the following multiple-choice questions.

Why does the man ask the woman if she lives off campus?
(A) To criticize her choice of housing
(B) To make polite conversation with a stranger
(C) To ask for directions to her house
(D) To find out if she can give him advice

Listen to **Track 1.12**.
Why does the woman say this?
(A) To share a story that illustrates why the man should listen to her advice
(B) To point out one reason that living off campus is worse than living on campus
(C) To prove that living alone is preferable to having roommates
(D) To explain why kitchen appliances are the most important feature of a house

Answer Explanation

After the man confirms that the woman lives off campus, he asks for her moving advice. Thus, the correct answer must be **Choice D**.

Answer Explanation

The woman's story illustrates the importance of making a list of what each housemate can bring. Because making a list is what she advised the man to do, the correct answer must be **Choice A**.

Purpose Questions

Listen to **Track 1.13**. Take notes using the template below as you listen to the conversation.

Key Terms
- intramural sports team
- volleyball
- roommates

Vocabulary
- intramural (adj): taking place within a single school or university
- awesome (adj): very good, excellent

Things to Consider

WHY are the speakers having the conversation?

Notes
_____
_____
_____

Answer the following multiple-choice questions.

1) Listen to **Track 1.14**.
   Why does the man say this?
   (A) To reveal that there are no winners in intramural sports
   (B) To argue that intramural sports are not competitive enough
   (C) To explain what makes intramural sports so popular
   (D) To convince the woman to join his intramural sports team

2) Listen to **Track 1.15**.
   Why does the woman say this?
   (A) To point out some differences between volleyball and other sports
   (B) To explain why she will join an intramural sports team
   (C) To illustrate some of the benefits of daily exercise
   (D) To argue that volleyball is the best form of exercise

Purpose Questions

Practice 2

Listen to **Track 1.16**. Take notes using the template below as you listen to the conversation.

Key Terms
- test and quiz scores
- class attendance

Vocabulary
- attendance (n): the act of regularly going to a certain event or location

Things to Consider

WHY are the speakers having the conversation?

Notes
_____
_____
_____

Answer the following multiple-choice questions.

3) Listen to **Track 1.17**.
   Why does the professor say this?
   (A) To criticize the student's apparent lack of motivation
   (B) To point out the reason for the student's low test scores
   (C) To explain the university's policies on class attendance
   (D) To argue that class attendance is more important than studying

4) Why does the professor probably include information only presented in class on her tests?
   (A) To increase the lengths of her tests
   (B) To encourage students to study in groups
   (C) To encourage students to attend class
   (D) To prevent students from cheating

Purpose Questions

Listen to **Track 1.18**. Take notes using the template below as you listen to the conversation.

Key Terms
economics tutor
general education requirements

Vocabulary
pick up (phrasal verb): acquire by study or experience; learn

Things to Consider

WHY are the speakers having the conversation?

Notes
_____
_____
_____

Answer the following multiple-choice questions.

1) Listen to **Track 1.19**.
   Why does the tutor probably say this?
   (A) To show that he is smarter than the student
   (B) To explain what he does in his free time
   (C) To explain why graduate school is so difficult
   (D) To show that he is a qualified economics tutor

2) Listen to **Track 1.20**.
   Why does the student say this?
   (A) To explain why she wants to study anthropology
   (B) To explain why she does not like economics
   (C) To point out major differences between anthropology and economics
   (D) To point out the benefits of studying multiple subjects

Purpose Questions

Listen to **Track 1.21**. Take notes using the template below as you listen to the conversation.

Key Terms

open-book test
limited time

Vocabulary

comprehend (v): understand
show up (phrasal verb): appear

Things to Consider

WHY are the speakers having the conversation?

Notes

_____
_____
_____

Answer the following multiple-choice questions.

1) Listen to **Track 1.22**.
   Why does the student say this?
   (A) To complain to the professor that the test seems too difficult
   (B) To tell the professor about her normal studying habits
   (C) To explain why she's asking the professor for advice
   (D) To request that the professor postpone the test

2) Listen to **Track 1.23**.
   Why does the student say this?
   (A) To criticize the professor for making his tests too easy
   (B) To question the purpose of preparing for open-book tests
   (C) To explain why she prefers open-book tests to regular tests
   (D) To compare the professor's tests to other tests that she has taken

Conversation Question Type 4: Inference

WHAT IS AN INFERENCE QUESTION?

Inference Questions may ask you to make an inference based on the information in the conversation, make a prediction about what a speaker will do after the conversation, or identify the speaker's attitude. Below are the three categories of inference questions that you might see on the conversation portion of the Listening test.

INFERENCE QUESTION FORMATS

Category 1 – Inference: An *inference* is a conclusion that is based on the facts of the conversation but not directly stated. In order to make an inference, you must pay attention to what the speaker suggests during a conversation. Common formats for **Inference Questions** include:

What does the speaker imply/suggest about _____ in the conversation?
What does the speaker mean when he/she says this?

Category 2 – Prediction: Prediction Questions ask you to identify what a speaker will do based on the information presented in the conversation. Thus, you must be able to infer a speaker's future actions based on what he or she says. Common formats for **Prediction Questions** include:

What will the student probably do after talking to the professor/advisor?

Category 3 – Attitude: The speaker's attitude is his or her feelings about the information For example, a speaker may express approval, disapproval, indifference, excitement, confusion, or surprise toward what is being discussed. Many times the speaker communicates an attitude indirectly. Common formats for **Attitude Questions** include:

What is the speaker's opinion of _____?
Which of the following best describes the speaker's attitude toward _____?

TIPS

Listening Tips: When listening for information that will help you make inferences and predictions, rely on your ability to find meanings that are "under" or "beneath" the speaker's words. Good notes may help you review what the speaker says.

Answer Tips: In questions about inferences, predictions, and attitudes, the correct answer will usually be stated indirectly. As such, these questions are much more difficult to answer than **Main Idea Questions**, **Detail Questions**, or **Purpose Questions**. When you encounter an **Inference**, a **Prediction**, or an **Attitude Question**, look at your notes if you cannot remember exactly what was said. Incorrect answer choices may:

- repeat the speaker's words with a different message
- be inaccurate based on what you hear in the conversation
- be irrelevant and not about anything mentioned in the conversation

Inference Questions

Listen to **Track 1.24**. Take notes using the template below as you listen to the conversation.

Key Terms
Victory Theater
northbound shuttle
theater department
Adams Avenue

Vocabulary
perpendicular (adj): situated at a 90 degree angle to a line, a plane, or a surface

Things to Consider

HOW do the speakers organize and present the conversation?
(Identify the speakers' attitudes and the implications of the conversation.)

Notes

FS asking for directions to Victory Theater (unfamiliar w/ campus → freshman)

MS gives her directions (shuttle → Adams Ave. → theater)   FS has to be there in 10 minutes

Answer the following multiple-choice questions.

1) Based on the conversation, what can be inferred about the woman?
   (A) She has never visited the university before.
   (B) She is good friends with the man.
   (C) She is a new student at the university.
   (D) She is a theater arts major.

2) What will the woman probably do next?
   (A) Board a northbound shuttle
   (B) Walk with the man
   (C) Skip her friend's performance
   (D) Walk to Victory Theater

Answer Explanation
The woman tells the man that she is "still learning her way around campus," so we can infer that she has not been attending the university for long. Based on this information, we can infer that the correct answer is **Choice C**.

Answer Explanation
The man tells the woman "to leave now," recommending that she take the "northbound shuttle [that is] coming right now." Thus, we can infer that the correct answer is **Choice A**.

Inference Questions

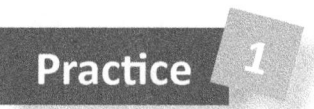

Listen to **Track 1.25**. Take notes using the template below as you listen to the conversation.

Key Terms
class attendance
tardiness

Vocabulary
diligent (adj): hardworking

Things to Consider

HOW do the speakers organize and present the conversation?
(Identify the speakers' attitudes and the implications of the conversation.)

Notes
_____
_____
_____

Answer the following multiple-choice questions.

1) For what reasons does the professor probably excuse the student's tardiness?
   Choose 2 answers.
   (A) The student needs to pass the professor's class in order to graduate.
   (B) The student will stay after class to make up for his tardiness.
   (C) The student has a reasonable excuse for his tardiness.
   (D) The student has proven to be intelligent and hardworking.

2) What best describes the professor's attitude toward the student's tardiness?
   (A) Furious
   (B) Concerned
   (C) Amused
   (D) Apathetic

Inference Questions

Listen to **Track 1.26**. Take notes using the template below as you listen to the conversation.

Key Terms
extension
research paper

Vocabulary
overwhelmed (adj): to have or be given too much of something

bite off more than you can chew (idiom): take on more responsibilities than you can manage.

Things to Consider

HOW do the speakers organize and present the conversation?
(Identify the speakers' attitudes and the implications of the conversation.)

Notes
_____
_____
_____

Answer the following multiple-choice questions.

3) Listen to **Track 1.27**.
   What does the professor mean when she says this?
   (A) The student should take more nutrition classes.
   (B) The student has signed up for too many classes.
   (C) The student should not eat during the professor's class.
   (D) The student needs to spend less time at the dining hall.

4) Based on the conversation, what can be inferred about the student?
   (A) He will drop out of the professor's class soon.
   (B) He frequently asks the professor for extensions on assignments.
   (C) He has not yet done any research for his paper.
   (D) He is nervous about asking the professor for an extension.

Inference Questions

Listen to **Track 1.28**. Take notes using the template below as you listen to the conversation.

Key Terms
- tour guide
- interview
- application
- short paper

Vocabulary
feedback (n): information on people's thoughts regarding the quality of a product or service

Things to Consider

HOW do the speakers organize and present the conversation?
(Identify the speakers' attitudes and the implications of the conversation.)

Notes
_____
_____
_____

Answer the following multiple-choice questions.

5) Based on the conversation, what can be inferred about the student?
   (A) She is outgoing and enjoys interacting with others.
   (B) She has held a job as a tour guide before.
   (C) She is not qualified to become a campus tour guide.
   (D) She is nervous about her upcoming interview.

6) What will the student probably do next?
   (A) Go to her interview for the tour guide position
   (B) Fill out the application for the tour guide position
   (C) Begin leading a campus tour for incoming freshmen
   (D) Talk to the advisor about upcoming campus activities

Inference Questions

Listen to **Track 1.29**. Take notes using the template below as you listen to the conversation.

Key Terms
lab partner
absent

Vocabulary
proposition (n): a plan or a suggestion
get a hold of (someone) (v): communicate with, contact, reach

Things to Consider

HOW do the speakers organize and present the conversation?
(Identify the speakers' attitudes and the implications of the conversation.)

Notes
_____
_____
_____

Answer the following multiple-choice questions.

7) What can be inferred about the student?
   (A) Her lab grade will suffer because she cannot complete the assignment.
   (B) Her lab partner has never been missing from lab before today.
   (C) She has never attended a science lab class before.
   (D) She does not like her lab partner, Dillon.

8) Listen to **Track 1.30**.
   What can be inferred from this?
   (A) The student cannot complete the lab assignment by herself.
   (B) Most students will fail the lab assignment.
   (C) The student will not have enough time to complete the lab assignment.
   (D) The entire class will work together to complete the lab assignment.

EXERCISE 1

As you listen to **Track 1.31**, take notes on the conversation between the university employee and the student. Then answer the multiple-choice questions that follow.

Key Terms
on-campus parking permit
off-campus parking lots
shuttle

Vocabulary
permit (n): a document or license that authorizes a person to do something

Things to Consider

WHAT is the conversation about?

WHAT details contribute to the main idea?

WHY are the speakers having the conversation?

HOW do the speakers organize and present the conversation?
(Identify the speakers' attitudes and the implications of the conversation.)

Notes

_____
_____
_____
_____
_____
_____
_____
_____
_____
_____

EXERCISE 1

Circle the correct answer or answers to each of the multiple-choice questions below.

1) Why does the student visit the university employee's office?
   (A) To learn about the university's public transportation system
   (B) To purchase an on-campus parking permit
   (C) To ask about the availability of off-campus parking
   (D) To complain about a parking ticket he received on campus

2) According to the university employee, when do most students purchase parking permits?
   (A) Near the end of summer
   (B) During the first week of school
   (C) During the second week of school
   (D) During finals week

3) Listen to **Track 1.32**.
   Why does the student say this?
   (A) To point out a difficulty of living off campus
   (B) To explain why he wants to sell his car
   (C) To point out that traffic enforcers are too strict
   (D) To explain why he needs a parking permit

4) Based on the conversation, what can be inferred about on-campus parking at the university?
   (A) Many students park on campus without buying a parking permit.
   (B) On-campus parking lots are located far from most classrooms.
   (C) There are many more students than there are available parking spaces.
   (D) Fewer students bought parking permits this year than in previous years.

5) How does the student solve his parking issue?
   (A) He convinces the university employee to sell him an on-campus parking permit.
   (B) He purchases an off-campus parking permit.
   (C) He decides to put his car up for sale.
   (D) He decides to leave his car at his house for the rest of the year.

EXERCISE 2

As you listen to **Track 1.33**, take notes on the conversation between the students. Then answer the multiple-choice questions that follow.

Key Terms

roommate
group project

Vocabulary

pulling his weight (idiom): doing his fair share of the task or project
bummed (slang): upset, disappointed
mope (v): think gloomily or sadly; brood

Things to Consider

WHAT is the conversation about?

WHAT details contribute to the main idea?

WHY are the speakers having the conversation?

HOW do the speakers organize and present the conversation?
(Identify the speakers' attitudes and the implications of the conversation.)

Notes

_____
_____
_____
_____
_____
_____
_____
_____
_____
_____

EXERCISE 2

Circle the correct answer or answers to each of the multiple-choice questions below.

1) Why does the woman want to speak with the man?
   (A) To find out if he is taking a certain class
   (B) To ask him for some dating advice
   (C) To see if he will help her finish a group project
   (D) To find out if he can help her find someone

2) What is the relationship between the man and Andrew?
   (A) They are working on a project together.
   (B) They are in a psychology class together.
   (C) They are roommates.
   (D) They are brothers.

3) Listen to **Track 1.34**.
   Why does the man say this about Andrew?
   (A) To explain why Andrew has not been attending class
   (B) To defend Andrew from the woman's criticism
   (C) To criticize Andrew for his lifestyle choices
   (D) To defend Andrew's decision to skip his classes

4) Listen to **Track 1.35**.
   What does the man mean when he says this?
   (A) Andrew is in charge of taking measurements for the group project.
   (B) Andrew has not completed his portion of the group project.
   (C) Andrew is too busy exercising to complete the group project.
   (D) Andrew has gained weight since he started working on the group project.

5) How does the man probably feel about the woman?
   (A) He believes that she is being too critical of Andrew.
   (B) He is sympathetic toward her desire to finish the group project.
   (C) He is concerned for her because of her recent break-up.
   (D) He believes that she should finish the group project without Andrew.

EXERCISE 3

As you listen to **Track 1.36**, take notes on the conversation between the recreation department employee and the student. Then answer the multiple-choice questions that follow.

Key Terms

rental
recreation department
student ID

Vocabulary

equipment (n): items that are meant to be used for a specific activity

Things to Consider

WHAT is the conversation about?

WHAT details contribute to the main idea?

WHY are the speakers having the conversation?

HOW do the speakers organize and present the conversation?
(Identify the speakers' attitudes and the implications of the conversation.)

Notes

___
___
___
___
___
___
___
___
___
___

EXERCISE 3

Circle the correct answer or answers to each of the multiple-choice questions below.

1) Why is the student talking to the recreation department employee?
   (A) To sign up for tennis lessons
   (B) To rent some athletic equipment
   (C) To reserve a tennis court
   (D) To apply to be a physical trainer

2) Listen to **Track 1.37**.
   Why does the recreation department employee say this?
   (A) To determine if the student is familiar with the rental system
   (B) To determine if the student has stolen equipment from the recreation department
   (C) To find out why the student is visiting the university's recreation department
   (D) To find out how the student learned of the equipment rental program

3) What must the student give the recreation department employee in order to check out tennis equipment?
   (A) His phone number
   (B) His name and address
   (C) Five dollars
   (D) His student ID

4) Why will the student return the equipment within three hours?
   (A) He has a class that starts in three hours.
   (B) He does not want to be charged late fees.
   (C) He will be tired after three hours of playing tennis
   (D) He wants to make sure that others get to use the equipment.

5) What will the recreation department employee probably do next?
   (A) Help the next student in line
   (B) Play tennis with the student
   (C) Get the tennis equipment for the student
   (D) Charge the student five dollars for the tennis equipment

EXERCISE 4

As you listen to **Track 1.38**, take notes on the conversation between the students. Then answer the multiple-choice questions that follow.

Key Terms

Lecture Hall 203
Psychology 1
Professor Duarte

Vocabulary

off the top of my head (idiom): without giving something deliberation or serious thought
courtyard (n): a completely or partially walled area without a roof
know (one's) stuff (slang): know what one is supposed to know

Things to Consider

WHAT is the conversation about?

WHAT details contribute to the main idea?

WHY are the speakers having the conversation?

HOW do the speakers organize and present the conversation?
(Identify the speakers' attitudes and the implications of the conversation.)

Notes

_____
_____
_____
_____
_____
_____
_____
_____
_____
_____

EXERCISE 4

Circle the correct answer or answers to each of the multiple-choice questions below.

1) Why does the man want to speak with the woman?
   (A) To find out how friendly a psychology professor is
   (B) To determine if a certain class is worth taking
   (C) To ask for direction to a location on campus
   (D) To find out how crowded a certain lecture hall will be

2) Listen to **Track 1.39**.
   Why does the woman say this?
   (A) To persuade the man to attend his lecture for Psychology 1
   (B) To explain how she know the lecture hall's location
   (C) To point out something that she and the man have in common
   (D) To prove that she knows more about psychology than the man does

3) According to the woman, why did the man probably walk past his lecture hall without noticing it?
   (A) He has bad eyesight, and he forgot to wear his glasses.
   (B) Someone distracted him by asking him questions.
   (C) He was looking at a campus map instead of his surroundings.
   (D) Some buildings on campus are not well labeled.

4) What is the woman's opinion of Professor Duarte?
   (A) He is kind and knowledgeable.
   (B) He is quiet and brilliant.
   (C) He is challenging but fair.
   (D) He is lazy and mean.

5) Based on the conversation, what can be inferred about the man?
   (A) He will miss his upcoming psychology lecture.
   (B) He is a relatively new student at the university.
   (C) He is good friends with the woman.
   (D) He does not like attending such a large university.

EXERCISE 5

As you listen to **Track 1.40**, take notes on the conversation between the librarian and the student. Then answer the multiple-choice questions that follow.

Key Terms

library
textbooks
Sociology 143

Vocabulary

in demand (n): desired by many people
suppose (v): assume that something is true

Things to Consider

WHAT is the conversation about?

WHAT details contribute to the main idea?

WHY are the speakers having the conversation?

HOW do the speakers organize and present the conversation?
(Identify the speakers' attitudes and the implications of the conversation.)

Notes

_____
_____
_____
_____
_____
_____
_____
_____
_____
_____
_____
_____

EXERCISE 5

Circle the correct answer or answers to each of the multiple-choice questions below.

1) Why does the female student approach the librarian?
   (A) To purchase one of the library's textbooks
   (B) To apply for a job at the library to help pay for her textbooks
   (C) To check the library's lost-and-found for one of her textbooks
   (D) To find out if the library has a copy of a certain textbook

2) Listen to **Track 1.41**.
   Why does the student say this?
   (A) To complain that the professor assigns too much reading
   (B) To explain why she needs to use the textbook
   (C) To point out one difficulty of being a university student
   (D) To clarify why sociology is her most difficult class

3) For how long can the female student use the textbook before she must return it?
   (A) One hour
   (B) Three hours
   (C) One day
   (D) Two weeks

4) What can be inferred about the female student?
   (A) She has not checked out a textbook from the library before.
   (B) She does not want to do the reading for her Sociology 143 class.
   (C) She has never been to the university's library before this visit.
   (D) She has spoken to the librarian on many occasions.

5) What will the librarian probably do next?
   (A) Retrieve a list of available textbooks for the student
   (B) Direct the student to the private study rooms
   (C) Retrieve the sociology textbook for the student
   (D) Show the student where to find the sociology textbook

EXERCISE 6

As you listen to **Track 1.42**, take notes on the conversation between the university employee and the student. Then answer the multiple-choice questions that follow.

Key Terms

university health care
on-campus health facilities

Vocabulary

comprehensive (adj): all-inclusive; including all aspects of something
antibiotic (n): a medicine that slows or stops the spread of microorganisms such as bacteria

Things to Consider

WHAT is the conversation about?

WHAT details contribute to the main idea?

WHY are the speakers having the conversation?

HOW do the speakers organize and present the conversation?
(Identify the speakers' attitudes and the implications of the conversation.)

Notes

_____
_____
_____
_____
_____
_____
_____
_____
_____
_____

EXERCISE 6

Circle the correct answer or answers to each of the multiple-choice questions below.

1) Why does the student visit the university's health center?
   (A) To receive treatment for a minor injury
   (B) To complain about the increasing cost of student health care
   (C) To sign up for the university's health care program
   (D) To give the university employee a completed student health care application

2) What does the student have to do to receive on-campus health care?
   Choose 2 answers.
   (A) Pay a fee
   (B) Get a physical exam
   (C) Get her parents' signatures
   (D) Fill out an application

3) Listen to **Track 1.43**.
   Why does the university employee say this?
   (A) To point out the reason that most students visit the urgent care center
   (B) To emphasize the university health center's convenient location
   (C) To reveal the negative aspects of student health care
   (D) To explain why the health center is always crowded

4) Why does the university health center's staff not perform complex surgeries?
   (A) The health center is currently understaffed.
   (B) Legal restrictions forbid complex medical procedures.
   (C) It has never been necessary to perform major surgery.
   (D) The health center lacks the necessary medical equipment.

5) Listen to **Track 1.44**.
   What can be inferred from this?
   (A) The student has already paid the fee.
   (B) The student cannot afford to pay the fee.
   (C) The fee is lower than the student expected.
   (D) The fee is lower than it was last year.

CHAPTER 2

Academic Lectures

Academic Lectures

EXPLANATION OF TASK

Each iBT TOEFL Listening section will include four to six academic lectures. These lectures will discuss topics that you are likely to encounter as a student at an American university. The topics are drawn from a range of academic fields, including psychology, biology, chemistry, the social sciences, and literature.

Each lecture is 3 to 5 minutes long. Because these lectures are supposed to replicate natural-sounding speech in an American university setting, the speakers may use English speech patterns such as repetition, digression from the main topic, false starts, pauses, and fillers (um, uh, eh, well). You will hear each lecture only once, but you are encouraged to take notes on the lecture information as you listen.

After you have listened to the lecture, you must answer six multiple-choice questions that relate to the lecture information. These questions will be related to the main idea, purpose, organization, or implications of the lecture. You may use your notes when answering the questions.

 Because this is the intermediate-level book in the series, the conversations in this book are shorter and use simpler language than those you will encounter on the iBT TOEFL.

LECTURE FORMAT

The excerpt that you listen to will likely be of a professor lecturing on a certain subject. However, you may also hear an excerpt of a professor answering a student's question, or a back-and-forth discussion between a professor and his or her students.

NECESSARY SKILLS

In order to successfully complete the academic lecture portions of the Listening section, you must be able to:

- comprehend vocabulary regarding a variety of academic topics
- take notes on academic material
- summarize spoken information
- recognize the main idea and details of a spoken academic lecture
- determine the purpose of a spoken academic lecture
- make inferences about the organization and content of a spoken academic lecture
- make inferences about the attitude of the speaker

Question Types

The iBT TOEFL Listening section consists of four main types of questions.

1 Main Idea Questions

Main Idea Questions will require you to identify the main topic of the lecture. Because the answers to these questions are drawn directly from the lecture content, taking notes may guide you when answering these questions.

2 Detail Questions

Detail Questions will require you to identify a detail, an example, or an explanation related to the main topic. Because the answers to these questions are drawn directly from the lecture content, taking notes may guide you when answering these questions.

3 Purpose Questions

Purpose Questions will require you to identify *why* the speaker makes a particular statement or asks a particular question. Therefore, when listening to the lecture, concentrate on fully comprehending the purpose of the lecture.

4 Inference Questions

Inference Questions will require you to make an inference, or assumption, based on the contents of the lecture. An inference question might ask you to identify the speaker's tone or the lecture's basic structure.

Academic Lecture Question Type 1: Main Idea

WHAT IS A MAIN IDEA QUESTION?

The *main idea*, or topic, is the overall subject of the lecture. Use caution when answering **Main Idea Questions**: the lecturer will not always directly state his main idea. Therefore, you may have to infer the main idea based on the details and examples provided by the speaker. There will be one **Main Idea Question** after each academic lecture.

HOW TO TAKE NOTES

When taking notes on an academic lecture, the main idea will likely be one of the first things you write down. As you listen to the lecture, ask yourself, "**WHAT** is the lecture about?" Doing so will make identifying and answering the **Main Idea Question** easier.

MAIN IDEA QUESTION FORMATS

Main Idea Questions will usually ask you to identify the main idea, subject, or topic of the lecture. Common formats for a **Main Idea Question** include:

> *What is the main topic of the lecture?*
> *What is the main purpose of the lecture?*
> *What is the lecture mainly about?*
> *What is the professor discussing in the lecture?*

TIPS

Listening Tips: When listening for **Main Idea Questions**, focus on information presented in the beginning of the lecture. This part of the lecture sometimes contains important words, phrases, and sentences that indicate the main idea of the lecture.

Answer Tips: In questions about the topic or main idea, the correct answer will deal with the general subject of the lecture. Incorrect answer choices may be:

- broader than the focus of the lecture
- details of the lecture, not the main idea
- erroneous according to the speaker
- about a subject not mentioned in the lecture

Main Idea Questions

Listen to **Track 2.01**. Take notes using the template below as you listen to the lecture.

Key Terms

Isaac Newton   motion
force   mass
principle of inertia

Vocabulary

inertia (n): a quality of remaining unchanged unless influenced by an outside force

expel (v): to eject or force something outward

Things to Consider

WHAT is the lecture about?

Notes

Issac Newton, laws of motion → how force/mass influence motion

(1) principle of inertia, (2) F = ma, (3) reaction → = & opposite reaction

Answer the following multiple-choice question.

What is the main topic of the lecture?
(A) The early life of Isaac Newton
(B) Laws in physics identified by Isaac Newton
(C) Mathematical formulas used in physics
(D) Government regulations for scientific research

Answer Explanation

The professor begins the lecture by stating that he is going to "introduce Isaac Newton's laws of motion," which are *laws in physics*. Therefore, the main idea of the lecture is summarized by **Choice B**.

Main Idea Questions

Listen to **Track 2.02**. Take notes using the template below as you listen to the lecture.

Key Terms
- blueprint
- light-sensitive paper
- mechanical drawing

Vocabulary
- dimension (n): a measurable aspect of something (length, width, height, or depth)
- tracing paper (n): thin, see-through drawing paper

Things to Consider

WHAT is the lecture about?

Notes
_____
_____
_____

Answer the following multiple-choice question.

1) What is the main topic of the lecture?
   (A) How to choose color for a building
   (B) An important copying technique for architects
   (C) The oldest architectural drawing in existence
   (D) A test taken by all architects

Main Idea Questions

Listen to **Track 2.03**. Take notes using the template below as you listen to the lecture.

Key Terms
- National Health Service (NHS)
- surgeries
- general practitioner (GP)
- specialist

Vocabulary
- comprehensive (adj): complete; all-inclusive
- emphasize (v): draw attention or give importance to something
- referral (n): a notice that directs a patient to a specialist

Things to Consider

WHAT is the lecture about?

Notes
_____
_____
_____

Answer the following multiple-choice question.

2) What is the main topic of the lecture?
   (A) The use of taxes to fund medical schools
   (B) The differences between generalist and specialist doctors
   (C) The problems with healthcare in the United States
   (D) The healthcare system of the United Kingdom

Main Idea Questions

Listen to **Track 2.04**. Take notes using the template below as you listen to the lecture.

Key Terms
- equator
- subtropical regions

Vocabulary
- deter (v): prevent something from happening
- latitude (n): a way of measuring a location's distance from the equator

Things to Consider

WHAT is the lecture about?

Notes
_____
_____
_____

Answer the following multiple-choice question.

3) What is the main topic of the lecture?
   (A) The reasons for high temperatures in tropical regions
   (B) The relationship between atmospheric pressure and temperature
   (C) The process of desert formation
   (D) The effects of rainfall on desert regions

Main Idea Questions

Practice 4

Listen to **Track 2.05**. Take notes using the template below as you listen to the lecture.

Key Terms
- folk music
- flamenco music
- Roma people

Vocabulary
staccato (adj or adv): (in music) each note being sharply separated from previous and following notes
incorporate (v): include

Things to Consider

WHAT is the lecture about?

Notes
_____
_____
_____

Answer the following multiple-choice question.

4) What is the main topic of the lecture?
   (A) A style of guitar playing that is fun and easy to learn
   (B) A type of folk music that probably originated in Spain
   (C) A genre of music often enjoyed by European royalty
   (D) A group of people that immigrated to Spain centuries ago

Academic Lecture Question Type 2: Detail

WHAT IS A DETAIL QUESTION?

Details are specific pieces of information that relate to a larger topic. These pieces of information can be facts, descriptions, reasons, or examples. **Detail Questions** will ask you to recall specific information from the lecture as it was stated by the speaker. There will be one to three **Detail Questions** in each academic lecture.

HOW TO TAKE NOTES

When taking notes on an academic lecture, the details will likely be spread throughout the lecture. Focus on writing down only details that relate to the main idea of the lecture. **Before taking notes, try to identify the main idea of the lecture**.

As you listen to the lecture, ask yourself, "**WHAT** details contribute to the main idea?" Doing so will make identifying and answering the **Detail Questions** easier.

DETAIL QUESTION FORMATS

Detail Questions will ask you to identify specific details, explanations, or examples that relate to the main idea of the lecture. Common formats for the **Detail Questions** include:

> *What does the professor say about _____ in the lecture?*
> *According to the professor, what is true about _____?*
> *What is said about _____ in the lecture?*
> *Who/What/Where/When/Why/How _____?*

Whereas **Main Idea Questions** always appear as multiple-choice questions with one correct answer, **Detail Question**s have one, two, or three correct answer choices.

TIPS

Listening Tips: When listening for details, notice information that contributes to the main idea of the lecture. This information may involve information such as numbers, dates, names, definitions, reasons, connections, choices, and processes.

Answer Tips: In questions about details, the correct answer will always restate facts, descriptions, reasons, and examples from the lecture. When you answer detail questions, try to recall exactly what was said by the speaker. Look at your notes if you cannot remember exactly what was said. Incorrect answer choices may:

- repeat some of the speaker's words but convey a different meaning
- use words that sound like, but are actually different from, the speaker's words
- be inaccurate or irrelevant based on what you hear in the lecture

Detail Questions

Listen to **Track 2.06**. Take notes using the template below as you listen to the lecture. Then answer the multiple-choice questions that follow.

Key Terms
- automation
- Plato
- education
- proofreading software

Vocabulary
automation (n): the state of machines doing work that was once done by people

reliance (n): trust in or dependence on someone or something

Things to Consider
WHAT is the lecture about?

WHAT details contribute to the main idea?

Notes
- automation in edu. = using tech. when learning
- Plato feared literacy → no more memorizing
- Automation pros: writing on comp. faster
- cons: too much reliance on proofing software → bad spelling, grammar

Answer the following multiple-choice questions.

According to the professor, what did Plato fear about the spread of literacy?
(A) It would not be accessible to all social classes.
(B) It would decrease people's abilities to memorize information.
(C) It would promote the spread of rumors and false information.
(D) It would render his role as a philosopher unnecessary

What usually happens when students write without using proofreading software?
(A) Their writing lacks organization and focus.
(B) They write much more quickly.
(C) They produce concise and elegant writing.
(D) Their writing contains many grammar and spelling errors.

Answer Explanation
The professor states that Plato thought that "writing information down would diminish people's abilities to memorize," so the correct answer must be **Choice B**.

Answer Explanation
According to the professor, when students "write without proofreading software, their writing is filled with mistakes." Thus, the correct answer must be **Choice D**.

Detail Questions

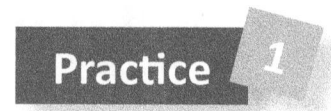

Listen to **Track 2.07**. Take notes using the template below as you listen to the lecture.

Key Terms
- the butterfly effect
- meteorologist
- weather prediction

Vocabulary
- **chaos theory (n):** a field in mathematics that studies physical systems that seem random, such as the weather
- **hypothesize (v):** to present an idea based on limited evidence

Things to Consider
WHAT is the lecture about?

WHAT details contribute to the main idea?

Notes
_____
_____
_____

Answer the following multiple-choice questions.

1) What idea does "the butterfly effect" refer to?
   (A) Seemingly insignificant actions can cause large events.
   (B) Chaos theory can only be explained using metaphors.
   (C) All events are somehow connected to one another.
   (D) Butterflies' migration paths influence weather patterns.

2) According to the professor, who came up with the term "butterfly effect"?
   (A) Someone who studies statistics
   (B) Someone who studies chaos theory
   (C) Some who studies insects
   (D) Someone who studies weather patterns

Detail Questions

Listen to **Track 2.08**. Take notes using the template below as you listen to the lecture.

Key Terms
- socialism
- Louis Blanc
- Pierre J. Proudhon
- Robert Owen

Vocabulary
- **industrialism (n):** an economic system based on factories
- **constitution (n):** a collection of principles or ideas that describe how a nation is governed

Things to Consider

WHAT is the lecture about?

WHAT details contribute to the main idea?

Notes
_____
_____
_____

Answer the following multiple-choice questions.

3) Based on the lecture, what is the most important goal of socialism?
   (A) Longer vacations for workers
   (B) The freeing of unjustly imprisoned people
   (C) Voting rights for everyone
   (D) Public ownership of property

4) What did the Welsh-born leader Robert Owen believe?
   (A) Establishment of private property is a theft from the community
   (B) Sharing property leads to a better society
   (C) The competition created by capitalism is healthy
   (D) Natural resources should not be owned by the public

Detail Questions

Listen to **Track 2.09**. Take notes using the template below as you listen to the lecture.

Key Terms

Kuiper belt
Neptune
Pluto
Kuiper belt objects (KBOs)

Vocabulary

debris (n): fragments of something that was broken or destroyed
elliptical (adj): semi-circular; oval-shaped

Things to Consider

WHAT is the lecture about?

WHAT details contribute to the main idea?

Notes

_____
_____
_____

Answer the following multiple-choice questions.

5) What do scientists believe is the origin of the Kuiper belt?
   (A) Materials left over from planetary formation
   (B) Gases released by the sun long ago
   (C) Materials from a collision between Pluto and Neptune
   (D) The merging of several large, gaseous planets

6) According to the professor, what is true about Pluto?
   (A) It is one of Neptune's moons.
   (B) It is a Kuiper belt object.
   (C) It will someday hit Earth.
   (D) It has an unknown orbit.

Detail Questions

Listen to **Track 2.10**. Take notes using the template below as you listen to the lecture.

Key Terms
- neoteny
- physical characteristics

Vocabulary
- **domesticate (v):** tame, train
- **snout (n):** the part of an animal's head that contains its nose and mouth
- **gills (n):** openings on a fish's head that allow it to breathe underwater

Things to Consider

WHAT is the lecture about?

WHAT details contribute to the main idea?

Notes

_____
_____
_____

Answer the following multiple-choice questions.

7) What neotenic trait of some salamanders is discussed in the lecture?
   (A) They walk on land when they reach adulthood.
   (B) They retain their gills when they reach adulthood.
   (C) They are exceptionally large when they are young.
   (D) They only hunt for food when they are young.

8) According to the lecture, which of the following are neotenic traits in humans?
   Choose 2 answers.
   (A) Small size
   (B) Large hands
   (C) Small ears
   (D) Large eyes

Academic Lecture Question Type 3: Purpose

WHAT IS A PURPOSE QUESTION?

The "purpose" of a statement is the speaker's intention; you must infer purpose based on what the speaker says. In some **Purpose Questions**, you will listen to part of the lecture again before answering. There are usually one or two **Purpose Questions** that accompany each academic lecture.

HOW TO TAKE NOTES

The speakers usually state their purpose early in the conversation and continue to imply it through what they say and ask. **When taking notes on the purpose of the lecture, try to quickly identify the main idea.**

As you listen to the conversation, ask yourself, "**WHY** did the speaker include this information?" Doing so will make identifying and answering **Purpose Questions** easier.

PURPOSE QUESTION FORMATS

Purpose Questions will usually ask you why the speaker made a certain claim. Common formats for **Purpose Questions** include:

Why does the professor explain _____?
Why does the professor ask the class about _____?
Why does the professor say this?
Why does the student ask/say _____?

TIPS

Listening Tips: When listening for the purpose of a lecture or statement, you must rely on your ability to draw logical conclusions to determine *why* a statement is being made. Your notes may help you piece information from the lecture together.

Answer Tips: The correct answers to **Purpose Questions** will often be stated indirectly. Thus, these questions are slightly more difficult to answer than **Main Idea** or **Detail Questions**. When answering **Purpose Questions**, look at your notes if you cannot remember exactly what the speakers said. Incorrect answer choices may:

- repeat some of the speaker's words but convey a different meaning
- use words that sound like but are actually different from the speaker's words
- be inaccurate based on what you hear in the lecture
- be irrelevant and not about anything mentioned in the lecture

Purpose Questions

Listen to **Track 2.11**. Take notes using the template below as you listen to the lecture.

Key Terms
Don Quixote
chivalric romance

Vocabulary
Don (adj): Spanish honorific title; "Sir"
don (v): put something on
peasant (n): a poor individual who makes a living by farming a small piece of land

Things to Consider
WHY does the speaker present the lecture information?

Notes
Don Q. plot → old man becomes knight (inspired by chivalric romances)

book is famous → both funny & tragic

Answer the following multiple-choice questions.

1) Listen to **Track 2.12**.
   Why does the professor say this?
   (A) To show how the events of *Don Quixote* have influenced modern literature
   (B) To criticize Cervantes for stealing ideas from chivalric romances
   (C) To summarize the all the major plot points of *Don Quixote*
   (D) To explain how Don Quixote transforms himself into a "knight"

2) According to the author, why is *Don Quixote* such an enduring novel?
   (A) It mixes elements of humor and misfortune.
   (B) It captures the political tension present in 17th-century Spain.
   (C) It is filled with funny and interesting characters.
   (D) It discusses life events that are experienced by almost everyone.

Answer Explanation
The excerpt on **Track 2.12** explains what *Don Quixote* does to "become one of the brave knights he has read so much about," so the correct answer must be **Choice D**.

Answer Explanation
The professor states that *Don Quixote* is an influential novel because "it blurs the lines between comedy and tragedy," so the correct answer must be **Choice A**.

Purpose Questions

Listen to **Track 2.13**. Take notes using the template below as you listen to the lecture.

Key Terms
- wheel
- chariot

Vocabulary
- revolutionize (v): cause a drastic change
- agriculture (n): the practice of farming
- chaotic (adj): describing a state of confusion or disorder

Things to Consider

WHY does the speaker present the lecture information?

Notes
_____
_____
_____

Answer the following multiple-choice questions.

1) Why does the professor mention the chariot?
   (A) To change the lecture topic to military history
   (B) To give an example of an early use for the wheel
   (C) To show why some ancient civilizations were more powerful than others
   (D) To point out a unique feature of Asian and European civilizations

2) Why did ancient American civilizations probably not use wheels?
   (A) They did not want to use their domesticated animals to pull heavy loads.
   (B) They did not have the natural resources to construct wheels.
   (C) They lacked large, tamed animals that could pull carts.
   (D) They did not need wheels in warfare.

Purpose Questions

Listen to **Track 2.14**. Take notes using the template below as you listen to the lecture.

Key Terms
- Temple Grandin
- slaughterhouse
- livestock

Vocabulary
- humane (adj): being kind to living organisms
- autism (n): a brain disability that affects social skills
- slaughter (v): killing animals for their meat
- overstimulation (n): the state of being excessively excited

Things to Consider

WHY does the speaker present the lecture information?

Notes
_____
_____
_____

Answer the following multiple-choice questions.

3) Listen to **Track 2.15**.
   Why does the professor say this?
   (A) To explain why the professor is able to relate to Grandin on a personal level
   (B) To summarize the most important events of Grandin's life
   (C) To explain how Grandin could relate to the feelings of stress and overstimulation experienced by livestock
   (D) To point out how many difficulties Grandin had to overcome while researching and working

4) Why does the professor mention the curved livestock path developed by Grandin?
   (A) To give an example of how Grandin made the killing of livestock more humane
   (B) To criticize Grandin for supporting the livestock industry
   (C) To describe the laws that Grandin changed that affect the livestock industry
   (D) To remind the class that Grandin has reshaped the animal rights movement

Purpose Questions

Practice 3

Listen to **Track 2.16**. Take notes using the template below as you listen to the lecture.

Key Terms
obsessive compulsive disorder (OCD)
obsessions
compulsions

Vocabulary
contamination (n): the state of being dirty, impure, or polluted
relapse (v): become worse after a period of improvement

Things to Consider
WHY does the speaker present the lecture information?

Notes
_____
_____
_____

Answer the following multiple-choice questions.

5) Listen to **Track 2.17**.
   Why does the professor say this?
   (A) To explain how OCD is treated
   (B) To explain the differences between obsessions and compulsions
   (C) To explain why OCD is such a serious disorder
   (D) To explain how OCD is diagnosed

6) Listen to **Track 2.18**.
   Why does the professor say this?
   (A) To explain how OCD affects the brain
   (B) To remind the class of the importance of hygiene
   (C) To give an example of a compulsion
   (D) To clarify the relationship between obsessions and stress

Purpose Questions

Listen to **Track 2.19**. Take notes using the template below as you listen to the lecture.

Key Terms
- rabies virus
- vector species
- mammals

Vocabulary
- **host (n):** an organism in which a parasite or virus lives
- **marsupial (n):** an order of mammals found mostly in Australia and New Guinea
- **fatal (adj):** causing death

Things to Consider

WHY does the speaker present the lecture information?

Notes
_____
_____
_____

Answer the following multiple-choice questions.

7) Why does the professor present the information in the lecture?
   (A) To promote the killing of wild mammal species that carry rabies
   (B) To describe symptoms of rabies in various animals and in humans
   (C) To inform public health students about the spread and control of rabies
   (D) To inform public health students about public education and vector animals

8) Why does the professor mention the Carolina opossum?
   (A) To explain how rabies is able to spread so quickly
   (B) To give an example of an animal that cannot transmit rabies
   (C) To argue that all household pests should be tested for rabies
   (D) To show how rabies affects an animal's actions and behaviors

Academic Lecture Question Type 4: Inferences

WHAT IS AN INFERENCE QUESTION?

Inference Questions may ask you to make an inference based on the information in the lecture, explain the organization of the lecture, or identify the speaker's attitude. Below are the four categories of inference questions that you might see on the lecture portion of the Listening test.

INFERENCE QUESTION FORMATS

Category 1 – Inference: An *inference* is a conclusion drawn from material but that is not directly stated. In order to make an inference, you must pay attention to what the speaker suggests during a lecture. Common formats for **Inference Questions** include:

> *What can be inferred about _____ in the lecture?*
> *What does the professor imply/suggest about _____ in the lecture?*
> *What does the professor mean by this statement?*

Category 2 – Organization: Organization Questions ask you to identify the order in which the lecture information is presented. Thus, **Organization Questions** ask you how the speaker presents the information, for example, as a cause and effect. Common formats for **Organization Questions** include:

> *How does the speaker organize the lecture information?*
> *How does the speaker clarify the points he/she made about _____ ?*

Category 3 – Attitude: The speaker's attitude is his or her feelings about the information. For example, a speaker may feel approval, disapproval, indifference, excitement, confusion, or surprise toward what is being discussed. Many times the speaker communicates an attitude indirectly.
Common formats for **Attitude Questions** include:

> *What is the professor's opinion of _____ ?*
> *What is the professor's attitude toward _____ ?*

Category 4 – Connecting Information: Some lectures will include a Connecting Information Chart. To complete it, you must be able to categorize information presented in the lecture. Thus, you must understand the lecture's main idea and details to complete these charts.

TIPS

Answer Tips: In questions about inferences, organization, and attitude, the correct answer will usually be given indirectly. As such, these questions are more difficult to answer than **Main Idea**, **Detail**, and **Purpose Questions**. When you answer **Inference Questions**, look at your notes if you cannot remember exactly what was said. Incorrect answer choices may:

- repeat the speaker's words with a different message
- be inaccurate based on what you hear in the lecture
- be irrelevant and not about anything mentioned in the lecture

Inference Questions

Listen to **Track 2.20**. Take notes using the template below as you listen to the lecture.

Key Terms
- alcoholism
- neurotransmitters
- heredity
- environmental influences

Vocabulary
- evaluate (v): determine the condition of something or someone
- peer pressure (n): influence from one's friends or acquaintances

Things to Consider

HOW does the speaker organize and present the lecture?
(Identify the organization methods, tone, and implications of the speaker.)

Notes

risk factors for alcohol = genetic, env., neuro.

alcohol a problem for generations

Answer the following multiple-choice questions.

Listen to **Track 2.21**.
What does the professor mean when he says this?
(A) Alcoholism is a bigger problem in some places than in others.
(B) Alcoholism has been an issue in many places for a long time.
(C) Alcoholism is not as big an issue as it used to be.
(D) Alcoholism has only recently been recognized as an issue.

How does the professor organize the lecture?
(A) He introduces an issue before discussing its possible causes.
(B) He criticizes the lack of available research on an important topic.
(C) He presents a problem and offers possible solutions.
(D) He emphasizes a problem by discussing one specific example in detail.

Answer Explanation

This is an **Inference Question**. If something spans generations, that means that it has extended over a long period of time, so we can conclude that the correct answer must be **Choice B**.

Answer Explanation

This is an **Organization Question**. The professor begins the lecture by discussing alcoholism, and then he discusses three common ways that alcoholism might develop in an individual, so the correct answer must be **Choice A**.

Inference Questions

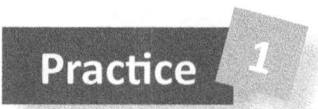

Listen to **Track 2.22**. Take notes using the template below as you listen to the lecture.

Key Terms
Voyager 1
solar system
space probe

Vocabulary
staggering (adj): enormous; surprising
vast (adj): immense, describing a large amount of something

Things to Consider

HOW does the speaker organize and present the lecture?
(Identify the organization methods, tone, and implications of the speaker.)

Notes
_____
_____
_____

Answer the following multiple-choice questions.

1) What can be inferred about *Voyager 1* from the lecture?
   (A) It can be viewed at night by using a telescope.
   (B) It is slowed down significantly by the pull of the Sun's gravity.
   (C) It has traveled further than any other man-made object.
   (D) It is still orbiting the moons of Jupiter and Saturn.

2) What will the professor probably talk about next?
   (A) How *Voyager 1* avoids hitting planets and space debris
   (B) Which planets *Voyager 1* will send photos of in the future
   (C) How *Voyager 1* travels at such high speeds
   (D) How *Voyager 1* communicates with Earth

Inference Questions

Listen to **Track 2.23**. Take notes using the template below as you listen to the lecture.

Key Terms
- macronutrient
- amino acids
- protein

Vocabulary
- **compound (n):** a substance composed of two or more elements that are bonded together
- **tissue (n):** the types of materials that animals and plants are made of

Things to Consider

HOW does the speaker organize and present the lecture?
(Identify the organization methods, tone, and implications of the speaker.)

Notes
_____
_____
_____

Answer the following multiple-choice questions.

3) What can be inferred about proteins?
   (A) They are much larger than amino acids.
   (B) They are created by scientists in laboratories.
   (C) They are found in very few food products.
   (D) They can be harmful to people if consumed.

4) What can be inferred about meat and dairy products?
   (A) They affect the human body in ways not understood by scientists.
   (B) They are not good sources of macronutrients.
   (C) They interrupt the creation of protein in humans.
   (D) They are among the best sources of amino acids.

Inference Questions

Practice 3

Listen to **Track 2.24**. Take notes using the template below as you listen to the lecture.

Key Terms
first organism
stomatolites

Vocabulary
accommodate (v): provide or create appropriate conditions for something or someone
microbe (n): a small, microscopic organism, such as a bacteria

Things to Consider

HOW does the speaker organize and present the lecture?
(Identify the organization methods, tone, and implications of the speaker.)

Notes

_____
_____
_____

Answer the following multiple-choice questions.

5) What can be inferred about the environmental conditions on Earth immediately after its formation?
(A) They were similar to today's environmental conditions.
(B) They were too extreme to accommodate life.
(C) They underwent a series of rapid changes.
(D) They were much different from what scientists had originally thought.

6) Listen to **Track 2.25**.
What can be inferred from this?
(A) Scientists may find evidence that life began more than 3.5-billion years ago.
(B) Scientists are not sure they have found the lowest level of stromatolites yet.
(C) Some stromatolite formations can take billions of years to form.
(D) Stromatolite fossils prove that no life existed more than 3.5 billion years ago.

Inference Questions

Practice 4

Listen to **Track 2.26**. Take notes using the template below as you listen to the lecture.

Key Terms
- proscenium stage
- theater-in-the-round
- open stage

Vocabulary
auditorium (n): the area of a theater where an audience sits

Things to Consider

HOW does the speaker organize and present the lecture?
(Identify the organization methods, tone, and implications of the speaker.)

Notes

_____
_____
_____

Complete the following table.

7) Place a check in each box where the stage type listed in the top row matches the description in the left column.

	Theater-in-the-round	Proscenium Stage	Open stage
Spectators sit around three sides of a raised platform that extends into an auditorium			
Spectators sit on all four sides of the stage			
Spectators can only see the front of the stage			

EXERCISE 1

As you listen to **Track 2.27**, take notes on the discussion between the professor and his students. Then answer the multiple-choice questions that follow.

Key Terms

rumination
depression
anxiety disorders

Vocabulary

injustice (n): absence of justice or fairness
strenuous (adj): requiring a considerable amount of force or energy
overwhelm (v): overpower, defeat

Things to Consider

WHAT is the lecture about?

WHAT details contribute to the main idea?

WHY does the speaker present the lecture information?

HOW does the speaker organize and present the lecture?

Notes

_____
_____
_____
_____
_____
_____
_____
_____
_____
_____

EXERCISE 1

Circle the correct answer or answers to each of the multiple-choice questions below.

1) What is the main topic of the lecture?
   (A) An event that causes a person to reconsider an opinion or belief
   (B) A mental process in which a person remembers an event over and over
   (C) A type of interaction in which one person becomes very upset
   (D) An medical procedure that reduces feelings of anxiety and depression

2) The psychological term "rumination" is a metaphor for which of the following?
   (A) The human digestive process
   (B) The feeling of hopelessness that results from depression
   (C) The sickness that results from consuming grass
   (D) The process of rechewing food

3) Listen to **Track 2.28**.
   Why does the professor say this?
   (A) To point out possible causes and effects of rumination
   (B) To transition the lecture topic to types of anxiety disorders
   (C) To illustrate the dangers of everyday social interactions
   (D) To point out the best ways to deal with social conflicts

4) According to the lecture, what is the difference between reflection and rumination?
   (A) Reflection has been around for much longer than rumination has.
   (B) Reflection is a group activity while rumination is done by oneself.
   (C) Reflection is a constructive way to think about something, while rumination is often psychologically harmful.
   (D) Reflection is a process that takes much longer to complete than the process of rumination.

5) According to the professor, how can people prevent rumination?
   (A) Write about whatever is bothering them in a journal or diary
   (B) Consult a medical professional, such as a doctor or a therapist
   (C) Continue to think about whatever issue is bothering them
   (D) Occupy their minds with physical or mental activities

6) What can be inferred about rumination from the lecture?
   (A) It can lead to personal insight.
   (B) It is triggered by an upsetting encounter or event.
   (C) It helps people forget other bad experiences.
   (D) It occurs when people cannot even one step to solve the problem.

EXERCISE 2

As you listen to **Track 2.29**, take notes on the business lecture. Then answer the multiple-choice questions that follow.

Key Terms

single proprietorship
stockholder   partnership
manager   corporation

Vocabulary

formality (n): something done to obey regulations or requirements

creditor (n): an individual or group that lend money with the expectation that it will be paid back with interest

Things to Consider

WHAT is the lecture about?

WHAT details contribute to the main idea?

WHY does the speaker present the lecture information?

HOW does the speaker organize and present the lecture?

Notes

_____
_____
_____
_____
_____
_____
_____
_____
_____
_____

EXERCISE 2

Circle the correct answer or answers to each of the multiple-choice questions below.

1) What is the main topic of the lecture?
   (A) Government regulation of business
   (B) How a corporation operates
   (C) Laws affecting the business world
   (D) The different types of business ownership

2) What is one benefit of a partnership over a single proprietorship?
   (A) A partnership can handle more business.
   (B) A partnership is less complicated legally.
   (C) A partnership requires fewer employees and sells cheaper products.
   (D) Partners are only responsible for their share of debt.

3) Which of the following are true of corporations?
   Choose 2 answers.
   (A) They are owned by stockholders.
   (B) They are difficult to invest in.
   (C) They are run by managers.
   (D) They are rarely financially successful.

4) Based on the information in the lecture, what can be inferred about single proprietorships and partnerships?
   (A) These types of businesses are usually more profitable than corporations.
   (B) Starting these types of businesses costs more than starting a corporation.
   (C) These types of businesses do not employ managers.
   (D) Founding and maintaining these types of businesses is financially risky.

5) Check the box where the industries listed in the left column matches the type of business ownership listed in the top row.

	Corporation	Single Proprietorship	Partnership
Banking and insurance			
Law and real estate			
Construction and food service			

EXERCISE 3

As you listen to **Track 2.30**, take notes on the geology lecture. Then answer the multiple-choice questions that follow.

Key Terms

- geothermal energy
- electricity
- magma
- hot springs

Vocabulary

radioactive (adj): giving off radiation (energy) or particles
harvest (v): collect a resource for use in the future

Things to Consider

WHAT is the lecture about?

WHAT details contribute to the main idea?

WHY does the speaker present the lecture information?

HOW does the speaker organize and present the lecture?

Notes

_____
_____
_____
_____
_____
_____
_____
_____
_____
_____

EXERCISE 3

Circle the correct answer or answers to each of the multiple-choice questions below.

1) What is the main topic of the lecture?
   (A) The extreme conditions that exist at the Earth's core
   (B) A process that turns steam into energy for electricity
   (C) A method of deriving energy from the Earth's heat
   (D) The various uses for hot springs throughout history

2) From what substance do people extract geothermal energy?
   (A) Hot, underground water
   (B) Hot, liquid magma
   (C) Underground fossil fuels
   (D) Rock from the Earth's core

3) Which of the following cause the Earth's core to maintain a temperature of 7,500 degrees Fahrenheit?
   Choose 2 answers.
   (A) The currents of vast underground oceans
   (B) The decay of radioactive elements
   (C) The residual heat from Earth's formation
   (D) The mixing of rock and magma

4) Listen to **Track 2.31**.
   Why does the professor say this?
   (A) To show how people in the past made use of geothermal energy
   (B) To explain why hot springs remain popular tourist destinations
   (C) To differentiate geothermal energy from other sources of energy
   (D) To introduce the topic of hygiene in ancient cultures

5) Listen to **Track 2.32**.
   What can be inferred from this?
   (A) The magma in Earth's crust and mantle is the hottest known material.
   (B) The most abundant material below the Earth's crust is magma.
   (C) The heat from magma makes Earth's mantle and crust hotter than its core.
   (D) The materials in Earth's core are denser than those in the mantle and crust.

6) What will the professor probably talk about next?
   (A) How ancient people used hot springs for indoor heating
   (B) How geothermal energy is converted into electricity
   (C) How magma travels from Earth's core to its mantle and crust
   (D) How geothermal energy is affecting the electricity supply.

EXERCISE 4

As you listen to **Track 2.33**, take notes on the political science lecture. Then answer the multiple-choice questions that follow.

Key Terms

protectionism
foreign competition
imports   subsidy
taxation   free trade

Vocabulary

promote (v): encourage the progress of something or someone; show support for

consumer (n): an individual who purchases goods and services

domestic (adj): inside a country; internal

Things to Consider

WHAT is the lecture about?

WHAT details contribute to the main idea?

WHY does the speaker present the lecture information?

HOW does the speaker organize and present the lecture?

Notes

_____
_____
_____
_____
_____
_____
_____
_____
_____
_____

EXERCISE 4

Circle the correct answer or answers to each of the multiple-choice questions below.

1) What is the main topic of the lecture?
   (A) Ways that free trade develops in a society
   (B) Methods used by governments to open domestic businesses
   (C) Ways that governments help domestic businesses succeed
   (D) Benefits of competition among businesses

2) Listen to **Track 2.34**.
   What can be inferred from this?
   (A) Taxing imported goods makes them more desirable to consumers.
   (B) Consumers often oppose tax raises on imported goods.
   (C) Domestic industries only make money by buying imported goods.
   (D) Protectionist policies ensure that consumers pay low prices for goods.

3) What are some protectionist policies that a government might use?
   Choose 2 answers.
   (A) Taxing imported goods
   (B) Restricting manufacturing among big businesses
   (C) Lowering taxes on consumers
   (D) Limiting the amount of imported goods

4) According to the professor, what is a subsidy?
   (A) Government money given to a struggling business
   (B) A tax placed on exported goods
   (C) A type of government that supports foreign industries
   (D) A government policy that protects consumers

5) Listen to **Track 2.35**.
   Why does the professor say this?
   (A) To explain why protectionist policies have been made illegal
   (B) To present a downside to a government's use of protectionism
   (C) To criticize America's dependence on imported goods
   (D) To differentiate free trade from other types of economies

6) According to the lecture, why does protectionism conflict with free trade?
   (A) Protectionism decreases business competition while free trade encourages business competition.
   (B) Protectionism is only used in the U.S. while free trade is applied internationally.
   (C) Protectionism is favored by most governments while free trade is regarded with suspicion.
   (D) Protectionism harms small businesses while free trade helps them grow.

EXERCISE 5

As you listen to **Track 2.36**, take notes on the discussion between the professor and his students. Then answer the multiple-choice questions that follow.

Key Terms

decimal system
sexagesimal numeral system

Vocabulary

Sumerians (n): ancient people who established the nation of Sumer in the Middle East approximately 6,000 years ago

Things to Consider

WHAT is the lecture about?

WHAT details contribute to the main idea?

WHY does the speaker present the lecture information?

HOW does the speaker organize and present the lecture?

Notes

_____
_____
_____
_____
_____
_____
_____
_____
_____
_____

EXERCISE 5

Circle the correct answer or answers to each of the multiple-choice questions below.

1) What is the main purpose of the lecture?
   (A) To criticize ancient civilizations for their complicated counting systems
   (B) To discuss the technological achievements of the ancient Sumerians
   (C) To praise ancient civilizations for their sophisticated mathematical equations
   (D) To introduce an ancient counting system still in use today

2) According to the lecture, what counting system do most people use today?
   (A) The fingers and toes system
   (B) The decimal system
   (C) The grouping system
   (D) The multiplication system

3) According to the professor, what civilization first developed the sexagesimal counting system?
   (A) The Sexagents
   (B) The Native Americans
   (C) The Sumerians
   (D) The Chinese

4) How do people use the sexagesimal numeral system in modern times?
   Choose 2 answers.
   (A) To measure distance
   (B) To measure time
   (C) To measure strength
   (D) To measure angles

5) Listen to **Track 2.37**.
   Why does the professor say this?
   (A) To demonstrate how the sexagesimal counting system may have originated
   (B) To test his students' abilities to perform simple mathematical operations
   (C) To determine whether or not the class was paying attention during his lecture
   (D) To show that the sexagesimal counting system is superior to the decimal system

6) What can be inferred about counting systems?
   (A) Many counting systems keep track of numbers using hands and fingers.
   (B) The sexagesimal counting system will become more popular than the decimal system.
   (C) Only the most technologically advanced ancient civilizations developed counting systems.
   (D) All counting systems were developed by cultures without written systems.

EXERCISE 6

As you listen to **Track 2.38**, take notes on the biology lecture. Then answer the multiple-choice questions that follow.

Key Terms

mutualism
honeydew
ants
aphids

Vocabulary

excrete (v): expel waste from the body
subdue (v): bring under control; overpower

Things to Consider

WHAT is the lecture about?

WHAT details contribute to the main idea?

WHY does the speaker present the lecture information?

HOW does the speaker organize and present the lecture?

Notes

_____
_____
_____
_____
_____
_____
_____
_____
_____
_____
_____

EXERCISE 6

Circle the correct answer or answers to each of the multiple-choice questions below.

1) What is the main topic of the lecture?
   (A) An overview of how various animals hunt for and gather food
   (B) A type of relationship in nature that benefits both parties involved
   (C) A species of insect with a unique method of developing
   (D) An introduction to the social structure of ant colonies

2) What is the main food source of aphids?
   (A) Young ants
   (B) Bark from trees
   (C) Chemicals released by ants
   (D) Sugar from plants

3) Listen to **Track 2.39**.
   Why does the professor say this?
   (A) To introduce the concept of domestication among insect species
   (B) To reconfirm that humans are the most intelligent species on Earth
   (C) To point out major biological differences between ants and humans
   (D) To show how mutualism applies to humans, cats, and dogs

4) Why do ants "domesticate" aphids?
   (A) To breed the aphids and the offspring as a food source
   (B) To keep the aphids as guard insects that protect ant colonies
   (C) To harvest a fluid that the aphids produce
   (D) To tame and calm the aphids

5) How do the ants prevent "domesticated" aphids from escaping?
   (A) The ants release chemicals that prevent aphids from leaving.
   (B) The ants build walls around the aphids, trapping them.
   (C) The ants carry aphids back if they stray.
   (D) The ants guard the aphids by constantly surrounding them.

6) How does the professor organize the lecture information?
   (A) He cites the opinions of others to prove his main idea.
   (B) He refutes a common misconception using scientific evidence.
   (C) He introduces a concept and elaborates on it using an example.
   (D) He uses charts and statistics to clarify a confusing idea.

CHAPTER 3

Actual Practices

Take notes as you listen to the lecture on **Track 3.01**. Then answer the multiple-choice questions that follow.

Anthropology

ancient Egypt papyrus
Nile River eye makeup
reeds

Things to Consider

WHAT is the lecture about?

WHAT details contribute to the main idea?

WHY does the speaker present the lecture information?

HOW does the speaker organize and present the lecture?

Notes

Circle the letter next to the correct answer or answers to each of the multiple-choice questions below.

1) What is the main topic of the lecture?
   (A) How Egyptians used the Nile to migrate to more hospitable climates
   (B) How Egyptians used the resources of the Nile to meet everyday needs
   (C) How Egyptians used the flooding of the Nile in agriculture
   (D) How Egyptians flourished because the Nile was a source of drinking water

2) Why does the professor state that vast deserts surround the Nile River?
   (A) To explain why most Egyptian resources came from the Nile
   (B) To show how geographically diverse the country of Egypt is
   (C) To explain why Egyptian culture developed in isolation from other cultures
   (D) To explain the hot climate in Egypt

3) How did Egyptians use the plants along the Nile River?
   (A) By harvesting them for crops
   (B) By weaving them for use as river rafts
   (C) By making medicines to treat various illnesses
   (D) By making clothing, paper and other necessities

4) How did Egyptians use rocks and minerals from the desert?
   (A) To improve the flavor of various foods
   (B) To make fertilizer for the flax crop
   (C) To make a unique black eye makeup
   (D) To create building materials

5) Listen to **Track 3.02**.
   Why does the professor say this?
   (A) To show that aspects of culture, such as makeup, may develop for practical reasons
   (B) To show that Egyptians were very concerned with using cosmetics to look younger
   (C) To demonstrate that Egyptians did not rely only on the Nile for resources
   (D) To transition to a discussion about modern science

6) What can be inferred about ancient Egypt based on the information in the lecture?
   (A) The annual flooding of the Nile made farming impossible in ancient Egypt.
   (B) The annual flooding of the Nile destroyed many Egyptian homes.
   (C) Ancient Egypt was underpopulated because few could withstand the heat.
   (D) Ancient Egypt would not have thrived without the Nile River.

Take notes as you listen to the conversation on **Track 3.03**. Then answer the multiple-choice questions that follow.

- critical analysis paper
- *The Great Gatsby*
- Greek tragedies
- tragic hero
- introduction

Things to Consider

WHAT is the conversation about?

WHAT details contribute to the main idea?

WHY are the speakers having the conversation?

HOW do the speakers organize and present the conversation?

Notes

_____
_____
_____
_____
_____
_____
_____
_____

Circle the letter next to the correct answer or answers to each of the multiple-choice questions below.

1) Why does the student visit the professor?
   (A) To ask the professor to proofread his paper
   (B) To get help with writing an introduction to his paper
   (C) To explain why he does not have a topic for his paper
   (D) To criticize the teacher's interpretation of *The Great Gatsby*

2) Listen to **Track 3.04**.
   Why does the professor say this?
   (A) To differentiate research papers from analysis papers
   (B) To identify a common problem among writers
   (C) To explain why the student received a bad grade
   (D) To anticipate what the student's problem is

3) The student believes that *The Great Gatsby* includes similarities to which of the following?
   (A) Greek tragedies
   (B) Superhero comics
   (C) Literary criticisms
   (D) Roman comedies

4) Listen to **Track 3.05**.
   What is suggested about Oedipus and Pentheus from this?
   (A) They are famous Greek authors.
   (B) They are characters from *The Great Gatsby*.
   (C) They are friends of the student.
   (D) They are characters from Greek tragedies.

5) Which of the following best describes the professor's attitude toward the student?
   (A) Confused
   (B) Bored
   (C) Supportive
   (D) Resentful

ACTUAL PRACTICE 1

Take notes as you listen to the lecture on **Track 3.06**. Then answer the multiple-choice questions that follow.

Psychology

- clinical depression
- brain chemistry
- nervous system
- oxytocin

Things to Consider

WHAT is the lecture about?

WHAT details contribute to the main idea?

WHY does the speaker present the lecture information?

HOW does the speaker organize and present the lecture?

Notes

_____
_____
_____
_____
_____
_____
_____
_____

Circle the letter next to the correct answer or answers to each of the multiple-choice questions below.

1) What is the main topic of the lecture?
   (A) The positive effects of reducing oxytocin levels in certain people
   (B) The symptoms and underlying causes of depression
   (C) The pros and cons on taking medication to treat depression
   (D) The environmental factors that can lead to depression

2) How many Americans suffer from clinical depression and anxiety at any given time?
   (A) 190 million
   (B) 19 million
   (C) 1.9 million
   (D) 5 million

3) Which of the following are symptoms of depression?

   Choose 2 answers.

   (A) Delusions and hallucinations
   (B) Difficulties sleeping
   (C) Excess energy
   (D) Feelings of hopelessness

4) Listen to **Track 3.07**.
   Why does the professor say this?
   (A) To explain why depression is often so difficult to treat
   (B) To illustrate the relationship between mood and emotion
   (C) To describe the symptoms of depression in greater detail
   (D) To emphasize the relationship between brain chemistry and stress levels

5) Why does the professor talk about brain chemistry?
   (A) To point out some flaws with current treatments for clinical depression
   (B) To differentiate clinical depression from other anxiety disorders
   (C) To explain some possible biological causes of clinical depression.
   (D) To demonstrate how clinical depression always causes permanent brain damage

6) The professor mentions a chemical called *oxytocin*, which increases feelings of comfort and security. What can be inferred about oxytocin?
   (A) Doctors regard oxytocin as the most important brain chemical.
   (B) Oxytocin levels increase when a person is isolated from others.
   (C) Many people with depression do not produce enough oxytocin.
   (D) Many doctors believe that consuming oxytocin cures depression.

Take notes as you listen to the lecture on **Track 3.08**. Then answer the multiple-choice questions that follow.

Philosophy

intelligence   environment
adapting   abstract thought

Things to Consider

WHAT is the lecture about?

WHAT details contribute to the main idea?

WHY does the speaker present the lecture information?

HOW does the speaker organize and present the lecture?

Notes
_____
_____
_____
_____
_____
_____
_____
_____
_____

Circle the letter next to the correct answer or answers to each of the multiple-choice questions below.

1) What is the main purpose of the lecture?
   (A) To discuss some definitions of "intelligence"
   (B) To determine how to measure animal intelligence
   (C) To differentiate abstract and concrete thought
   (D) To prove that humans are the most intelligent organisms

2) Why does the professor state that the term "intelligence" has many definitions?
   (A) To explain why humans are more intelligent that animals
   (B) To emphasize that different professions assign different characteristics to intelligence
   (C) To differentiate qualities of human intelligence from qualities of animal intelligence
   (D) To show why only philosophers discuss the term "intelligence"

3) What is the professor's example of adapting to one's environment?
   (A) Finding water in the desert
   (B) Starting a fire in a rainstorm
   (C) Building a shelter in the snow
   (D) Using GPS to find a way to the store

4) Listen to **Track 3.09**.
   What does the professor suggest when he says this?
   (A) Dolphins are probably more creative than ants.
   (B) An animal must demonstrate the ability for abstract thought to be considered intelligent.
   (C) Communicating with dolphins and ants would prove that they are the most intelligent animals.
   (D) Communication barriers prevent humans from determining animals' levels of intelligence.

5) How does the professor define "abstract thoughts"?
   (A) As concrete objects that can be objectively measured
   (B) As ideas or concepts that cannot be perceived with the senses
   (C) As the foundation of a moral philosophy of good versus evil
   (D) As another term for the phenomenon of "daydreaming"

6) What does the professor imply at the end of the discussion?
   (A) Intelligence is the only important factor for an animal's survival.
   (B) Philosophers always need concrete definitions for abstract terms.
   (C) The ability for abstract thought is the most important determiner of intelligence.
   (D) Sometimes describing a term is more useful than defining it.

Take notes as you listen to the conversation on **Track 3.10**. Then answer the multiple-choice questions that follow.

> job fair   dress nicely
> school website   resume

Things to Consider

WHAT is the conversation about?

WHAT details contribute to the main idea?

WHY are the speakers having the conversation?

HOW do the speakers organize and present the conversation?

Notes
_____
_____
_____
_____
_____
_____
_____
_____

Circle the letter next to the correct answer or answers to each of the multiple-choice questions below.

1) Why does the student talk with the university employee?
   (A) To apply for an on-campus job opening
   (B) To learn how to prepare for job interviews
   (C) To get information about an upcoming job fair
   (D) To ask the university employee to proofread her resume

2) What is the student's major?
   (A) Education
   (B) Accounting
   (C) Business
   (D) Psychology

3) Listen to **Track 3.11**.
   Why does the student probably say this?
   (A) She worries that she is asking too many questions.
   (B) She is becoming annoyed by the university employee.
   (C) She talks to the university employee daily.
   (D) She wants to speak with a different university employee.

4) According to the university employee, how should the student prepare for the job fair?
   Choose 2 answers.
   (A) By talking to her professors
   (B) By dressing well
   (C) By bringing her resume
   (D) By bringing her school transcript

5) Based on the information in the conversation, what can be inferred about job fairs?
   (A) They can benefit both students and local businesses.
   (B) They only benefit students majoring in business or accounting.
   (C) They are often major expenses for local businesses.
   (D) They are great places to make new friends.

ACTUAL PRACTICE 2

Take notes as you listen to the lecture on **Track 3.12**. Then answer the multiple-choice questions that follow.

English Literature

mystery writer
Agatha Christie

predictable
suspense

Things to Consider

WHAT is the lecture about?

WHAT details contribute to the main idea?

WHY does the speaker present the lecture information?

HOW does the speaker organize and present the lecture?

Notes

_____
_____
_____
_____
_____
_____
_____
_____

Circle the letter next to the correct answer or answers to each of the multiple-choice questions below.

1) What is the main topic of the lecture?
   (A) Agatha Christie's long and successful career as a writer
   (B) The importance of England's most influential mystery writers
   (C) The debate surrounding the quality of Agatha Christie's writing
   (D) The formulaic and poorly written novels of Agatha Christie

2) Why does the professor list how many copies of Agatha Christie's book have been sold?
   (A) To show that many readers have poor taste in literature
   (B) To suggest that people like to read about the lives of rich people
   (C) To imply that critics of her work are jealous of her success
   (D) To show that her books are very popular

3) According to the lecture, which of the following are criticisms leveled against Christie's novels?
   Choose 2 answers.
   (A) They often have predictable plots.
   (B) They are too focused on police and court procedures.
   (C) They support hurtful racial stereotypes.
   (D) They are too focused on the lives of the rich.

4) Listen to **Track 3.13**.
   What does the professor suggest when he says this?
   (A) Christie repeatedly uses the same plot in the same way.
   (B) Christie changed plot details to make each story original.
   (C) Christie's supporters believe that she actually used many different plots.
   (D) Christie made her plots predictable so readers could figure out the ending.

5) What does the professor suggest when he claims that Agatha Christie "does not seem dazzled by rich people"?
   (A) Agatha Christie thought that rich people were better than poor people.
   (B) Agatha Christie was not impressed when rich people wore too much jewelry.
   (C) Agatha Christie enjoyed staying in the homes of rich friends.
   (D) Agatha Christie thought that rich people were much the same as other people.

6) Why does the professor believe that Agatha Christie set so many of her mystery novels in rich country homes?
   (A) To show that there was more crime in the country than in the city
   (B) To demonstrate her ability to describe the beautiful English countryside
   (C) To create a setting where the characters could believably stay until the mystery was solved
   (D) To honestly convey the country life that she and her friends enjoyed

Take notes as you listen to the lecture on **Track 3.14**. Then answer the multiple-choice questions that follow.

Education

child
art
scribbling stage
pre-schematic stage
schematic stage

Things to Consider

WHAT is the lecture about?

WHAT details contribute to the main idea?

WHY does the speaker present the lecture information?

HOW does the speaker organize and present the lecture?

Notes

Circle the letter next to the correct answer or answers to each of the multiple-choice questions below.

1) What is the main purpose of the lecture?
   (A) To train preschool teachers to identify talented young artists
   (B) To explain which art supplies are appropriate for which age levels
   (C) To encourage parents to give their children art materials
   (D) To suggest that artistic development reflects cognitive development

2) What might a child in the pre-schematic stage draw?
   (A) Many figures that are the same size, shape, and color
   (B) A picture made up entirely of circles, without any lines
   (C) A figure with a circular face, legs, and possibly arms
   (D) A picture that would be exhibited in museum galleries and exhibitions

3) What might a child in the schematic stage draw?
   (A) Pictures with planned scenes and landscapes
   (B) Pictures of people without bodies or faces
   (C) Pictures of circles, without lines
   (D) Pictures of sports cars and animated characters

4) Why does the professor describe children in the schematic stage as drawing as though they have "X-ray vision"?
   (A) To show that children in the schematic stage think that they have super powers
   (B) To show that children at this stage are very concerned about broken bones
   (C) To explain that children in this stage may draw the inside of things
   (D) To point out that some children are already interested in medical science

5) What does the professor imply about the importance of art supplies to the cognitive development of young children?
   (A) Children will not develop cognitively without access to art materials.
   (B) Children should study art more than they should study reading and writing.
   (C) Children's access to art supplies will help teachers measure their development.
   (D) The best schools will always have the best art supplies and the smartest children.

6) Why does the professor divide a child's artistic development into different stages?
   (A) To show what kinds of art materials are best for each age group of children
   (B) To help teachers plan lessons for art class for young children
   (C) To describe typical patterns of growth in thinking
   (D) To show how to help children keep up with their age group in drawing skills

Take notes as you listen to the conversation on **Track 3.15**. Then answer the multiple-choice questions that follow.

final project   Greek history

Things to Consider

WHAT is the conversation about?

WHAT details contribute to the main idea?

WHY are the speakers having the conversation?

HOW do the speakers organize and present the conversation?

Notes

Circle the correct answer or answers to each of the multiple-choice questions below.

1) Why does the student visit the professor?
   (A) To give a presentation for a class project
   (B) To review the requirements for a large assignment
   (C) To retake an exam that he did poorly on
   (D) To ask about the correct translation of a Greek text

2) Listen to **Track 3.16**.
   Why does the professor say this?
   (A) To congratulate the student for his preparedness
   (B) To imply that the student is doing poorly in class
   (C) To state that the student asks too many questions
   (D) To emphasize the importance of the final project

3) Which of the following are components of the student's final project?
   Choose 2 answers.
   (A) A historical reenactment
   (B) A research paper
   (C) A presentation
   (D) A short story

4) For the translation portion of the project, why must the student turn in the original text along with his translation?
   (A) So the professor can determine if the student's translation is plagiarized
   (B) So the professor can check the accuracy of the student's translation
   (C) So the student can read the original text aloud to the class
   (D) So the student can submit his translation to be published

5) Based on the conversation, what class of the student's does the professor probably teach?
   (A) The Cultures of Ancient Greece
   (B) Medieval Latin Literature
   (C) Linguistics
   (D) The Archaeology of Ancient Egypt

Take notes as you listen to the lecture on **Track 3.17**. Then answer the multiple-choice questions that follow.

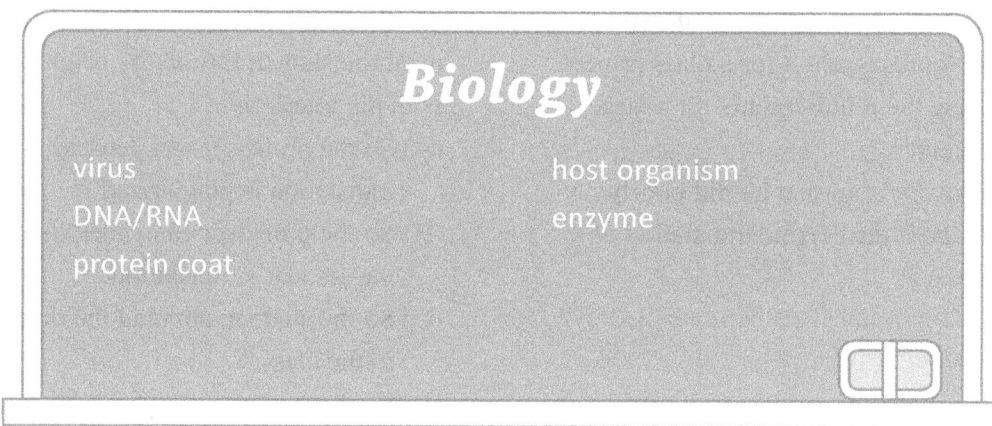

Things to Consider

WHAT is the lecture about?

WHAT details contribute to the main idea?

WHY does the speaker present the lecture information?

HOW does the speaker organize and present the lecture?

Notes

_____
_____
_____
_____
_____
_____
_____
_____

Circle the letter next to the correct answer or answers to each of the multiple-choice questions below.

1) What is the main topic of the lecture?
   (A) Small, simple organisms that need other organisms to reproduce
   (B) Differences between the structures of DNA and RNA
   (C) The process that leads to the formation of human cells
   (D) Similarities between viruses and bacteria

2) According to the professor, what is the "main part" of a virus?
   (A) Its protective protein coating
   (B) Its outer coating of fat that protects it
   (C) Its DNA or RNA
   (D) The enzymes it uses to reproduce

3) Why is it not possible for a virus to reproduce without a host cell?
   (A) A virus does not have the genetic code necessary for reproduction.
   (B) A virus lacks a protective protein coating.
   (C) A virus is too large to reproduce without a host cell.
   (D) A virus lacks the enzymes necessary to reproduce without a host cell.

4) Why does the professor compare a virus to an architect?
   (A) The virus makes the DNA or RNA code, which is like an architect's blueprints.
   (B) The virus makes scale models of the new cells for the host cell to copy.
   (C) The virus uses its protective protein coating to make a plan for new cells.
   (D) The virus uses its layer of protective fat to mold new cells and replicate itself.

5) Why does the professor compare the enzymes of a host cell to construction workers?
   (A) The enzymes of the host cell build the new virus.
   (B) The enzymes of the host cell break down the protective protein of the virus.
   (C) The enzymes of the host cell build a wall around a virus.
   (D) The enzymes of the host cell stop the virus from reproducing.

6) Listen to **Track 3.18**.
   What does the professor suggest when he says this?
   (A) Viruses only target very large cells.
   (B) Viruses often harm their host organisms.
   (C) Viruses are usually destroyed before they can reproduce.
   (D) Viruses reproduce slowly in their host organisms.

Take notes as you listen to the lecture on **Track 3.19**. Then answer the multiple-choice questions that follow.

Modern Dance

George Balanchine
ballet
Russia

Things to Consider

WHAT is the lecture about?

WHAT details contribute to the main idea?

WHY does the speaker present the lecture information?

HOW does the speaker organize and present the lecture?

Notes

_____
_____
_____
_____
_____
_____
_____
_____
_____
_____

Circle the letter next to the correct answer or answers to each of the multiple-choice questions below.

1) What is the main topic of the lecture?
   (A) A choreographer who is often criticized for his lack of formal training
   (B) A dancer who rigorously trained in Russian ballet
   (C) A choreographer who revolutionized ballet
   (D) A dancer who only performed in Broadway shows and Hollywood movies

2) What characteristics did George Balanchine value in dancers?
   Choose 2 answers.
   (A) Acting skills
   (B) Daintiness
   (C) Athleticism
   (D) Long legs

3) How were Balanchine's ballets different from ballets of the past?
   (A) Balanchine's ballets are based on the plays of William Shakespeare.
   (B) Balanchine's ballets are based on stories from Greek Myth.
   (C) Balanchine's ballets are based on traditional Russian folk tales.
   (D) Balanchine's ballets are abstract and do not tell a story.

4) Listen to **Track 3.20**.
   Why does the professor say this about George Balanchine?
   (A) To show that Balanchine understood traditional ballet
   (B) To show that Balanchine was an outsider who did not like ballet
   (C) To show that Balanchine was copying ballets from Russia and France
   (D) To show that Balanchine preferred ballroom dancing to ballet

5) Why does the professor end the lecture by explaining some common criticisms of Balanchine's works?
   (A) To emphasize that dancers no longer appreciate Balanchine's works
   (B) To show how views of ballet have changed in recent decades
   (C) To argue that Balanchine never understood the fundamentals of ballet
   (D) To point out how underappreciated Balanchine's work is today

6) What does this lecture imply about the art of ballet?
   (A) It is influenced by the past but still changes over time.
   (B) It should follow the rules established by great artists of the past.
   (C) It needs to change everything about the art or become boring.
   (D) It should only be about the physical strength of the dancers.

ACTUAL PRACTICE 4

Take notes as you listen to the conversation on **Track 3.21**. Then answer the multiple-choice questions that follow.

> extra credit presentation
>
> research paper

Things to Consider

WHAT is the conversation about?

WHAT details contribute to the main idea?

WHY are the speakers having the conversation?

HOW do the speakers organize and present the conversation?

Notes

_____
_____
_____
_____
_____
_____
_____
_____

Circle the letter next to the correct answer or answers to each of the multiple-choice questions below.

1) Why does the student go to talk with the professor?
   (A) To ask for more time to complete an extra credit assignment
   (B) To ask the professor to help her complete a research paper
   (C) To turn in a late assignment to improve her grade
   (D) To ask about an upcoming extra credit opportunity

2) Listen to **Track 3.22**.
   Why does the professor say this?
   (A) To congratulate the student for having the highest grade in the class
   (B) To explain why the professor questions the student's desire for extra credit
   (C) To point out to the student that the professor does not have a good memory
   (D) To explain why the professor will not be offering any extra credit opportunities

3) Listen to **Track 3.23**.
   Why does the professor say this?
   (A) He appreciates the student's desire for a good grade.
   (B) He has determined what will be included in the extra credit assignment.
   (C) He looks up to the student as a role model.
   (D) He is determined to give the student a "B" in the class.

4) According to the professor, when will students give their extra credit presentations?
   (A) Next week
   (B) On the last day of class
   (C) In two weeks
   (D) On the day of the final exam

5) Listen to **Track 3.24**.
   What is the student's attitude when she says this?
   (A) Hesitant
   (B) Nostalgic
   (C) Optimistic
   (D) Confused

Take notes as you listen to the lecture on **Track 3.25**. Then answer the multiple-choice questions that follow.

Things to Consider

WHAT is the lecture about?

WHAT details contribute to the main idea?

WHY does the speaker present the lecture information?

HOW does the speaker organize and present the lecture?

Notes

_____
_____
_____
_____
_____
_____
_____
_____

Circle the letter next to the correct answer or answers to each of the multiple-choice questions below.

1) What is the main topic of the professor's lecture?
   (A) The accounts of people who were kidnapped
   (B) The use of brainwashing by politicians
   (C) The differences between brainwashing and thought-control
   (D) The steps involved in changing a person's beliefs

2) Listen to **Track 3.26**.
   What can be inferred from this?
   (A) People attempt to brainwash others for social, political, and religious reasons.
   (B) Brainwashing used to be much more common than it is today.
   (C) Religious cults brainwash people more than any other group.
   (D) Brainwashing is not usually regarded as a serious crime.

3) What is usually the first step in brainwashing?
   (A) Keeping the victim well-fed and well-rested
   (B) Providing the victim with opportunities to contact friends and family
   (C) Keeping the victim hungry, tired, and alone
   (D) Threatening the victim with torture and punishment

4) What is the last step in the brainwashing process?
   (A) Convince the victim that there is no hope of survival
   (B) Offer the victim a chance to feel safe and loved
   (C) Reunite the victim with family and friends
   (D) Remind the victim of his or her original beliefs and values

5) According to the lecture, brainwashing works because people have which need?
   (A) To feel cared for and accepted
   (B) To please friends and family
   (C) To forget about past events
   (D) To learn valuable new information

6) What can you infer about human personality and identity from the lecture?
   (A) Brainwashing changes a person's identity, but not his or her personality.
   (B) There is no relationship between personality and identity.
   (C) Personality and identity are not concrete and can be changed.
   (D) People's personalities and identities are formed at birth.

Take notes as you listen to the lecture on **Track 3.27**. Then answer the multiple-choice questions that follow.

Nutritional Science

- gluten
- wheat-based products
- celiac disease
- FODMAPs

Things to Consider

WHAT is the lecture about?

WHAT details contribute to the main idea?

WHY does the speaker present the lecture information?

HOW does the speaker organize and present the lecture?

Notes

Circle the letter next to the correct answer or answers to each of the multiple-choice questions below.

1) What is the main purpose of the lecture?
   (A) To criticize people who consume excessive amounts of gluten
   (B) To address a common misconception about gluten intake
   (C) To discuss the causes of celiac disease
   (D) To examine the success of some popular American diet plans

2) According to the professor, what percentage of people have a disease that prevents them from digesting gluten properly?
   (A) About 5%
   (B) About 50%
   (C) About 1%
   (D) About 10%

3) Which of the following provides the best description of FODMAPs?
   (A) A group of carbohydrates that are difficult for the body to process
   (B) A carbohydrate that causes symptoms such as sleepiness and memory loss
   (C) A group of carbohydrates responsible for causing celiac disease
   (D) A group of food products high in essential nutrients such as fiber and calcium

4) Listen to **Track 3.28**.
   Why does the professor say this?
   (A) To explain why so many people experience symptoms that they mistakenly attribute to gluten intolerance
   (B) To criticize people for consuming too many foods that are high in carbohydrates
   (C) To recommend that all people remove apples, avocados, wheat, and tofu from their diets
   (D) To point out foods that can lead to the development of celiac disease

5) According to the professor, what is the relationship between gluten intolerance and FODMAPs?
   (A) People with gluten intolerance should consume more products containing FODMAPs.
   (B) Gluten is a key component in all products containing FODMAPs.
   (C) Consuming FODMAPs leads to the development of gluten intolerance.
   (D) The symptoms of gluten intolerance may be caused by FODMAPs.

6) What does the professor's lecture suggest about people who self-diagnose medical conditions or food allergies?
   (A) They may save their own lives without going to the doctor.
   (B) They may save money by avoiding unnecessary doctor's appointments and lab tests.
   (C) They may be unnecessarily removing important nutrients from their diet.
   (D) They should remove avocados and apples from their diet.

ACTUAL PRACTICE 5

Take notes as you listen to the conversation on **Track 3.29**. Then answer the multiple-choice questions that follow.

> graduate biology major
> upper-division on track
> general education requirements

Things to Consider

WHAT is the conversation about?

WHAT details contribute to the main idea?

WHY are the speakers having the conversation?

HOW do the speakers organize and present the conversation?

Notes

_____
_____
_____
_____
_____
_____
_____
_____
_____

Circle the letter next to the correct answer or answers to each of the multiple-choice questions below.

1) Why does the student visit the advisor?
   (A) To see if the university will offer any biology labs next year
   (B) To switch his major from biology to academic advising
   (C) To confirm that he can graduate at the end of next year
   (D) To register for some general education classes

2) Why does the advisor ask for the student's name and student ID number?
   (A) To help the student fill out an application to switch majors
   (B) To make sure that student's name is spelled correctly on his diploma
   (C) To respond to the student's complaint that there are not enough general education classes
   (D) To access the student's transcript in the university's computer system

3) Listen to **Track 3.30**.
   What does the student imply when he says this?
   (A) He has to take more classes than he had thought in order to graduate.
   (B) He is afraid that he will fail his general education classes.
   (C) He does not think that the university offers the classes that he needs to take.
   (D) He has accidentally registered for the wrong classes.

4) According to the advisor, what class can the student take to fulfill two general education requirements?
   (A) A biology lab
   (B) An art history class
   (C) An upper-division biology class
   (D) A women's studies class

5) Listen to **Track 3.31**.
   What best describes the student's attitude toward the advisor when he says this?
   (A) Sarcastic
   (B) Attentive
   (C) Surprised
   (D) Appreciative

Take notes as you listen to the lecture on **Track 3.32**. Then answer the multiple-choice questions that follow.

Literature

situational irony
subvert expectations

Things to Consider

WHAT is the lecture about?

WHAT details contribute to the main idea?

WHY does the speaker present the lecture information?

HOW does the speaker organize and present the lecture?

Notes

Circle the letter next to the correct answer or answers to each of the multiple-choice questions below.

1) What is the main topic of this lecture?
   (A) The use of dramatic irony in literature
   (B) Common plot structures of television shows
   (C) Situations that go against expectations
   (D) The differences between tragedy and comedy

2) What can be inferred about irony from the beginning of the professor's lecture?
   (A) Irony occurs very often in media and in our daily lives.
   (B) Irony is a cruel form of humor and hurts people's feelings.
   (C) Irony was first used very recently.
   (D) Irony is only depicted in fictional situations.

3) How does the woman prepare for the trivia competition?
   (A) She watches quiz shows on television.
   (B) She takes on-line courses in history and popular culture.
   (C) She participates in other contests for practice.
   (D) She buys and studies books on trivia.

4) What "mystery prize" does the woman in the story win?
   (A) A book store gift certificate
   (B) A collection of trivia books
   (C) An expensive vacation
   (D) A collection of gift wrapping paper

5) Listen to **Track 3.33**.
   Why does the professor say this?
   (A) To introduce a new type of irony to the class
   (B) To provide more examples of situations with unexpected results
   (C) To show that most examples of situational irony involve public safety
   (D) To make the students laugh and forget the lesson

6) What can be inferred about comedy in general from the lecture?
   (A) Comedy is more popular with most audiences than tragedy.
   (B) Trivia competitions are similar to comedies.
   (C) Comedy often subverts our expectations to make us laugh.
   (D) Comedy is much harder to perform than tragedy.

Take notes as you listen to the lecture on **Track 3.34**. Then answer the multiple-choice questions that follow.

European History

Industrial Revolution
craftspeople
textile mills

Luddites
General Ludd
British government

Things to Consider

WHAT is the lecture about?

WHAT details contribute to the main idea?

WHY does the speaker present the lecture information?

HOW does the speaker organize and present the lecture?

Notes

_____
_____
_____
_____
_____
_____
_____
_____

Circle the letter next to the correct answer or answers to each of the multiple-choice questions below.

1) What is the main topic of the lecture?
   (A) A group of revolutionaries who rejected certain aspects of industrial manufacturing
   (B) The social and economic changes that resulted from the Industrial Revolution
   (C) A controversial war hero known as General Ludd
   (D) British resistance to the rise of industrialism in France

2) Why did the Luddites destroy industrial equipment?
   (A) To avoid having to use dangerous machinery
   (B) To create more work for equipment manufacturing companies
   (C) To honor the memory of General Ludd
   (D) To ensure that factories would have to keep skilled textile craftspeople

3) What international event was happening during the Luddite revolution?
   (A) The British were at war with Spain.
   (B) The British were invading Germany.
   (C) The British were settling Canada.
   (D) The British were at war with France.

4) Why were Luddites sent to penal colonies in Australia?
   (A) To build a skilled labor force for the new colony
   (B) To keep them out of British military forces
   (C) To keep them from demonstrating in England
   (D) To supply the British Army with new uniforms

5) Although the Luddite movement lasted only five years, how is its influence still felt?
   (A) Ludd Day is still celebrated as a holiday in England.
   (B) "Luddite" is still associated with a mistrust of technology.
   (C) England is still at war with France.
   (D) People who make clothes are called "Luddites."

6) What does the modern appeal of Luddites suggest about society?
   (A) People still respect skilled laborers.
   (B) Not enough people understand British history.
   (C) Some people fear changes in technology.
   (D) Most people today support changes in technology.

Take notes as you listen to the conversation on **Track 3.35**. Then answer the multiple-choice questions that follow.

> Greek tragedy
> *catharsis*
>
> emotional relief
> *Titanic*

Things to Consider

WHAT is the conversation about?

WHAT details contribute to the main idea?

WHY are the speakers having the conversation?

HOW do the speakers organize and present the conversation?

Notes

_____
_____
_____
_____
_____
_____
_____
_____

Circle the letter next to the correct answer or answers to each of the multiple-choice questions below.

1) Why does the student visit the professor?
   (A) To criticize the professor's incorrect use of a term
   (B) To show the professor that he understands Greek tragedy
   (C) To explain a confusing concept to the professor
   (D) To ask the professor to clarify a confusing concept

2) Why does the professor ask the student to name a sad film?
   (A) To illustrate the idea that all emotions are subjective
   (B) To help illustrate the concept of *catharsis*
   (C) To point out differences between Greek tragedies and modern films
   (D) To discuss the saddest movies

3) Listen to **Track 3.36**.
   What does the student mean when he says this?
   (A) He has just realized that he is speaking to the wrong professor.
   (B) He does not know where the professor's classroom is located.
   (C) He is not paying attention to the professor.
   (D) He is confused about the professor's statement.

4) According to the professor, what is the purpose of *catharsis*?
   (A) To help people better understand the events of a play or a film
   (B) To make the events of plays and films seem more believable
   (C) To find relief by releasing strong feelings of pity and fear
   (D) To persuade audiences to cheer for the villain of a play or a film

5) Based on the conversation, what can be inferred about *catharsis*?
   (A) It is an experience that spans generations and cultures.
   (B) It did not exist before the release of the film *Titanic*.
   (C) It can lead to feelings of depression and anxiety.
   (D) It can only be experienced by those viewing Greek tragedies.

Take notes as you listen to the lecture on **Track 3.37**. Then answer the multiple-choice questions that follow.

Physics

atoms
nucleus
protons
neutrons
electrons
fusion

Things to Consider

WHAT is the lecture about?

WHAT details contribute to the main idea?

WHY does the speaker present the lecture information?

HOW does the speaker organize and present the lecture?

Notes

Circle the letter next to the correct answer or answers to each of the multiple-choice questions below.

1) What is the main topic of the lecture?
   (A) The differences between the various particles found within an atom
   (B) The relationship between the speed and the size of an atom
   (C) How scientists can describe the structure of an atom despite its small size
   (D) The process in which two atoms merge together to create a heavier element

2) Which of the following particles are present in the nucleus of an atom?
   Choose 2 answers.
   (A) Electron
   (B) Proton
   (C) Neutron
   (D) Hydrogen

3) Listen to **Track 3.38**.
   Why does the professor say this?
   (A) To point out a peculiar feature of atomic fusion
   (B) To explain why fusion is important to energy production
   (C) To explain why iron is such an abundant element
   (D) To point out reasons for the Sun's brightness

4) According to the professor, where does the process of atomic fusion commonly occur?
   (A) On spaceships
   (B) Within active stars
   (C) Inside electrons
   (D) In empty space

5) Why do scientists hope to control the process of atomic fusion?
   (A) To create new elements for research purposes
   (B) To better understand how the universe formed
   (C) To harvest the energy created during fusion
   (D) To disprove claims that fusion is actually impossible

6) What topic will the class probably discuss next?
   (A) Star formation
   (B) Properties of heavy elements
   (C) Fundamental forces
   (D) The process of fission

Take notes as you listen to the lecture on **Track 3.39**. Then answer the multiple-choice questions that follow.

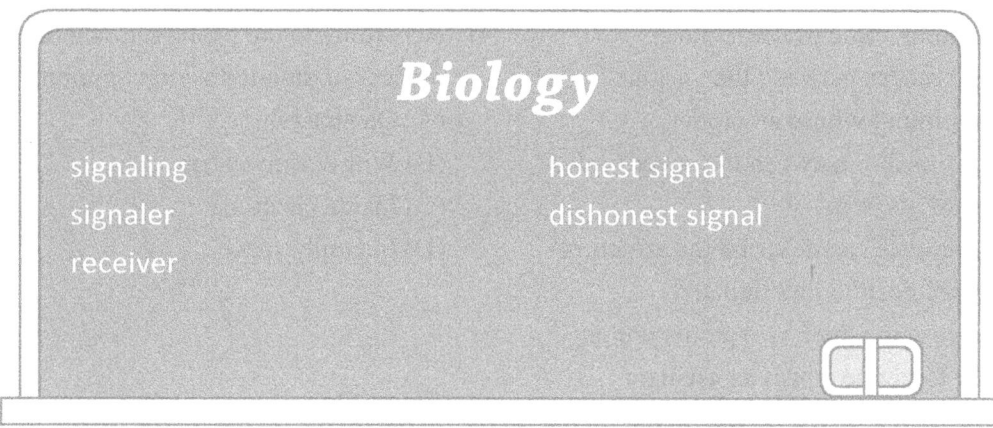

Things to Consider

WHAT is the lecture about?

WHAT details contribute to the main idea?

WHY does the speaker present the lecture information?

HOW does the speaker organize and present the lecture?

Notes

Circle the letter next to the correct answer or answers to each of the multiple-choice questions below.

1) What is the main idea of this lecture?
   (A) An ecosystem's food chain
   (B) Effective hunting strategies of predators
   (C) Relationships within bird flocks
   (D) Forms of animal communication

2) Why do some bird flocks choose an "alert bird"?
   (A) To warn the flock of impending climate changes
   (B) To warn the flock of predators
   (C) To locate the best feeding and resting locations
   (D) To guard the nests while the other birds sleep

3) Why do some birds use dishonest signals?
   (A) To confuse birds that they do not like
   (B) To hide food from other birds
   (C) To protect their own flock from predators
   (D) To show predators where there are other flocks to attack

4) What kinds of signals do animals primarily send?
   (A) Simple and complex signals
   (B) Honest and dishonest signals
   (C) Food and water signals
   (D) Predator and prey signals

5) Listen to **Track 3.40**.
   What can be inferred about signaling among alert birds from this?
   (A) Honest signals are more common than dishonest signals.
   (B) Dishonest signals always benefit predators.
   (C) Alert birds emit honest and dishonest signals at random.
   (D) Predators are never deceived by alert birds' dishonest signals.

6) What can you infer from the fact that birds use honest and dishonest signals?
   (A) Wild animals cannot be trusted and should not be kept as pets.
   (B) Animals know the difference between right and wrong.
   (C) Animal communication is more complicated than may seem.
   (D) Hunters need more sophisticated calls to attract birds to shoot.

Take notes as you listen to the conversation on **Track 3.41**. Then answer the multiple-choice questions that follow.

European history major
petition
credit

anthropology
archaeology

Things to Consider

WHAT is the conversation about?

WHAT details contribute to the main idea?

WHY does the speaker present the lecture information?

HOW do the speakers organize and present the conversation?

Notes
_____
_____
_____
_____
_____
_____
_____
_____
_____

Circle the letter next to the correct answer or answers to each of the multiple-choice questions below.

1) Why does the student visit the advisor?
   (A) To see if he can retake a class that he did poorly in
   (B) To see if he can become a teaching assistant for one of his classes
   (C) To see if he can complete an anthropology minor before he graduates
   (D) To see how many classes he has to take to complete his major

2) What is the name of the archaeology class that the student is taking?
   (A) Rebellion and Revolution
   (B) Excavating Ancient Britain
   (C) Digging for the Truth
   (D) Conquest in the West

3) Listen to **Track 3.42**.
   Why does the student say this?
   (A) To point out one reason that he finds the "Excavating Ancient Britain" class so interesting
   (B) To explain why the "Excavating Ancient Britain" class should count toward his major
   (C) To point out the differences between history and archaeology to the advisor
   (D) To explain why he believes that the "Excavating Ancient Britain" class is too difficult for him

4) What is the student's attitude when he is told that one of his classes does not count toward his major?
   (A) Confused and somewhat upset
   (B) Uncaring and somewhat rude
   (C) Calm and accepting
   (D) Sad and shy

5) What will the student probably do next?
   (A) Drop out of the "Excavating Ancient Britain" class
   (B) Change his major from European history to anthropology
   (C) Locate the professor of the "Excavating Ancient Britain" class
   (D) Take the form that the advisor gave him to the head of the history department.

Take notes as you listen to the lecture on **Track 3.43**. Then answer the multiple-choice questions that follow.

Art History

- photographer
- Richard Avedon
- fashion
- Duchess
- social issues
- mental health hospital
- Duke

Things to Consider

WHAT is the lecture about?

WHAT details contribute to the main idea?

WHY does the speaker present the lecture information?

HOW does the speaker organize and present the lecture?

Notes

Circle the letter next to the correct answer or answers to each of the multiple-choice questions below.

1) What is the main topic of the lecture?
   (A) A photographer famous for photographing natural landscapes
   (B) A photographer famous for photographing household pets
   (C) A photographer famous for his war photography
   (D) A photographer famous for photographing fashion and celebrities

2) What are some important characteristics of Richard Avedon's fashion photography?
   Choose 2 answers.
   (A) His photographs emphasized durable, long-lasting clothing styles.
   (B) His models often appeared to be moving.
   (C) He preferred to take color photographs of models.
   (D) His photographs suggested stories.

3) What was unique about Richard Avedon's photography of mental hospital patients?
   (A) The patients were photographed exercising and playing games.
   (B) Avedon photographed patients receiving electric shock therapy.
   (C) The patients appeared calm and at peace in the photographs.
   (D) The patients in the photographs appear to be miserable.

4) Why did the professor include the detail of Richard Avedon lying to the Duke and Duchess of Windsor about his taxi hitting a dog?
   (A) To show that Richard Avedon had a cruel sense of humor
   (B) To give an example of how far Richard Avedon would go to get a good picture
   (C) To explain why the Duke and Duchess of Windsor established an animal shelter
   (D) To emphasize Richard Avedon's commitment to animal rights

5) What conclusions may be drawn about Richard Avedon's photographic career from this lecture?
   (A) Richard Avedon only cared about photographing the rich and famous.
   (B) Richard Avedon specialized in photographing animals and the mentally ill.
   (C) Richard Avedon was interested in photographing a wide variety of subjects.
   (D) Richard Avedon built his career around pet photography.

6) What can you infer about photography from the lecture on Richard Avedon?
   (A) Some photography can inspire social change.
   (B) Anyone can be a great photographer if they have the right equipment.
   (C) Mental patients are usually uncooperative photographic subjects.
   (D) Animals make the best photographic subjects.

Take notes as you listen to the lecture on **Track 3.44**. Then answer the multiple-choice questions that follow.

World History

agricultural production   M.S. Swaminathan
Green Revolution   famine
Norman Borlaug   yield
short-stemmed wheat

Things to Consider

WHAT is the lecture about?

WHAT details contribute to the main idea?

WHY does the speaker present the lecture information?

HOW does the speaker organize and present the lecture?

Notes

_____
_____
_____
_____
_____
_____
_____
_____

Circle the letter next to the correct answer or answers to each of the multiple-choice questions below.

1) What is the main topic of the lecture?
   (A) A farming technique used on algae and seaweed that is reducing world hunger
   (B) The pros and cons of some important 20th-century agricultural innovations
   (C) A farming technique that proved effective everywhere but Southeast Asia
   (D) The factors that led to an increase in world famine

2) Listen to **Track 3.45**.
   What can be inferred from this?
   (A) Famine is no longer an issue in any country.
   (B) Famine often leads to the migration of human populations to more stable environments.
   (C) International crises can lead to important innovations that can save or improve lives.
   (D) Many countries are unwilling to send disaster relief to countries that are in need.

3) According to the professor, what did the innovations of plant geneticists during the latter half of the 20th century lead to?
   (A) An increased production of wheat and rice
   (B) Reduced social tensions in developing nations
   (C) Taller wheat plants with lighter seed pods
   (D) A decrease in the use of agricultural chemicals

4) What was one consequence of using science to increase grain production?
   (A) The need for more manual labor by farmers in developing countries
   (B) The increased use of fish as a pest control device in rice paddies
   (C) The increased local production of agricultural chemicals and farming equipment
   (D) The increased dependence on imported seeds and chemicals

5) Why does the professor say that the Green Revolution "was *creating* entirely new problems"?
   (A) To show how new plants and technology were damaging family farms and crop diversity
   (B) To show that the new plants and technologies were creating more leisure time for farmers
   (C) To explain how agricultural production in several countries diminished
   (D) To explain why the United Nations supported the Green Revolution

6) What can be inferred from the fact that the Green Revolution also created problems?
   (A) Scientists should never try to alter agricultural practices.
   (B) Plant geneticists should be looking for other sources of grain.
   (C) Scientific innovation often has unforeseen consequences.
   (D) Farmers will often resist technological changes.

Take notes as you listen to the conversation on **Track 3.46**. Then answer the multiple-choice questions that follow.

picking a major
narrow down options

aptitude test

Things to Consider

WHAT is the conversation about?

WHAT details contribute to the main idea?

WHY are the speakers having the conversation?

HOW do the speakers organize and present the conversation?

Notes

_____
_____
_____
_____
_____
_____
_____
_____
_____

Circle the letter next to the correct answer or answers to each of the multiple-choice questions below.

1) Why does the student talk to the advisor?
   (A) To retake an aptitude test
   (B) Toa ask for help with planning her schedule
   (C) To receive help with deciding on an area of study
   (D) To switch majors from math to chemistry

2) Listen to **Track 3.47**.
   Why does the advisor say this?
   (A) To point out how helpful advisors are
   (B) To criticize the student's indecisiveness
   (C) To explain the difficulties of being an advisor
   (D) To calm and reassure the student

3) Why does the advisor recommend that the student take an aptitude test?
   (A) To determine her academic strengths
   (B) To improve her grade in a class
   (C) To find out what university she should attend
   (D) To discover the cause of her anxiety

4) Based on the information in the conversation, what can be inferred about the student?
   (A) She does not like taking science classes.
   (B) She is anxious to declare a major.
   (C) She has taken an aptitude test before.
   (D) She does not like attending the university.

5) What will the student probably do next?
   (A) Go to her next class
   (B) Drop out of the university
   (C) Decide on a major
   (D) Sign up for the aptitude test

Take notes as you listen to the lecture on **Track 3.48**. Then answer the multiple-choice questions that follow.

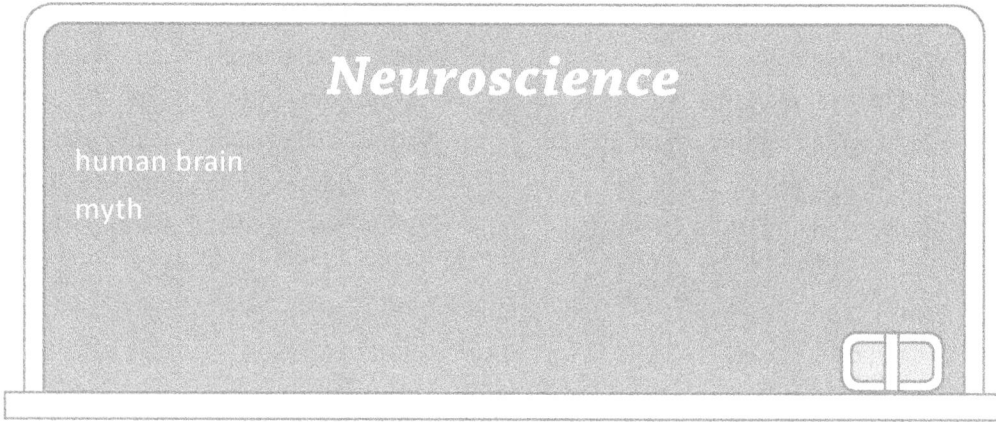

Things to Consider

WHAT is the lecture about?

WHAT details contribute to the main idea?

WHY does the speaker present the lecture information?

HOW does the speaker organize and present the lecture?

Notes

_____
_____
_____
_____
_____
_____
_____
_____

Circle the letter next to the correct answer or answers to each of the multiple-choice questions below.

1) What is the main purpose of the lecture?
   (A) To provide evidence for a controversial theory
   (B) To dismiss a commonly held scientific belief
   (C) To explain why brain scans are so useful
   (D) To point out the function of different parts of the brain

2) Why does the professor set out to disprove the myth that we only use 10% of our brains?
   (A) To prove that 90% of our brain is almost never being used
   (B) To imply that human beings are intellectually lazy
   (C) To encourage students to analyze scientific-sounding claims
   (D) To show how our unused brain capacity could solve all the world's problems

3) Listen to **Track 3.49**.
   Why does the professor say this?
   (A) To illustrate the relationship between radiation and electrons
   (B) To point out the difficulties of explaining scientific concepts to non-scientists
   (C) To explain why scientists study the color of the sky
   (D) To show that seemingly simple questions often have complex answers

4) According to the professor, why is the idea that humans only use 10% of their brains so appealing?
   (A) It proves that brain scans are the most effective way to study the brain.
   (B) It implies that humans have undiscovered mental capabilities.
   (C) It disproves the idea that education is necessary for success.
   (D) It explains why people become smarter as they grow older.

5) How does the professor organize the lecture?
   (A) He explains a myth and then discredits it using scientific evidence.
   (B) He presents a theory and then supports it using real-life examples.
   (C) He describes a process using examples from several academic fields.
   (D) He refutes a claim by having the students analyze a theory.

6) What can you infer from the professor's final question to the students?
   (A) There are other facts that refute the brain usage myth.
   (B) Disproving the brain usage myth is still a difficult task for scientists.
   (C) Most students still believe that people only use 10% of their brains.
   (D) The professor needs help remembering the facts.

Take notes as you listen to the lecture on **Track 3.50**. Then answer the multiple-choice questions that follow.

Nutritional Science

- starvation
- glucose
- ketone
- autophagy
- infections
- organ failure

Things to Consider

WHAT is the lecture about?

WHAT details contribute to the main idea?

WHY does the speaker present the lecture information?

HOW does the speaker organize and present the lecture?

Notes

_____
_____
_____
_____
_____
_____
_____
_____

Circle the letter next to the correct answer or answers to each of the multiple-choice questions below.

1) What is the main topic of this lecture on starvation?
   (A) The risks of a low calorie, high protein diet
   (B) The differences between hunger and starvation
   (C) The biology of the process of starvation
   (D) The best diets for weight loss

2) When are people considered to be "starving"?
   (A) When they have lost about 30% of body mass
   (B) When they have not eaten in more than two days
   (C) When their hair and teeth begin to fall out
   (D) When they have lost about 90% of body mass

3) Listen to **Track 3.51**.
   Why does the professor say this?
   (A) To explain the relationship between the digestive tract and the circulatory system
   (B) To transition to a discussion of muscle growth and development
   (C) To explain how people process food under normal circumstances
   (D) To point out the benefits of a high-glucose diet

4) What is the name of the process in which the body consumes muscle to attain energy?
   (A) Ketone
   (B) Autophagy
   (C) Fatty acid consumption
   (D) Muscle failure

5) Why does the professor describe different ways that starvation leads to death?
   (A) To explain how extreme starvation affects the body
   (B) To show that the body can convert muscle tissue into glucose
   (C) To suggest that a healthy diet and good sleeping habits can reverse starvation
   (D) To emphasize that starvation is more common than most people realize

6) How does the professor organize the lecture?
   (A) He presents evidence for a controversial theory.
   (B) He gives the historical background for a biological process.
   (C) He describes a term using metaphors and analogies.
   (D) He describes the stages of a biological process.

ACTUAL PRACTICE 9

Take notes as you listen to the conversation on **Track 3.52**. Then answer the multiple-choice questions that follow.

> eyewitness accounts   Krakatoa eruption
> *The Eruption of Krakatoa and Subsequent Phenomena*

Things to Consider

WHAT is the conversation about?

WHAT details contribute to the main idea?

WHY are the speakers having the conversation?

HOW do the speakers organize and present the conversation?

Notes

_____
_____
_____
_____
_____
_____
_____
_____

Circle the letter next to the correct answer or answers to each of the multiple-choice questions below.

1) What issue is the student having with his research paper?
   (A) He cannot find any primary sources.
   (B) He cannot think of a topic.
   (C) He believes his topic is too broad.
   (D) He is having trouble writing a conclusion.

2) Where does the professor recommend that the student look for *The Eruption of Krakatoa and Subsequent Phenomena*?
   (A) The professor's office
   (B) The university's bookstore
   (C) The university's library
   (D) The Internet

3) Listen to **Track 3.53**.
   Why does the professor say this?
   (A) To explain why she assigned the research paper
   (B) To show that she sympathizes with the student
   (C) To criticize the lack of resources at the university's library
   (D) To point out a downside of becoming a history professor

4) How many primary sources does the professor tell the student to include in his research paper?
   (A) At least one
   (B) At least two
   (C) At least three
   (D) At least four

5) Based on the conversation, what can be inferred about the professor?
   (A) She was on Krakatoa during the volcanic eruption.
   (B) She is reluctant to help the student with his research paper.
   (C) She is not concerned about the differences between primary and secondary sources.
   (D) She has researched the volcanic eruption on Krakatoa before.

Take notes as you listen to the lecture on **Track 3.54**. Then answer the multiple-choice questions that follow.

Marine Biology

- deep sea
- hydrothermal vents
- magma
- toxins
- bacteria
- digestive systems

Things to Consider

WHAT is the lecture about?

WHAT details contribute to the main idea?

WHY does the speaker present the lecture information?

HOW does the speaker organize and present the lecture?

Notes

_____
_____
_____
_____
_____
_____
_____
_____
_____

Circle the letter next to the correct answer or answers to each of the multiple-choice questions below.

1) What is the main topic of the lecture?
   (A) The formation of the bottom of the ocean
   (B) Some differences between the ocean's surface and its depths
   (C) A unique deep-sea ecosystem
   (D) The food chain in the deep sea

2) Why is the water emerging from hydrothermal vents filled with minerals?
   (A) The intense pressure from the ocean water above forms mineral clusters.
   (B) The ocean floor absorbs sunlight and changes it into minerals.
   (C) Human mining activities have caused minerals to leak into hydrothermal vents.
   (D) The vents are fed by mineral-rich subsurface water.

3) Listen to **Track 3.55**.
   Why does the professor say this?
   (A) To describe the appearance of hydrothermal vents
   (B) To explain why researchers study hydrothermal vents
   (C) To compare hydrothermal vents to skyscrapers
   (D) To describe how scientists first discovered hydrothermal vents

4) What substance do the creatures living near hydrothermal vents survive on?
   (A) Tube worms
   (B) Hydrogen sulfide
   (C) Subsurface magma
   (D) Minerals found on the ocean floor

5) What does the professor suggest about the bacteria that make life possible near hydrothermal vents?
   (A) They are among the most common bacteria found on Earth.
   (B) They are mostly found in environments that are toxic to other organisms.
   (C) They eventually kill the aquatic organism that they live inside of.
   (D) They exist in the stomachs of all aquatic species.

6) Listen to **Track 3.56**.
   What can be inferred from this?
   (A) Most deep-sea creatures do not live for long because of their harsh environment.
   (B) Scientists hope that humans will soon be able to live in the deep sea.
   (C) Deep-sea creatures have evolved special adaptations to survive in extreme environments.
   (D) Scientists do not understand how deep-sea creatures live in their harsh environments.

Take notes as you listen to the lecture on **Track 3.57**. Then answer the multiple-choice questions that follow.

Art History

James Turrell
light
optical illusions
sky spaces
Breathing Light
Rodan Crater

Things to Consider

WHAT is the lecture about?

WHAT details contribute to the main idea?

WHY does the speaker present the lecture information?

HOW does the speaker organize and present the lecture?

Notes

Circle the letter next to the correct answer or answers to each of the multiple-choice questions below.

1) What is the main purpose of the lecture on James Turrell?
   (A) To show that light itself can be an artistic medium
   (B) To show the importance of light in museum art displays
   (C) To study the effect of light on visual art
   (D) To argue that James Turrell should be more famous

2) Listen to **Track 3.58**.
   Why does the professor say this?
   (A) To imply that all good art reproduces natural lighting
   (B) To explain how an artist's choice of colors affects the audience's emotions
   (C) To criticize artists who use too many dark colors
   (D) To introduce the relationship between light and the visual arts

3) According to the professor, how did James Turrell begin his career?
   (A) He filled a room with very bright light.
   (B) He experimented with projecting images.
   (C) He created colored light from special lamps.
   (D) He painted and lit up an empty hotel in California.

4) Listen to **Track 3.59**.
   What does the professor mean when she says this?
   (A) People often become lost in Turrell's exhibits.
   (B) Viewing Turrell's works can be disorienting.
   (C) Most people do not understand the purpose of Turrell's work.
   (D) Viewing Turrell's work causes memory loss and dizziness.

5) According to the professor, what is James Turrell's masterpiece?
   (A) He shone light in such a way that people could float.
   (B) He created a wall out of light.
   (C) He excavated and lit up an ancient volcano.
   (D) He lit up a small island with 3-D images.

6) Based on the information in the lecture, what can be inferred about the art of James Turrell?
   (A) Turrell is more concerned with our perception of light than with images.
   (B) Turrell is not as important as more traditional California painters and sculptors.
   (C) Turrell's art is simple for viewers to understand.
   (D) Turrell's art makes viewers feel restful and at peace.

Take notes as you listen to the conversation on **Track 3.60**. Then answer the multiple-choice questions that follow.

class registration   English placement exam

Things to Consider

WHAT is the conversation about?

WHAT details contribute to the main idea?

WHY are the speakers having the conversation?

HOW do the speakers organize and present the conversation?

Notes

_____
_____
_____
_____
_____
_____
_____
_____

Circle the letter next to the correct answer or answers to each of the multiple-choice questions below.

1) Why does the student talk to the advisor?
   (A) To take a placement exam
   (B) To find out how to register for a class
   (C) To transfer some class credits from a different university
   (D) To apply to the university

2) Listen to **Track 3.61**.
   Why does the student say this?
   (A) To ask for details about the contents of the exam
   (B) To tell the advisor his opinion about the process
   (C) To confirm with the advisor that he knows what he should do
   (D) To tell the advisor of his plans for the next two hours

3) Where will the student take the English entrance exam?
   (A) The university's library
   (B) The university's central plaza
   (C) The advisor's office
   (D) The university's main auditorium

4) According to the advisor, how long does it take to complete the English placement exam?
   (A) About half an hour
   (B) About one hour
   (C) About two hours
   (D) All day

5) What can be inferred about the student?
   (A) He has not registered for university classes before.
   (B) He will fail the English placement exam.
   (C) He took college-level writing classes in high school.
   (D) He will not take the placement exam.

ACTUAL PRACTICE 10

Take notes as you listen to the lecture on **Track 3.62**. Then answer the multiple-choice questions that follow.

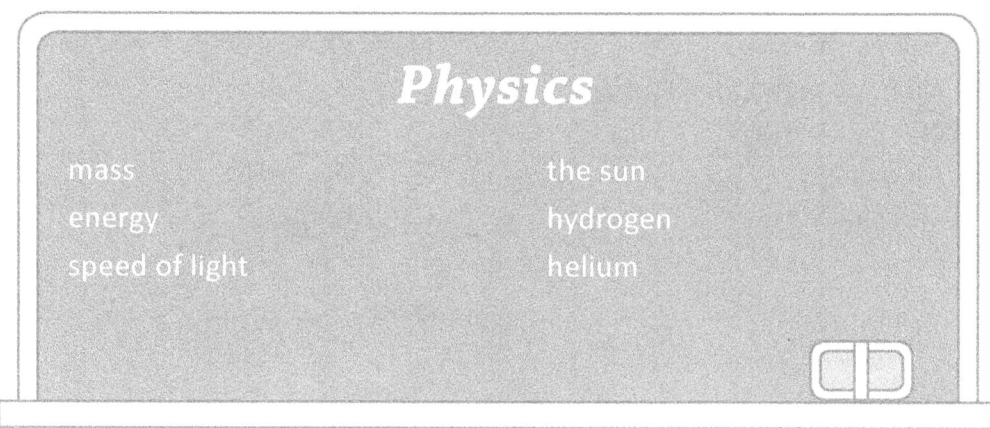

Things to Consider

WHAT is the lecture about?

WHAT details contribute to the main idea?

WHY does the speaker present the lecture information?

HOW does the speaker organize and present the lecture?

Notes

___
___
___
___
___
___
___
___

Circle the letter next to the correct answer or answers to each of the multiple-choice questions below.

1) What is the main topic of the lecture?
   (A) The differences between experimental and theoretical physics
   (B) The relationship between matter and energy
   (C) The equation for calculating the speed of light
   (D) The environmental conditions on the surface of the sun

2) Listen to **Track 3.63**.
   What can be inferred about the professor from this?
   (A) She expects the class to be familiar with the equation.
   (B) She has already talked about the equation with the class.
   (C) She decided to become a professor because of this equation.
   (D) She will include information about the equation on the class' next test.

3) Listen to **Track 3.64**.
   Why does the professor say this?
   (A) To hint at the equation's versatility
   (B) To shift the discussion to heat and magnetic energies
   (C) To contrast different forms of energy
   (D) To imply that the equation contains mathematical errors

4) What does the variable "c" stand for in the equation "$E=mc^2$"?
   (A) The conversion constant
   (B) The size of a particle
   (C) The speed of sound
   (D) The speed of light

5) Listen to **Track 3.65**.
   Why does the professor say this?
   (A) To point out the problems with the equation "$E=mc^2$"
   (B) To correct a mistake that she made earlier in the lecture
   (C) To show that the sun and the Earth are very similar
   (D) To introduce a real-world application of the equation "$E=mc^2$"

6) According to the professor, what does the fusion of hydrogen atoms in the sun demonstrate?
   (A) The differences between light and energy
   (B) The relationship between energy and the speed of light
   (C) The process by which matter changes into energy
   (D) The absorption of energy by matter

Actual Test

CHAPTER 4

Actual Test Information

In this section, you will listen to a series of academic lectures and campus-related conversations. After each lecture and conversation, you will answer a series of multiple-choice questions about what you have just heard. Multiple-choice questions are worth one point each, and chart-based, "organizing information" questions are worth two points each.

Because this is the intermediate book in *KALLIS' iBT TOEFL Listening* Series, the lectures and conversations here are shorter and simpler than the ones that you will encounter when you take the official iBT TOEFL. Here, each lecture and conversation will last from one to three minutes.

When you take the official iBT TOEFL, you will have 60 to 90 minutes to listen to the lectures and conversations and to answer all the corresponding questions. Because of the reduced lecture and conversation lengths in this book, you should spend no more than 45 minutes completing the Actual Test portion of this book.

	Very Poor	Poor	Good	Very Good	Excellent
Points	1 - 10	11 - 16	17 - 23	24 - 29	30 - 34
Scale	1 - 9	10 - 14	15 - 21	22 - 26	27 - 30

ACTUAL TEST

Take notes as you listen to the lecture on **Track 4.01**. Then answer the multiple-choice questions that follow.

Latin American History

- Latin America
- Woman's Revolutionary Law
- Zapatistas
- southern Mexico

Notes

Listening 1

Circle the letter next to the correct answer or answers to each of the multiple-choice questions below.

1) What is the main topic of this lecture?
   (A) A comparison of the Sandinistas and the Zapatistas
   (B) The successes of some Latin American dictators
   (C) The United States' interest in securing Latin American trade
   (D) A successful revolution from Latin American history

2) According to the professor, what happens frequently in Latin American history?
   (A) Successful revolutions
   (B) Long and successful democracies
   (C) Long and successful monarchies
   (D) Long and cruel dictatorships

3) Listen to **Track 4.02**.
   Why does the professor say this?
   (A) To show that the Zapatistas wanted to start a bloody, violent revolution
   (B) To show why the Mexican Army attacked the Zapatistas
   (C) To show how the Zapatistas destroyed the environment
   (D) To show that the Zapatistas did not want a violent war

4) Why does the professor claim that the Zapatistas did not want to start a Communist revolution?
   (A) To explain why the Zapatistas were protecting the rights of women
   (B) To prove that the Zapatistas wanted to eliminate the Mexican government
   (C) To show how the Zapatistas were different from other groups in Latin America
   (D) To suggest that the Zapatistas were working with the American government

5) According to the professor, which of the following rights are guaranteed in the "Women's Revolutionary Law?"
   Choose 2 answers.
   (A) The right to fight in the revolution
   (B) The right to an education
   (C) The right to decide how many children to have
   (D) The right to leave Mexico and emigrate to the United States

6) What does the professor imply about the history of the nations of Latin America?
   (A) There is a tradition of democracy and stability in these nations.
   (B) Political control has often been maintained through force.
   (C) The rights of women are always protected.
   (D) The indigenous people in each nation of Latin American enjoy autonomy.

ACTUAL TEST

Take notes as you listen to the conversation on **Track 4.03**. Then answer the multiple-choice questions that follow.

> housing application
> State University
> Redwood College
> Oak College
> Cypress College
> Sequoia College

Notes

Circle the letter next to the correct answer or answers to each of the multiple-choice questions below.

1) What do the student and the advisor mainly discuss?
   (A) The differences between on-campus dormitories and apartments
   (B) The quickest way to get to the student's classes
   (C) The purpose of the different colleges at the university
   (D) The differences between the various majors offered at the university

2) According to the advisor, how do most students choose a college?
   (A) Based on the student's extracurricular interests
   (B) Based on the college's location
   (C) Based on the student's major
   (D) Based on the student's name

3) Listen to **Track 4.04**.
   Why does the advisor ask this?
   (A) To recommend a college for the student to consider
   (B) To tell the student how many other students have that major
   (C) To tell the student what classes to sign up for
   (D) To tell the student what professors he will have

4) What college does the advisor recommend for the student?
   (A) Oak College
   (B) Redwood College
   (C) Cypress College
   (D) Sequoia College

5) What will the student do next?
   (A) Take a tour of campus
   (B) Register for his classes
   (C) Sign up for the psychology major
   (D) Walk to Redwood College

ACTUAL TEST 3

Take notes as you listen to the lecture on **Track 4.05**. Then answer the multiple-choice questions that follow.

Biology

- horseshoe crab
- Federal Drug Administration (FDA)
- Limulus Amebocyte Lysate (LAL)
- coagulate
- batch
- pathogens

Notes

Listening 3

Circle the letter next to the correct answer or answers to each of the multiple-choice questions below.

1) What is the main purpose of the lecture?
   (A) To show students how evolution affects different populations at different times
   (B) To show students how different animals have differently colored blood
   (C) To explain why the blood of horseshoe crabs is an important scientific resource
   (D) To explain why the blood of horseshoe crabs is blue instead of red

2) Why do researchers use LAL, the compound extracted from horseshoe crab blood?
   (A) To test medicine for safety
   (B) To detect toxins in certain types of sea food
   (C) To detect the presence of pollution in seawater
   (D) To test blood in the laboratory

3) Why does the professor refer to the LAL in the blood of horseshoe crabs as a "lifesaver" for humans?
   (A) To point out that LAL is used in lifesaving devices
   (B) To explain how LAL is used to replace human blood
   (C) To show that LAL supplements the human immune system
   (D) To emphasize that LAL testing prevents the sale of unsafe drugs

4) Listen to **Track 4.06**.
   Why does the professor say this?
   (A) To give thanks to the horseshoe crabs for their contribution to human health
   (B) To point out that the horseshoe crabs usually recover from the procedure
   (C) To point out that horseshoe crabs are not an endangered species
   (D) To point out that horseshoe crabs are donated to other organizations

5) Check each box where the term in the left column matches the description in the top row.

	This neutralizes pathogens	This fights and destroys pathogens	This forms a barrier around some poisons
Human Immune System			
Horseshoe Crab Immune system			

ACTUAL TEST 4

Take notes as you listen to the lecture on **Track 4.07**. Then answer the multiple-choice questions that follow.

American Literature

- Maxine Kingston
- Chinese immigrants
- Cantonese legends
- ghosts
- perceptions
- memoir

Notes

Listening 4

Circle the letter next to the correct answer or answers to each of the multiple-choice questions below.

1) What is the main topic discussed in the lecture?
   (A) The unfair treatment of Chinese immigrants in California
   (B) A book that analyzes Chinese and American ghost stories
   (C) A unique account of an immigrant's childhood in America
   (D) The rise of female authors in 20th-century America

2) What different elements does Maxine Hong Kingston include in her memoir?
   Choose 2 answers.
   (A) She uses plots from Chinese opera.
   (B) She uses Cantonese legends.
   (C) She uses her mother's stories.
   (D) She uses Hollywood movie plots.

3) What are two examples of the "ghosts" that Kingston mentions in the title of the book?
   Choose 2 answers.
   (A) Characters from cartoons that she watched as a child in California
   (B) People she never met from China who are characters in the book
   (C) People who dress up on Halloween and try to frighten immigrants
   (D) Maxine and other Chinese immigrants, as seen by other Americans

4) Why does Maxine Hong Kingston include stories about characters from China that she never met?
   (A) To show how different her life experiences growing up in America are
   (B) To suggest there is a strong connection between her experience and theirs in China
   (C) To remind the readers that this is a book about Chinese immigrants and their descendants
   (D) To show that China has a rich culture that has much to contribute to America

5) Listen to **Track 4.08**.
   What does the professor suggest when she says this?
   (A) Kingston often confuses fantasy with reality.
   (B) Kingston believes that memory is usually wrong.
   (C) Most people forget most of their childhoods.
   (D) Perceptions change as a person grows and develops.

6) What does the professor suggest about the stories that Kingston's mother told her?
   (A) Their messages were ambiguous.
   (B) Kingston did not believe that they were true.
   (C) They were usually long and complicated.
   (D) They were about Kingston's mother's childhood.

ACTUAL TEST 5

Take notes as you listen to the conversation on **Track 4.09**. Then answer the multiple-choice questions that follow.

- graduate school
- applications
- psychology major
- work experience
- GRE
- letters of recommendation

Notes

Circle the letter next to the correct answer or answers to each of the multiple-choice questions below.

1) What do the student and the advisor mainly discuss?
   (A) The best universities for the student to transfer to
   (B) Where to look for internships on campus
   (C) The differences between psychology and neurology degrees
   (D) How to prepare for applying to graduate schools

2) Listen to **Track 4.10**.
   Why does the student say this?
   (A) To explain how he has prepared for neuroscience graduate programs
   (B) To point out the differences between cognitive science and neuroscience
   (C) To prove that he should already have received a graduate degree by now
   (D) To compare his class schedule to the schedules of other students

3) Listen to **Track 4.11**.
   What does the advisor mean when she says this?
   (A) The student's professors should be able to show him where the career center is.
   (B) The student's professors should be able to suggest some available internships.
   (C) His professors will fill out his graduate school applications for him.
   (D) His professors will point out any mistakes that he makes during his internship.

4) Why does the advisor recommend that the student visit the tutoring center?
   (A) To ask for some letters of recommendation
   (B) To receive help in his cognitive science classes
   (C) To ask about internship opportunities as a tutor
   (D) To receive help preparing for the GRE

5) What is NOT recommended by the advisor as a way of preparing for graduate school?
   (A) Seeking internship opportunities
   (B) Studying for the GRE
   (C) Switching majors
   (D) Asking for letters of recommendation

ACTUAL TEST 6

Take notes as you listen to the lecture on **Track 4.12**. Then answer the multiple-choice questions that follow.

Cosmology

- cosmic microwave background (CMB)
- radio receiver
- Bell Laboratories
- Big Bang
- deep space
- heat energy

Notes

Circle the letter next to the correct answer or answers to each of the multiple-choice questions below.

1) What is the main topic of this lecture?
   (A) The different theories explaining the origin of the universe
   (B) The reasons that microwaves are so important to technological developments
   (C) The discovery of leftover energy from the origin of the universe
   (D) The many uses of radio receivers in astronomy

2) When do scientists believe the Big Bang occurred?
   (A) About 140 billion years ago
   (B) About 1.4 million years ago
   (C) About 4 million years ago
   (D) About 14 billion years ago

3) What conclusion did some 20th-century mathematicians and scientists reach about the Big Bang?
   (A) There must be heat energy remaining from the Big Bang.
   (B) The heat from the Big Bang explosion had disappeared.
   (C) The Big Bang explosion was not very hot.
   (D) The heat from the Big Bang explosion was too hot to measure.

4) Listen to **Track 4.13**.
   Why does the professor say this?
   (A) To infer that scientists should find more efficient ways to make new discoveries
   (B) To explain why cosmology is the most difficult field in science
   (C) To criticize scientists for not conducting enough experiments
   (D) To emphasize the difficulty of detecting the cosmic microwave background

5) Listen to **Track 4.14**.
   What does the professor suggest when she says this?
   (A) Scientists are known for making mathematical errors.
   (B) Many important scientific discoveries are made unintentionally.
   (C) Accidents during scientific experiments can be very dangerous.
   (D) There were many cases of CMB discovery.

6) How did scientists eventually detect the presence of the cosmic microwave background?
   (A) Using a powerful telescope
   (B) Using a radio receiver
   (C) Using a microwave detector
   (D) Using a giant thermometer

APPENDIX

Listening Scripts

CHAPTER 1

TRACK 1.01

Narrator: Listen to a conversation between a student and a professor.
Female Student (FS): Hi, Professor Walton. Do you have time for me to ask you something?
Male Professor (MP): Certainly, Cassie.
FS: Well, I'm kind of confused about the assignment you gave us today in class.
MP: Okay. What part is confusing?
FS: So we're supposed to watch one of our favorite movies, and I know you want us to watch it critically. But what I don't understand is what aspect of the movie you want us to be critical of. Like, do you want us to analyze the movie's story, the acting, the cinematography, or what?
MP: Well, that's really for you to decide. Do you read any movie reviews in your free time?
FS: Yeah, I read them sometimes.
MP: And in the reviews that you read, do the critics always analyze the same aspects of film? You know, does a film critic only critique the acting in every film he or she reviews.
FS: Well, no. I guess the critic analyzes different things based on the strengths and weaknesses of the film.
MP: And that's exactly what I want you to do. Be a film critic.
FS: Okay, I think I see what you mean. Thanks for the help.
MP: Any time.
Narrator: Now get ready to answer the question.

TRACK 1.02

Narrator: Listen to a conversation between a student and a university employee.
Male University Employee (ME): Hi, there. What can I help you with?
Female Student (FS): Hi. Well, this may sound kind of dumb, but I was wondering if you could help me set up my student email account. I'm terrible with computers.
ME: I'd be glad to help you. And don't worry, a lot of students have trouble setting up a student email account. So to begin the setup process, go to the university website's home page.
FS: Oh, wait a minute. Let me write this down so I don't forget what to do. (Student takes out paper and pen) Okay, go ahead.
ME: Alright. So once you're on the university home page, you'll see a tab at the top of the screen called "Student Center." Click on that.
FS: Okay, got it.
ME: And on the top of the "Student Center" page, you'll see a little box that says "Student Email." Click the button below that; the button should say "Sign Up," I think. From there, you'll just have to create a username and a password, and you'll be all set.
FS: Great, Thanks for all your help.
ME: My pleasure. Have a good afternoon.
Narrator: Now get ready to answer the question.

TRACK 1.03

Narrator: Listen to a conversation between a student and a professor.
Female Student (FS): Hi, Professor Brooks. You wanted to speak with me?
Male Professor (MP): Yes, Holly. Thanks for staying after class to talk. As you know, this is a very small class, and one of the biggest benefits of a small class is being able to voice your opinions. But here we are, three weeks into class, and I haven't heard you make a single comment.
FS: I know. I'm sorry, professor. I just get really nervous. I feel like everyone else has all these insightful things to say, and I just never know what to add.
MP: Well, Holly, I'm sure you have something to say. Your writing is among the best in the class. And, though I hate to say it, your grade will suffer if you don't speak up more in class.
FS: But I really enjoy your class, and I want to get an "A." It's just that I feel like anything I say might sound stupid.
MP: You're very articulate and insightful, and you're speaking among friends here. I'm sure your comments and opinions will be welcome in class.
FS: Maybe you're right. I'll try to participate more.
Narrator: Now get ready to answer the question.

TRACK 1.04

Narrator: Listen to a conversation between two students.
Female Student (FS): Hey, Jude.
Male Student (MS): Hey, Tammy. What's up?
FS: Well, you do a lot of group projects for your business major, right?
MS: Yeah, I guess so. Why do you ask?
FS: I just got assigned my first group project, and no one in my group, myself included, knows where to work on group projects.
MS: What do you mean?
FS: Well, the library's too quiet to work in a group—you know, since the whole group has to talk about ideas and stuff together. And the coffee shop is always too crowded. I don't think there are ever five open seats for everyone in my group.
MS: Well, have you been to the library's basement level?
FS: The library has a basement?
MS: Yeah. If you walk down the stairs from the library's first floor, you'll find a study room with lots of big tables. And down there you don't have to be as quiet as in the rest of the library. It's perfect for group projects.
FS: Oh, perfect. I'm going to check that out right now. Thanks for the heads up!
MS: No problem.
Narrator: Now get ready to answer the question.

TRACK 1.05

Narrator: Listen to a conversation between a student and an advisor.
Male Advisor (MA): Good afternoon. How can I help you?
Female Student (FS): Well, this is my first semester at the university, and I'm kind of having trouble with the classes.
MA: I'm sorry to hear that. Could you explain what you mean by "having trouble"?
FS: I guess what I mean is—well, this may sound whiny—all the classes are so impersonal. I mean, all my introductory chemistry lectures are in huge lecture halls with hundreds of students, and most of my professors are never available for questions or anything. I always thought college was going to be a lot of small classes and one-on-one discussions with professors.
MA: Ah, I see the problem. Eventually, your classes will become much smaller, and you'll get to talk to your professors more. But that doesn't usually happen until you start taking upper-division classes. Introductory classes are always large and impersonal.
FS: So upper-division classes are much smaller?
MA: Absolutely. And the professors are much more likely to interact with the students, too.
FS: That's good to hear. Thanks for the help.
MA: No problem. Come see me anytime you have similar academic questions.
Narrator: Now get ready to answer the question.

TRACK 1.06

Narrator: Listen to a conversation between a student and a university employee.
Female University Employee (FE): Good morning.
Male Student (MS): Hi. I was hoping that you could tell me how the meal points system works here. I know I have 15,000 meal points for the semester, but I don't really understand what that means.
FE: No problem. So there are two main dining halls, one on-campus grocery store, and two on-campus cafés. You can use your meal points to purchase food and drink at any of these locations.
MS: I didn't know the meal points worked at the café. I've been paying for things with cash there all semester!
FE: Oh, no. I'm sorry to hear that. Well, from now on you can just get coffee or whatever else you want there with meal points.
MS: I'll be sure to remember that. And how much money is each meal point worth. 15,000 meal points seems like a lot.
FE: Each meal point is worth ten cents. So really, it's like you have a food allowance of 1,500 dollars for each semester. So, for example, it takes 80 meal points to eat at the dining hall, so each dining hall trip costs eight dollars.
MS: Okay, that makes a lot more sense. Thanks for your help.
Narrator: Now get ready to answer the questions.

TRACK 1.07

Narrator: Listen to a conversation between a student and a librarian.

Female Student (FS): Excuse me, (*reads librarian's nametag*) Mr. Davis. I'm having a lot of trouble finding a certain book, so I was hoping you could help me find it.

Male Librarian (ML): Well, I'll certainly see what I can do. Who's the author?

FS: Her name is Hildegard of Bingen. I guess she's this religious writer from Medieval Europe.

ML: Yes, that's right. She was a brilliant writer and composer. In what class are you studying her?

FS: It's this religious studies class on monastic life in Medieval Europe. It's taught by Professor Dayton.

ML: I see. Jodie Dayton is a great lecturer. I'm glad to hear she's teaching that class. Sorry, I got off topic there. What book by Hildegard are you looking for?

FS: Professor Dayton told us to read some excerpts from a book called *Know the Ways of the Lord*, but I can't find it anywhere.

ML: I know what the problem is. We carry that book, but it's under the original Latin title, *Scivias*. You see, *Scivias* is an abbreviation for the full Latin title. I'll show you where it is. Follow me.

FS: No wonder I couldn't find it. Thanks for your help.

Narrator: Now get ready to answer the questions.

TRACK 1.08

Narrator: Listen to a conversation between two students.

Male Student (MS): You're in charge of running the on-campus garden, right?

Female Student (FS): I am indeed.

MS: Oh, great. Hi, my name is Tony. I want to volunteer to help out in the garden sometime.

FS: Awesome. We're always looking for new volunteers. What inspired you to help out?

MS: Well, I worked as a landscaper over the summer. And my favorite part of that was getting to arrange and plant flowers and bushes. Then I heard about the on-campus garden earlier this year, so I figured I'd see if I could help you guys out.

FS: That's great. I'm glad to hear you have some experience with planting and landscaping.

MS: Well, my dad owns his own landscaping business, so I've grown up around this kind of stuff. But I haven't done much gardening, so I'm sure there's lots I can learn.

FS: Well, me and the other volunteers meet at the garden every Saturday at 9 am. You should come by this weekend and I'll show you around.

MS: That sounds great. I'm already looking forward to it.

Narrator: Now get ready to answer the questions.

TRACK 1.09

Narrator: Listen to a conversation between two students.

Male Student (MS): Hey, Anna, I saw you perform with "Vocal Chords" last night in the dining hall. You guys were great, but I didn't know you were in an a cappella group.

Female Student (FS): Oh you did? Thanks! I joined at the beginning of this year. It's a lot of fun. The performances are great because they're so laid back, and everyone involved is really nice.

MS: That sounds awesome. You know, I did choir in high school, and I've been looking for a way to practice my singing.

FS: I didn't know you sing. Yeah, you should definitely try out for "Vocal Chords." It'd be really fun to have you in the group.

MS: That's what I was thinking. But I'm a little out of practice, and I'd like some time to get back into singing—you know, practice my scales and stuff.

FS: That's a good idea, but you'd better practice quickly —we're having tryouts in two weeks.

MS: Oh, wow. I guess I'd better start preparing, then. I have to go to class now, but I'd like to ask you more about "Vocal Chords" later.

FS: Sounds great. Let's meet up after your class, then.

Narrator: Now get ready to answer the questions.

TRACK 1.10

Narrator: Listen to a conversation between a student and a librarian.

Female Student (FS): Hi. Could you help me with something?

Male Librarian (ML): Well, I certainly hope so. What seems to be the problem?

FS: Well, I was using one of the private study rooms, and someone came in and told me that he had reserved it and that I needed to leave. But I've never heard of people reserving the study rooms. I thought they were kind of a first-come, first-served thing.

ML: Oh, no. Most students reserve the study rooms hours, or sometimes even days, in advance.

FS: Oh, okay. I guess that guy who told me to leave wasn't lying then. Well, I still want to use those rooms to study in. I like how they're never noisy, and they're always really clean. So how can I reserve a study room?

ML: You just have to go on the university library website, and on the left side of the website's home page, there will be a tab called "Study Rooms." Just click on that tab, and the website will guide you through the reservation process.

FS: Sounds easy. Thanks for your help!

Narrator: Now get ready to answer the questions.

TRACK 1.11

Narrator: Listen to a conversation between two students.

Male Student (MS): Hey, Donna. You live in a house off campus, right?

Female Student (FS): Yeah, I live over on Walnut Street. Why do you ask?

MS: Well, I live in the dorms now, but I'm going to move into a house off campus next year with some guys from the baseball team, and I was wondering if you could tell me if there's anything I should do to prepare for living off campus.

FS: Oh, yeah. I guess there are a few differences between living on and off campus. How many people are you living with?

MS: It's going to be me and two other guys.

FS: Well, one good thing to do is make a list of everything you'll need for the house—you know, kitchen stuff, furniture, a television—and have each person put their name next to what they can bring. That way you'll have everything you need when you move in.

MS: That's a great idea!

FS: When my housemates and I moved into our current house, we didn't make a list like that, and we ended up with three sets of silverware and no microwave. (*Both laugh*)

Narrator: Now get ready to answer the questions.

TRACK 1.12

Narrator: Why does the woman say this?

FS: When my housemates and I moved into our current house, we didn't make a list like that, and we ended up with three sets of silverware and no microwave. (*Both laugh*)

TRACK 1.13

Narrator: Listen to a conversation between two students.

Male Student (MS): Hey, Darla!

Female Student (FS): Hi, Matt. What's up?

MS: Not much. I was thinking of starting an intramural sports team this semester. Do you want to help me form a team?

FS: I don't know. I'm not really that good at sports.

MS: That's okay. I mean, we'd just be competing against other students. Nobody really cares who wins or anything.

FS: Well, I guess that's true. What sport are you going to sign up for?

MS: I was thinking volleyball.

FS: Well, volleyball is a lot of fun. And both of my roommates played volleyball in high school.

MS: Oh, that's awesome! They should join the team, too!

FS: Yeah, I'll ask them if they want to join as well.

MS: So you'll play, too?

FS: Yeah, I guess so. Volleyball is a lot of fun, and I could always use some more exercise.

MS: Great! I'm going to go get the form for creating an intramural volleyball team. Can you ask your roommates if they want to be on our team now? I want to get a team together as soon as possible.

FS: Sure. How about I meet you back here in 15 minutes with their answers?

MS: Perfect. See you soon.

Narrator: Now get ready to answer the questions.

TRACK 1.14

Narrator: Why does the man say this?

MS: That's okay. I mean, we'd just be competing against other students. Nobody really cares who wins or anything.

TRACK 1.15

Narrator: Why does the woman say this?

FS: Yeah, I guess so. Volleyball is a lot of fun, and I could always use some more exercise.

TRACK 1.16

Narrator: Listen to a conversation between a student and a professor.

Male Student (MS): Excuse me, professor. Do you have a minute to talk?

Female Professor (FP): Of course.

MS: Well, my grade in your class is kind of bad right now. I think I have a "C" or a "C minus." And I was wondering if you could recommend anything that might help me improve my grade.

FP: Ah, yes. Well, right now it seems like your project grade is fine. If I'm not mistaken, it's your test and quiz scores that are lowering your grade so much.

MS: That's true, but I study for all of your tests, and I feel like I understand all the material. I just don't know why I'm doing so poorly on them.

FP: Well, you know I don't take attendance in this class, but I can't help but notice that you've missed quite a few of my classes. A lot of my test material is on information that's only mentioned in class, not in the reading.

MS: Oh. I see.

FP: So start showing up to every class, and I think you'd be surprised by how much better you do on tests and quizzes.

MS: Okay, professor. I'll be sure to do that.

Narrator: Now get ready to answer the questions.

TRACK 1.17

Narrator: Why does the professor say this?

Female Professor: Well, you know I don't take attendance in this class, but I can't help but notice that you've missed quite a few of my classes. A lot of my test material is on information that's only mentioned in class, not in the reading.

TRACK 1.18

Narrator: Listen to a conversation between a student and a tutor.

Male Tutor (MT): Hi. Are you Angelica?

Female Student (FS): Yep, that's me.

MT: Hi. My name's Travis. So you're looking for some tutoring help in economics, right?

FS: Yeah, that's right. I have to take Economics 1 for my general education requirements, and it's turning out to be way harder than I thought.

MT: Alright. Well, I'm here to give you some help in economics. So, for starters, let me give you a bit of background about myself. I'm a graduate student in accounting, but I've had to take a lot of economics classes, too.

FS: Oh, awesome. If you're a graduate student, you must really know your stuff.

MT: Well, after six years of studying all this business and accounting, I certainly hope I've picked up a thing or two. And how about you. What's your major?

FS: Right now I'm undeclared, but I'm thinking of going into anthropology. I find the development of different cultures really interesting, and there's not much math or economics involved in anthropology. (*Both chuckle*)

MT: I guess economics isn't for everyone, but anthropology sounds really interesting. Anyway, I guess we should get started on some tutoring….

Narrator: Now get ready to answer the questions.

TRACK 1.19

Narrator: Why does the tutor probably say this?

MT: So, for starters, let me give you a bit of background about myself. I'm a graduate student in accounting, but I've had to take a lot of economics classes, too.

TRACK 1.20

Narrator: Listen to part of the conversation. Then answer the question.

FS: Right now I'm undeclared, but I'm thinking of going into anthropology. I find the development of different cultures really interesting, and there's not much math or economics involved in anthropology.

Narrator: Why does the student say this?

FS: I find the development of different cultures really interesting, and there's not much math or economics involved in anthropology.

TRACK 1.21

Narrator: Listen to a conversation between a student and a professor.

Female Student (FS): Hey, Professor Morrissey. I have some questions about next week's test.

Male Professor (MP): Oh, the test on chapters six through nine. What would you like to know?

FS: Well, I know it's an open-book test, but I've never taken one of those before. So I'm not really sure if I should try to prepare for it differently than other tests.

MP: Well, I say you should start by making sure you comprehend the major concepts from each chapter, and bookmark any concepts that are confusing or difficult to remember. That way, if those difficult concepts show up on the test, you'll know exactly where to look for them.

FS: Okay. I will definitely do that. But why should I study at all if I get to use the book during the test. I mean, I'll have all the information right in front of me.

MP: You may have access to all the information, but you only have a limited amount of time. You can't use your book for every question, or you'll never be able to finish the test.

FS: Oh, yeah. I guess that's a good point.

Narrator: Now get ready to answer the questions.

TRACK 1.22

Narrator: Why does the student say this?

FS: Well, I know it's an open-book test, but I've never taken one of those before. So I'm not really sure if I should try to prepare for it differently than other tests.

TRACK 1.23

Narrator: Why does the student say this?

FS: But why should I study at all if I get to use the book during the test. I mean, I'll have all the information right in front of me.

TRACK 1.24

Narrator: Listen to a conversation between two students.

Female Student (FS): Excuse me. Sorry to bother you, but do you know where the Victory Theater is?

Male Student (MS): Yeah, it's across campus, by the theater department.

FS: Oh, okay. Sorry to keep bugging you, but can you tell me where the theater department is? I'm still learning my way around campus.

MS: Yeah, no problem. So the quickest way to get there is by taking the shuttle. So you'll want to get on the next northbound shuttle, and take it until you get to Adams Avenue. Get off there, and cross the bridge that's perpendicular to Adams Avenue. Once you're across the bridge, you should be able to see the theater department. Victory Theater should be just a little ways to the left.

FS: Great, thanks for the directions. Do you think I can get there in 10 minutes? My friend is in a show that starts really soon.

MS: Maybe. You'll definitely want to leave now, though. And, hey, what perfect timing: I see a northbound shuttle coming right now.

FS: Perfect. Thanks for the directions!

MS: No problem.

Narrator: Now get ready to answer the questions.

TRACK 1.25

Narrator: Listen to a conversation between a student and a professor.

Male Student (MS): See you tomorrow, Professor Adams.

Female Professor (FP): Actually, Dan. Can I talk to you for a minute.

MS: Uh, yeah. What's up?

FP: Well, I'm a little worried about your attendance in this class.

MS: But I haven't missed a class all semester.

FP: That may be true. But you're late to almost every lecture.

MS: Oh, I was hoping you didn't notice.

FP: Nope. I've definitely noticed. You seem like a smart, diligent student. Why aren't you coming to class on time?

MS: Well, I have a class that ends ten minutes before this class starts, and it's all the way across campus. Even when I run here, I'm still a few minutes late.

FP: I see. Well, I suppose your tardiness is somewhat understandable. But why don't you ever leave that class a bit early to get here on time? I mean, it's a little alarming that you're late to *every one* of my classes.

MS: I tried to leave early once, but the professor called me out in front of the whole class. It was pretty embarrassing.

FP: I see. Well, I wouldn't do this for most students, but I guess I can forgive your tardiness.

Narrator: Now get ready to answer the questions.

TRACK 1.26

Narrator: Listen to a conversation between a student and a professor.

Female Professor (FP): Hey, Mario. How are you doing? You look pretty tired.

Male Student (MS): Yeah, I am. I'm taking six classes this semester, and all the reports and assignments are really cutting into my sleep schedule.

FP: Sounds like you've bitten off a bit more than you can chew.

MS: You know, I'm starting to think you might be right. That's kind of why I came to talk to you today. I know our research paper is due at the end of next week, but

I'm overwhelmed with work right now. I have two labs due on that same day. So, well…

FP: You're looking for an extension on the research paper?

MS: Yeah. And I would never normally ask for special treatment like this or anything. I just really want to turn in a quality paper.

FP: I understand. You're a diligent student, and you're asking for this extension well before the due date, so I'll give you an extra week.

MS: Thank you so much, professor! I've already done all the research, so I guarantee it'll be a great paper.

FP: I look forward to reading it.

Narrator: Now get ready to answer the questions.

TRACK 1.27

Narrator: Listen to part of the conversation. Then answer the question.

MS: Yeah, I am. I'm taking six classes this semester, and all the reports and assignments are really cutting into my sleep schedule.

FP: Sounds like you've bitten off a bit more than you can chew.

Narrator: What does the professor mean when she says this?

FP: Sounds like you've bitten off a bit more than you can chew.

TRACK 1.28

Narrator: Listen to a conversation between a student and an advisor.

Male Advisor (MA): Good morning. How can I help you?

Female Student (FS): Well, I always see students giving on-campus tours to incoming freshmen. And the tour guides always look like they're having fun—you know, they're always laughing and smiling.

MA: We do get a lot of comments from student tour guides saying how much fun it is to interact with the incoming students.

FS: Well, I was wondering, what does someone have to do to apply for one of these tour guide positions?

MA: Ah, I thought that might be your question. Well, applying to be a tour guide is a three-step process. First, you'll need to fill out a simple form. It just asks for your name, major, basic stuff like that. (*Advisor hands the application to student*) Here, this is the form.

FS: Great. So I'll fill this out. Then what are the other two steps?

MA: So after we've reviewed your application, we'll call you to set up an interview. And then, after the interview, we'll have you write a short paper.

FS: Awesome. I'll come back later with this application filled out.

MA: Sounds good. After that, we can schedule an interview.

Narrator: Now get ready to answer the questions.

TRACK 1.29

Narrator: Listen to a conversation between a student and a laboratory instructor.

Female Student (FS): Excuse me, David. I have a bit of a problem

Male Laboratory Instructor (MI): Hey, Monica. What's up?

FS: Well, my lab partner isn't here today, and I don't really know what to do.

MI: Ah, I see. Who's your lab partner?

FS: Dillon.

MI: That's right. Have you tried calling him or texting him?

FS: Yeah, but he won't respond. I've left him a bunch of messages and voicemails.

MI: Hmmmm. Well, today's lab is pretty difficult and requires a lot of work. So I'd say you have two choice for finishing the lab: you can either try to get ahold of Dillon later, and both of you can come to tomorrow's lab and do the experiment there. Or you can join another lab group now, do the experiment there, and tell Dillon that he'll have to do the same with a lab group tomorrow.

FS: Okay. Since I can't reach Dillon at all, I'll just join a lab group now and tell Dillon that he has to do the same tomorrow.

MI: Sounds good. But make sure you tell Dillon Otherwise he could end up failing the lab.

FS: I'll be sure to let him know.

Narrator: Now get ready to answer the questions.

TRACK 1.30

Narrator: What can be inferred from this?

MI: Hmmmm. Well, today's lab is pretty difficult and requires a lot of work. So I have two propositions that will allow you to finish the lab…

TRACK 1.31

Narrator: Listen to a conversation between a student and a university employee.

Male Student (MS): Hello. Is this where I go to buy an on-campus parking permit?

Female University Employee (FE): This is the right place, but we're currently out of parking permits.

MS: What? But it's only the second week of school. How could they have already sold out?

FE: Well, to be honest with you, we sold out before school even started. Usually, students buy their parking permits when they come to campus to register for classes toward the end of summer, so a couple weeks before school starts.

MS: Well, what am I supposed to do with my car, then? I've been parking it in local neighborhoods, but I have to move it every few days so I don't get a parking ticket.

FE: Don't worry, you're not completely out of options. In fact, the university also owns a couple of off-campus parking lots, and those still have spaces available.

MS: Well, how far away from campus are they?

FE: About two miles away from the dorms, but there's a shuttle that goes to the parking lot pretty regularly. And the off-campus parking lot is a lot cheaper.

MS: Oh, okay. I guess this off-campus parking could be okay. How much does it cost to park there for the school year?

FE: It's 210 dollars for the year.

MS: Wow. That's like 300 dollars cheaper than a year of on-campus parking.

FE: Yeah, it's a pretty good deal. Would you like to purchase a yearlong pass for the off-campus parking lots?

MS: Yes, please. Can I pay with my debit card?

Narrator: Now get ready to answer the questions.

TRACK 1.32

Narrator: Why does the student say this?

MS: I've been parking it in local neighborhoods, but I have to move it every few days so I don't get a parking ticket.

TRACK 1.33

Narrator: Listen to a conversation between two students.

Female Student (FS): Hey, Matt. Do you have a minute to talk?

Male Student (MS): Hey, Lisa. Yeah, I have some time before my next class. What's up?

FS: You're still roommates with Andrew, right?

MS: I sure am. Why do you ask?

FS: Well, I'm working on a group project with him and a couple other people in our psychology class. And—don't get me wrong—Andrew's a really cool guy, but—

MS: He's not pulling his weight on the project, is he?

FS: Yeah, that's exactly the problem! And he hasn't been to class in over a week, so I can't talk to him about it personally.

MS: Yeah, his girlfriend broke up with him, so he's been pretty bummed lately. Honestly, he spends most of his time moping around the dorm, eating instant ramen while he complains about his life.

FS: Oh, I'm sorry to hear that. But, to be honest, I don't want to get an "F" on this project because of his broken heart.

MS: (*Chuckles*) As cold as that sounds, I understand where you're coming from. Well, since I'm his roommate and all, I guess I'll try to talk to him. You know, give him the whole "It's better to have loved and lost…" speech. I'll also remind him of his academic responsibilities. I mean, it's like you said: he shouldn't cause you to fail just because he's sad.

FS: Thanks, I really appreciate your help. I feel bad for Andrew, but this project needs to get done.

MS: It's no problem. I'll let you know when I've talked to him.

Narrator: Now get ready to answer the questions.

TRACK 1.34

Narrator: Why does the man say this about Andrew?

MS: Yeah, his girlfriend broke up with him, so he's been pretty bummed lately. Honestly, he spends most of his time moping around the dorm, eating instant ramen while he complains about his life.

TRACK 1.35

Narrator: Listen to part of the conversation. Then answer the question.

FS: And—don't get me wrong—Andrew's a really cool guy,

but—

MS: He's not pulling his weight on the project, is he?

Narrator: What does the man mean when he says this?

MS: He's not pulling his weight on the project, is he?

TRACK 1.36

Narrator: Listen to a conversation between a student and a recreation department employee.

Male Student (MS): Excuse me, is this where I can rent sports equipment?

Female Recreation Department Employee (FE): Yes, you've come to the right place.

MS: Great. I was hoping to check out a couple of tennis rackets and tennis balls.

FE: That should be no problem. Have you rented equipment from the recreation department before?

MS: Well, I've been to the gym many times, but no, I've never rented anything before.

FE: Okay. Let me explain the rental system then. All you have to do is give me your student ID, and I'll give you whatever equipment you need. Once I have your ID, you have three hours with the equipment. After three hours, come back here to return the equipment, and I'll give you your student ID back. Or, if you want, you can re-check out the equipment.

MS: What if I'm gone for more than three hours?

FE: Then I have to charge you five dollars per piece of equipment that's returned late.

MS: Ah, okay. In that case, I'll definitely be back within three hours.

FE: Great. Any more rental-related questions?

MS: Nope, I think I got it. Here is my ID. (*Takes out student ID and hands it to employee*)

FE: (*Takes student ID*) Alright. So I have your ID, let me go get your equipment. Oh, and if you find that anything doesn't work or is starting to break, just bring it back here and I'll replace it.

MS: Sounds good. Thanks for your help.

FE: No problem at all. I'll be right back with your equipment.

Narrator: Now get ready to answer the questions.

TRACK 1.37

Narrator: Listen to part of the conversation. Then answer the question.

FE: That should be no problem. Have you rented equipment from the recreation department before?

MS: Well, I've been to the gym many times, but no, I've never rented anything before.

Narrator: Why does the recreation department employee say this?

FE: Have you rented equipment from the recreation department before?

TRACK 1.38

Narrator: Listen to a conversation between two students.

Male Student (MS): Excuse me, do you know where Lecture Hall 203 is? I don't really know my way around campus yet.

Female Student (FS): Hmmmm, Lecture Hall 203. I don't know off the top of my head, but I might still be able to help you. What class do you have there?

MS: Psychology 1.

FS: Oh, okay. I know what lecture hall you're talking about. It's one of the bigger lecture halls on campus. In fact, Lecture Hall 203 is where I took Psychology 1, too.

MS: Awesome. I was starting to think I'd never find it. I've already asked three other people, and none of them could help me.

FS: Well, I guess it's a good thing that I'm a psychology major.

MS: I'll say.

FS: So you're actually pretty close to the lecture hall now. Just keep walking north, turn left at the big courtyard ahead, and you should be able to see Lecture Hall 203 from there.

MS: You're kidding! I must've walked right by it. I was over there just a few minutes ago.

FS: Yeah, the lecture halls here really aren't that well labeled. Hopefully it's easy to find now that you know what to look for.

MS: Thank you for the directions. I was worried I was going to be late for the first day of class.

FS: It's no problem. Just out of curiosity, who's teaching Psychology 1 this semester?

MS: Oh, let me check. (*Student gets out his class schedule*) Ah, here it is. The professor's last name is Duarte.

FS: Oh, good. that's the same professor who taught my Psychology 1 class. He's really nice, and he definitely knows his stuff.

MS: Oh, good. Well, thanks again for your help.

FS: No problem.
Narrator: Now get ready to answer the questions.

TRACK 1.39

Narrator: Listen to part of the conversation. Then answer the question.
FS: Oh, okay. I know what lecture hall you're talking about. It's one of the bigger lecture halls on campus. In fact, Lecture Hall 203 is where I took Psychology 1, too.
Narrator: Why does the woman say this?
FS: In fact, Lecture Hall 203 is where I took Psychology 1, too.

TRACK 1.40

Narrator: Listen to a conversation between a student and a librarian.
Male Librarian (ML): Good morning. What can I do for you?
Female Student (FS): Well, my friend told me that the library keeps copies of all the textbooks for students to use.
ML: Well, almost all the textbooks. We try to keep a stock of textbooks for students who can't afford, or simply don't want to buy, the expensive textbooks they need for their classes.
FS: Oh, great. Can you see if you have the textbook for Sociology 143.
ML: Yes. Let me see. (*Librarian types information into computer*) Yes, we have one copy available right now. Would you like to check it out?
FS: Yes, please. I really need to catch up on the reading for that class.
ML: Okay. And, before I go grab that book for you, do you know the policy for checking out class textbooks?
FS: Isn't it the same as for regular library books? You check it out for two weeks at a time?
ML: Actually, no. Because class textbooks are always in such high demand, we can only let you use the book for a three-hour period, once per day. And the book has to stay in the library, so no taking it back to your dorm room or anything.
FS: Oh, that's too bad. Well, I guess I'll have to read quickly. (*Chuckles*) I knew this whole "free textbooks at the library" thing was too good to be true.
ML: Yes. I suppose all good things come at a price. Well, I'll go get that sociology textbook for you right now.
FS: Thank you very much.
Narrator: Now get ready to answer the questions.

TRACK 1.41

Narrator: Listen to part of the conversation. Then answer the question.
ML: Yes, we have one copy available right now. Would you like to check it out?
FS: Yes, please. I really need to catch up on the reading for that class.
Narrator: Why does the student say this?
FS: I really need to catch up on the reading for that class.

TRACK 1.42

Narrator: Listen to a conversation between a student and a university employee.
Female Student (FS): Excuse me. Is this where I come to sign up for the university's health care program?
Male University Employee (ME): That's correct. I can help you set that up. Do you know how the university's health care program works?
FS: Not really. Can you explain it?
ME: Certainly. So all you have to do to sign up is fill out this application (*University Employee hands Student an application*) and pay a one-time fee. Once you've done those two things, you'll be covered for the rest of the academic year.

Most students purchase the university's health care, even if they already have health insurance. After all, you can only use the on-campus health facilities if you sign up for the university's health care program. And the nearest urgent care center is six miles away, while the university health center is located right in the middle of campus.
FS: Okay, that sounds good. But how comprehensive is the coverage that I'm paying for? You guys can't perform surgery and stuff here, can you?
ME: Well, our on-campus medical staff can perform simple procedures, like stitching up minor wounds. And our staff can prescribe antibiotics and some medication, in case you get sick. But we don't have the proper medical equipment for more complicated procedures.
FS: Well, hopefully I won't need any major surgeries. So I guess I'll just sign up now. How much does it cost to get insured for the school year?

ME: It's a one-time fee of 310 dollars.
FS: Oh, awesome. I'll gladly pay that amount.
ME: Sounds good. Once you've give me the completed application and the payment, I'll put your information into our system right away.
FS: Thanks.
Narrator: Now get ready to answer the questions.

TRACK 1.43

Narrator: Listen to part of the conversation. Then answer the question.
ME: Most students purchase the university's health care, even if they already have health insurance. After all, you can only use the on-campus health facilities if you sign up for the university's health care program. And the nearest urgent care center is six miles away, while the university health center in located right in the middle of campus.
Narrator: Why does the university employee say this?
ME: And the nearest urgent care center is six miles away, while the university health center in located right in the middle of campus.

TRACK 1.44

Narrator: Listen to part of the conversation. Then answer the question.
ME: It's a one-time fee of 310 dollars.
FS: Oh, awesome. I'll gladly pay that amount.
Narrator: What can be inferred from this?
FS: Oh, awesome. I'll gladly pay that amount.

CHAPTER 2

TRACK 2.01

Narrator: Listen to a lecture in a physics class.
Male Professor (MP): Today, I'm going to introduce Isaac Newton's laws of motion. These laws explain how force and mass affect motion. Being familiar with these laws will be crucial to understanding many of our experiments later on.

Newton's first law states that a moving object will continue to move in the same direction at the same speed unless an outside force affects it. This law also states that an object at rest will stay at rest unless a force acts on it. Newton's first law is known as the principle of inertia.

Newton's second law states that acceleration is the result of a force acting on a mass. So the more massive an object is, the more force it takes to accelerate that object. This law is so important because Newton determined the exact relationship between force, mass, and acceleration using the formula "F = ma," where "F" is the force, "m" is the object's mass, and "a" is the acceleration.

The third law states that for each action there's an equal and opposite reaction. And this law is best understood using an example. Rockets take off by expelling gases. The downward motion of the gases creates a reaction of the rocket upward that helps it overcome gravity and fly into space.
Narrator: Now get ready to answer the question.

TRACK 2.02

Narrator: Listen to a lecture in an architecture class.
Female Professor (FP): Last class we discussed mechanical drawings, which are scale drawings that show how something functions or how something should be constructed.

Although you'll create most of your mechanical drawings on the computer this semester, we'll spend the next couple of classes learning about blueprints. A blueprint is really just a copy of a mechanical drawing. These copies are called "blueprints" because the process produces white lines on a blue background.

One of the main functions of blueprints is to guide construction workers and managers. Blueprint copies provides each worker with identical information about the dimensions and position of each piece needed for a project.

To create a blueprint, you must first make the original drawing on a material that allows light to pass through it, so tracing paper is ideal for these original drawings. Then you place the tracing paper with the original drawing on top of light-sensitive paper and shine a bright light on it.

Next you remove the original drawing and wash the tracing paper in water. The water causes the light-sensitive paper to turn blue wherever it was exposed to light. The paper that was underneath your lines doesn't turn blue because the lines prevented the light from hitting the paper. This process produces a copy that has white lines on a blue background.

Narrator: Now get ready to answer the question.

TRACK 2.03

Narrator: Listen to a lecture in a medical science class.

Female Professor (FP): As you know, the United States has no comprehensive national system for providing healthcare. But the United Kingdom does.

The United Kingdom has a healthcare system called the National Health Service—NHS for short—that gives free medical care to all citizens. The NHS receives most of its funding from the general taxes that all citizens pay.

So how does this NHS system work? Well, everyone in the United Kingdom registers with a doctor called a general practitioner. People can register with any general practitioner, or "GP," of their choice. Most GPs see patients in offices called "surgeries."

People call their GPs whenever they need medical care. When a GP feels that a patient needs specialized care, the GP refers the patient to a specialist. Patients cannot consult specialists without a referral from a GP. All specialists in the United Kingdom work in hospitals. When a specialist has completed a patient's treatment, the specialist sends the patient back to the GP.

Both GPs and specialists are paid by the National Health Service. In addition, the NHS provides many community support services, including nurses, ambulances, and certain types of home care.

The NHS holds down the cost of health care by emphasizing primary care and by limiting the number of hospitals. The number of doctors is also controlled by budget limits. The NHS controls where GPs can practice to make certain that medical care is available in all geographic areas.

Narrator: Now get ready to answer the question.

TRACK 2.04

Narrator: Listen to a lecture in a meteorology class.

Male Professor (MP): On this diagram of Earth, you'll notice two thick bands have been drawn around the Earth at 30 degrees latitude both north and south of the equator. Most of the world's deserts are located between these two bands.

To find out how these deserts formed, we need to start at the equator. Equatorial regions receive more sunlight, and this sunlight heats up the air. This heated air rises into the atmosphere, losing moisture and cooling off along the way.

Next, this cool, dry air drifts north and south of the equator, and eventually descends before reaching the 30-degree latitude mark. As this dry air descends, it becomes pressurized. Being under high pressure causes the air to heat up again. Then the high-pressure air sits over this subtropical region, dropping little to no moisture and even drawing moisture from the surrounding region because of the air's heat and dryness. This dry, high-pressure air even deters winds that could bring rain to the region because winds move toward low-pressure regions, not high-pressure ones. If this warm, dry air sits over a region long enough, a desert will form.

But this isn't the only reason for desert formation. Now let's talk about rain shadow.

Narrator: Now get ready to answer the question.

TRACK 2.05

Narrator: Listen to a lecture in a music history class.

Female Professor (FP): Folk music traditions are styles that developed among ordinary people. It was poor people's music, not music for kings and queens. A great example is flamenco music from southern Spain. Most experts agree that flamenco music originated with the ethnic Roma people of Spain, who are sometimes called "Gypsies." Flamenco also may reflect Arab and Jewish cultural influences.

As you'll know if you've ever listened to or seen it performed, the most striking aspect of flamenco is its boldness and intensity. Flamenco integrates guitars, dancers, and singers. The guitars are plucked and tapped rhythmically, dancers stomp and clap at lightning speed, singers cry out desperate emotions, and the listeners clap, stamp their feet, and shout. The music can be complex. Sometimes it incorporates measures of 12 beats each, sometimes the singers and guitars are using different rhythms, and sometimes the musicians improvise, as in jazz.

Flamenco techniques for the guitar take many years of practice to learn. As in classical guitar, there is more plucking than strumming. The fingers of the right hand pluck scales on the strings rapidly—for as many as 16 notes a beat. In flamenco, frequently after plucking a string, the finger rests on the next string very briefly. The effect is to stop that string's vibration, creating an overall staccato sound.

Narrator: Now get ready to answer the question.

TRACK 2.06

Narrator: Listen to part of a lecture in an education class.
Male Professor (MP): So today I want to discuss the pros and cons of automation in education. In other words, I want to talk about whether students' increasing reliance on computers and other technologies generally helps or harms learning.

So to start, the belief that new technologies harm one's ability to learn is not new. About 2,500 years ago, Plato expressed his fear that writing information down would diminish people's abilities to memorize that same information. After all, if people can read something at any time, why would they bother memorizing it? Ultimately, literacy has shaped societies into what they are today, but Plato may have had a point: people's ability and willingness to memorize information has almost certainly declined.

Now let's look at a modern example: the pros and cons of automation when writing a research paper. Let's start with the pros. Because of the wealth of information on the Internet, conducting research for a paper has never been easier. And typing a paper on a word processor is much faster than any other method of recording information. But there are also cons to relying on a computer when writing a paper. Many students rely on spelling- and grammar-proofreading software to correct their writing. Yet by doing so, a student doesn't actually learn proper spelling or grammar. Thus, when students have to write without proofreading software, their writing is often filled with mistakes.

Narrator: Now get ready to answer the questions.

TRACK 2.07

Narrator: Listen to a lecture from a mathematics class.
Female Professor (FP): Since this concept will come up quite a bit when we discuss chaos theory, I want to start today's lecture with the butterfly effect. The butterfly effect is a metaphor that illustrates a hugely important concept in the study of chaos theory. And this major concept is that a seemingly small event in one place can cause a chain of events that lead to a major event somewhere else.

Now this idea might become a little easier to understand once you know where the term "butterfly effect" comes from. In the mid-20th century, a meteorologist, which is the name for someone who studies weather patterns, suggested that tiny events could cause big ones. He hypothesized that the flapping of a butterfly's wings in South America could cause a series of events that would lead to tornadoes hitting Texas days later. In other words, a small and seemingly insignificant event can lead to a large event.

And, as strange as it seems, the concept can be supported by evidence. For example, the butterfly effect could metaphorically explain why it's so hard to predict the weather. After all, a minor change in atmospheric conditions—atmospheric conditions being factors like cloud density and wind patterns—can end up greatly influencing the weather.

Narrator: Now get ready to answer the questions.

TRACK 2.08

Narrator: Listen to a lecture in a political science class.
Male Professor (MP): Today we continue our exploration of different political-economic systems with socialism.

The term "socialism" first appeared in Europe in the 1800s. At that time, thinkers who favored socialism claimed it was a more natural economic system than capitalism. The early socialists believed that public ownership would solve issues such as poverty and social unrest. And during the early- and mid-1800s, socialist writers and speakers were very vocal with their beliefs. The French socialist writer Pierre J. Proudhon argued that the establishment of private property was actually a form of theft from the community. And Welsh-born socialist leader Robert Owen believed that the sharing of property created social harmony and progress, contrasting with the competition and conflict created by capitalism and industrialism.

Such ideas influenced political movements

that attempted to strengthen the working class. For example, let's look at French socialist leader Louis Blanc. During the mid-1800s, he helped create nationally funded trade unions and cooperatives that were meant to give social and political strength to the working class. Unfortunately, these organizations were mismanaged by the government, and they quickly collapsed. But many of his socialistic ideas persisted, and by the 20th century, dozens of countries had included references to socialism in their constitutions.

So now let's fast-forward and look at the condition of some modern socialist states.

Narrator: Now get ready to answer the questions.

TRACK 2.09

Narrator: Listen to a lecture in an astronomy class.

Female Professor (FP): The Kuiper belt is a large band of space debris that's located beyond Neptune and encircles the outer portion of our solar system. Astronomers think that this debris is left over from the formation of the solar system itself. Kuiper belt objects, or "KBOs" as they are known to astronomers, consist mostly of various ices. Astronomers are unsure exactly how many of these KBOs orbit beyond Neptune, but they estimate that there are at least 70,000 KBOs with diameters of at least 60 miles.

In fact, the biggest KBO is Pluto, which was downgraded from a planet to a dwarf planet in 2006. Most KBO's orbit the sun in circular orbits beyond Neptune, but some have much more erratic and elliptical orbits.

The Kuiper belt is named after the Dutch-born American astronomer Gerard P. Kuiper. He speculated that comet-sized objects may have orbited beyond Neptune, but he thought that gravity and interactions with the outer planets had pushed these objects out of the solar system long ago. Then, in 1992, over 50 years after Kuiper's speculation, the English-born American astronomer David Jewitt and the Vietnamese-born astronomer Jane Luu made the first discovery of a KBO other than Pluto.

Narrator: Now get ready to answer the questions.

TRACK 2.10

Narrator: Listen to a lecture in a biology class.

Male Professor (MP): Today we'll be looking at the biology of animal domestication. And one of the major characteristics of, well, pretty much every domesticated animal is neoteny. So can anyone tell me what neoteny is or give an example of it?

Male Student (MS): Well, I don't really know how it applies to domesticated animals. But doesn't neoteny happen in some salamander species? Like, don't some species have both lungs and gills?

MP: Yes. When salamanders are young, they're aquatic, so they breathe using gills. But as adults, they breathe using lungs, on land. So neoteny is when the adult animals in a species keep some of the physical characteristics of the young.

So in neoteny, some traits of the adults are, well, child-like. So what are some physical characteristics typical of human babies?

MS: A small nose, big eyes, and... well, babies are smaller than adults.

MP: Very good. Those are all neotenic qualities in humans, and the ones you described are true of most mammal species. (*To female student*) Oh, yes. You have a question?

Female Student (FS): Aren't all those qualities that Tom just listed features of many breeds of dog. Like, pugs are pretty small and have flattened faces and short snouts. And, well, most dogs have bigger eyes than wolves do.

MP: Good observation. Dogs have many neotenic features, probably as a result of domestication…

Narrator: Now get ready to answer the questions.

TRACK 2.11

Narrator: Listen to a lecture from a European literature class.

Male Professor (MP): Before we begin reading *Don Quixote*, the classic novel by Miguel de Cervantes, I want to give you guys a little background information. Written and set in Spain in the early 1600s, the novel tells of the adventures, victories, and defeats of aged nobleman Alanso Quixano, who renames himself "Don Quixote." In the beginning of the novel, Don Quixote does nothing but sit at home and read chivalric romances, which are stories where brave, honorable knights save beautiful women from danger. So really, chivalric romances are the classic "knight in shining armor" stories.

Anyway, Don Quixote reads these romances, and he decides to become one of the brave knights he has read so much about. So he dons an old suit of armor; rides an old, skinny horse named Rocinante; and recruits a peasant named Sancho Panza to be his assistant, or squire. Then, he rides off to help the needy and bring justice to Spain.

Now one thing that makes *Don Quixote* so memorable and influential is the way it blurs the lines between comedy and tragedy. I mean, just think about the potential for comedy and tragedy in the novel's plot: an old man who tries to bring justice to the world by dressing up as a knight has the potential to be very funny and very tragic.

Narrator: Now get ready to answer the questions.

TRACK 2.12

Narrator: Why does the professor say this?
MP: So he dons an old suit of armor; rides an old, skinny horse named Rocinante; and recruits a peasant named Sancho Panza to be his assistant, or squire. Then, he rides off to help the needy and bring justice to Spain.

TRACK 2.13

Narrator: Listen to a lecture in an ancient history class.
Male Professor (MP): You know, it would be pretty reasonable to think that the wheel has been around for a really, really long time. I mean, it's a simple device that has revolutionized agriculture, transportation, warfare, and, well, pretty much every aspect of daily life.

So it often surprises people to learn that, as far as we know, the wheel was not invented until about 6,000 years ago. That's about the same time that some civilizations began writing information down. Most archaeologists agree that the wheel developed independently in several European and Middle Eastern civilizations at about the same time.

One of the most common uses for the wheel among these early civilizations was for the chariot, a horse-pulled cart most often used in battle. In battle, chariots were the tanks of their day: they were the biggest things on the battlefield, and they proved to be very successful. After all, imagine how terrifying it would be to see a large, horse-drawn chariot charging at you in the midst of a crowded, chaotic battlefield.

And while the wheel quickly spread throughout Europe, Asia, and parts of Africa shortly after it was first invented, very few ancient North and South American civilizations ever invented anything that functions like a wheel. Most archaeologists agree that this is because North and South America lacked any domesticated animals that were large enough to pull humans, supplies, or agricultural equipment, meaning that the wheel would not have had much obvious use.

Narrator: Now get ready to answer the questions.

TRACK 2.14

Narrator: Listen to a lecture in a bioethics class.
Female Professor (FP): Today we're going to discuss the humane treatment of animals. And I want to start by discussing one of the greatest figures in the fight for the humane treatment of livestock: Mary Temple Grandin. Grandin is an autistic woman and a doctor of animal sciences who has used her autism to help make the process of slaughtering livestock considerably more humane.

Diagnosed with autism at the age of two, Grandin claims she often feels anxious and stressed, and she's easily alarmed by loud noises and bright lights. After observing livestock and how they react to the bright lights, loud noises, and rough handling that they experience as they are led to be slaughtered, Grandin felt that she could relate to their feelings of stress and anxiety from overstimulation. As a result, Grandin introduced a number of changes to make the slaughter of livestock more humane. For example, she designed a curved, walled path that livestock can follow to the slaughterhouse. This curved path ensures that the livestock can't see the slaughterhouse in front of them, and it eliminates excessive light and noise.
So in short, Grandin overcame many of the social and neurological challenges associated with autism, and she managed to revolutionize the treatment of livestock in the process.

Narrator: Now get ready to answer the questions.

TRACK 2.15

Narrator: Why does the professor say this?
FP: Diagnosed with autism at the age of two, Grandin claims she often feels anxious and stressed, and she's easily alarmed by loud noises and bright lights.

TRACK 2.16

Narrator: Listen to a lecture from a psychology class.

Male Professor (MP): Now let's take a closer look at the anxiety disorder known as Obsessive Compulsive Disorder—OCD. So, you might think that OCD has something to do with cleaning or hand-washing, am I right? That is a common misconception, that OCD is always about fear of germs. Actually, the "O" part of OCD, the "obsessive" part, means that the person has repetitive fearful thoughts. These fearful thoughts take many forms in different people. An OCD sufferer's fear might have to do with having dirty hands, or it could be something like, "What if I accidentally cause my family's death?" "What if I push a child in front of a bus?" Or, "What if I cheat on this test?" OCD sufferers have all kinds of unwanted thoughts. OCD fears do not go away; they cause the sufferer constant dread.

The "C" part of OCD stands for "compulsive," meaning actions that the person feels must be taken due to their obsessive thoughts. The person might feel that he or she has to check that the stove is turned off over and over, for example, or clean off some contamination, or say something in an exact way, or avoid something. Again, the compulsive actions do not make sense. Sometimes the compulsive acts make the sufferer seem very stubborn and demanding, because sufferers may insist on actions that seem pointless or rude to others. Underneath, what's going on is that they feel desperate to prevent their fears from coming true. Yes, Josh, you had a question?

Male Student (MS): I was just wondering if people with OCD realize that the things they are doing do not make sense? Or do they think that what they are thinking and doing is logical?

MP: That's a great question. OCD sufferers feel they cannot control their fears, and even so, they do know that their fears are irrational. They realize that. OCD sufferers are often told to "just think about something else," which is something they can't do. Or, they keep their fears secret, instead of seeking help.

Narrator: Now get ready to answer the questions.

TRACK 2.17

Narrator: Why does the professor say this?

MP: So, you might think OCD has something to do with cleaning or hand-washing, am I right?

TRACK 2.18

Narrator: Why does the professor say this?

MP: Sometimes the compulsive acts make the sufferer seem very stubborn and demanding, because they may insist on actions that make life difficult for themselves and their loved ones.

TRACK 2.19

Narrator: Listen to a lecture from a biology class.

Female Professor (FP): We've known about the deadly rabies virus for 5,000 years. And since the 1800s, thanks to the groundbreaking work of Louis Pasteur, we've had a cure. Although the treatment and vaccine are effective, the virus must be stopped before it reaches the brain. If the virus reaches any mammal's brain, it's fatal.

Because this virus is so dangerous, it's important for public health officials to educate people about the vectors—that is, the points where the virus moves from animal hosts to human beings. Rabies only lives in mammals. For example, the Carolina opossum, a common backyard visitor throughout the United States, cannot carry the virus. Its marsupial blood isn't hot enough.

The most common vector animal are bats. There are thousands of bat species, and all can carry the virus and infect people. Next on the list are raccoons and skunks. Any unusual contact with these three species, especially if biting is involved, should be reported as a medical emergency.

Potentially, any mammal can carry the virus, including cows, wild dogs, and even rabbits. The key to controlling rabies is to educate people about the vector species and emphasize the need for immediate medical treatment.

Narrator: Now get ready to answer the questions.

TRACK 2.20

Narrator: Listen to a lecture in a psychology class.

Male Professor (MP): Alcoholism is an issue that spans both cultures and generations. One reason that alcoholism remains problematic is that there are so many risk factors associated with it. So today I'd like to break down the risk factors of developing an alcohol dependency into genetic, environmental, and physiological components.

Research shows that heredity plays an important role in alcoholism. The Collaborative Studies on the Genetics of Alcohol, or COGA for short, is a long-term study that has evaluated thousands of individuals in an attempt to associate certain genes with alcohol dependency. So far, researchers have isolated three chromosomes that are linked to an increased risk of alcohol dependency.

But environment also plays a role in the development of alcoholism. Environmental influences may include income level, family stability, peer pressure, and community acceptance of drinking.

Other research focuses on understanding how alcohol affects the brain's neurotransmitters, which are the chemicals that carry messages among nerve cells. Drinking alcohol changes levels of neurotransmitter activity, and these levels don't immediately return to normal when drinking stops. As a result, problem drinkers may not "feel right" when they stop drinking because their neurotransmitters have adapted to alcohol.

Narrator: Now get ready to answer the questions.

TRACK 2.21

Narrator: What does the professor mean when he says this?

MP: Alcoholism is an issue that spans both cultures and generations.

TRACK 2.22

Narrator: Listen to a lecture in an astronomy class.

Male Professor (MP): When asked about humanity's greatest space-related achievements, most people will mention the Mars rovers and, of course, *Apollo 11*'s Moon landing. And, although I regard these as incredible accomplishments, I believe that they can't compare to the decades-long journey of *Voyager 1*. So who here can tell me a bit about *Voyager 1*?

Female Student (FS): Isn't *Voyager 1* the space probe that took the first close-up photographs of Jupiter and Saturn?

MP: Yes, very good. Way back in 1979 and 1980, *Voyager 1* photographed these planets and their moons as it traveled past them. Since passing by Jupiter and Saturn, *Voyager 1* has been making its way further and further into deep space. And amazingly, in August of 2012, *Voyager 1* became the first spacecraft to leave our solar system.

Now let me put the vast distances that *Voyager 1* has traveled in perspective: the Moon is about 250,000 miles away from Earth, the Sun is about 93 million miles from Earth, and, believe it or not, *Voyager 1* is about 12 billion miles from Earth. So if it takes the light from the Sun about 8 minutes to travel the 93 million miles to Earth, it takes that same light about *18 hours* to reach *Voyager 1*. So now let's discuss how *Voyager 1* sends and receives data from such staggering distances....

Narrator: Now get ready to answer the questions.

TRACK 2.23

Narrator: Listen to a lecture in a nutritional science class.

Female Professor (FP): I will spend the next few lectures talking about macronutrients. Macronutrients are the nutrients your body requires a lot of to function. The first macronutrient we'll discuss is protein.

So protein does a lot more than simply build up muscle tissue. In fact, proteins are the second most plentiful substances in the human body, with water being the most plentiful. In addition to forming muscles, protein is necessary for the formation of hair, nails, and eyes. And on top of that, every cell in the human body has some protein in it.

Now that you have some idea of what proteins do, let me explain what protein actually is. Protein is formed from long chains of simple compounds called "amino acids." Although there are over 50 known amino acids, the proteins in our body are made from different combinations of about 20 amino acids. The human body can produce some of these 20 amino acids on its own, but nine of these essential amino acids must be obtained through what we eat. Meat and dairy products contain all the amino acids the human body needs to survive. And vegetables, grains, and beans have some amino acids, but not all of the amino acids that our bodies require.

Narrator: Now get ready to answer the questions.

TRACK 2.24

Narrator: Listen to a lecture in a biology class.

Male Professor (MP): So does anyone have any questions before we conclude today's lecture?
Female Student (FS): When did the first organisms appear on Earth?
MP: Now that question puzzled scientists for a long time. Although no one can say for certain when exactly life started here on Earth, fossil evidence indicates that life existed at least 3.5-billion years ago. And that's pretty amazing when you think about it. The Earth formed about 4.5-billion years ago, and then it took nearly a billion years for the Earth's crust to harden from hot, liquid rock into solid rock. So really, it seems as though life began as soon as Earth's conditions could accommodate it. (*To male student*) Yes, I see there's a question in the back row.
Male Student (MS): So what kind of organism was the earliest form of life?
MP: Well, the earliest we know of are single-celled microbes that gathered into large colonies. These colonies used energy from the sun as their food source, like plants do today. And these microbial colonies would slowly stack on top of each other, taking on the appearance of little rock-like towers. These "towers" are called stromatolites. And these stromatolites provide the fossil evidence telling us that life began *at least* 3.5-billion years ago.
Narrator: Now get ready to answer the questions.

TRACK 2.25

Narrator: What can be inferred from this?
Male Professor: And these stromatolites provide the fossil evidence telling us that life began *at least* 3.5-billion years ago.

TRACK 2.26

Narrator: Listen to a lecture in a theatre class.
Female Professor (FP): There are three basic stage types used in modern theater.

The "proscenium stage" is the most common type of stage, and it can only be viewed from the front. A rectangular frame called a proscenium arch surrounds this type of stage. Also, you'll usually see curtains attached to the proscenium arch, and as you guys probably know, the curtains may be drawn in order to hide the stage in between acts of a play or during scenery changes. Directors can use elaborate sets on a proscenium stage.

Another popular style of stage is the "open stage." Open stages have seats around three sides of a raised platform that extends into the auditorium. Directors and set designers working on open-stage productions must carefully plan a performance so that the actions of every actor can be seen from all three sides at the same time. So in an open-stage production, you will probably only see large pieces of scenery and props at the back of the stage so they don't block the audience's view.

In a "theater-in-the-round," viewers sit on four sides of the stage. The scenery used in a theater-in-the-round must be low enough to allow the performance area to be seen from every side. Scene changes are made in view of the audience, and the performers in a theater-in-the-round production have to make their entrances and exits through the auditorium.

Narrator: Now get ready to answer the questions.

TRACK 2.27

Narrator: Listen to a lecture in a psychology class.
Male Professor (MP): So I'd like to focus for a moment on rumination. You may be aware that the verb "ruminate" has two meanings. One is what cows, goats, sheep and some other animals do when they eat grass. They chew it, swallow it, keep it in a special stomach, then partially throw it up and chew it again. So to "ruminate" on something is to chew it up completely more than once.

But rumination also serves as a metaphor for thinking about the same thing over and over again. In other words, metaphorically, our minds are re-chewing experiences we've had. For example, perhaps a friend has said something mean. Perhaps we ourselves said something we regret. Perhaps we think for hours about what we *should have* said. But research shows that thinking about the same injustice or embarrassment over and over can lead to depression and anxiety disorders. (*To female student*) Yes, you had a question?
Female Student (FS): Yeah, I was wondering, doesn't thinking about something a lot help us figure out what to do about it? I mean, reflection is good, isn't it?
MP: You bring up a very good point. When used informally, the term "to ruminate" might just mean to reflect

on something—that is, to gain insight into something by considering it for a bit. In the field of psychology, however, to ruminate means to almost uncontrollably think about upsetting feelings and their causes.

When doing this kind of ruminating, you may remember other bad experiences. You may end up feeling really hopeless and overwhelmed by negative emotions. You may have a harder time forgiving others, or yourself.

So, researchers suggest that to break the cycle of rumination, people should distract themselves. They should do something that completely occupies their thoughts, such as a crossword puzzle or strenuous exercise. Then when they have calmed down, they should decide on at least one step they can take to solve the problem.

Narrator: Now get ready to answer the questions.

TRACK 2.28

Narrator: Why does the professor say this?

MP: For example, perhaps a friend has said something mean. Perhaps we ourselves said something we regret. Perhaps we think for hours about what we *should have* said. But research shows that thinking about the same injustice or embarrassment over and over can lead to depression and anxiety disorders.

TRACK 2.29

Narrator: Listen to a lecture in a business class.

Female Professor (FP): I want to focus today's lecture on three main types of business ownership in the United States: single proprietorships, partnerships, and corporations. Keep in mind that there are other, less common types of business ownership, but we'll discuss those in a later class.

Single proprietorships are businesses owned by one person. This owner makes all the company's decisions and gets all of the profits. Proprietors can start a business with a small amount of money and few legal formalities. But the owner is also completely responsible for any debt that the business accumulates. So when a single proprietor's business takes on debt, a creditor can take the owner's personal belongings, not just those associated with the business. Single proprietorships are the most common form of business ownership in farming, construction, and food service.

Partnerships consist of two or more owners who share the responsibilities and profits of a business. Partners sign a legal agreement that specifies the amount of work and money each person contributes as well as the percentage of profits each receives. Partnerships can usually handle more business than a single proprietor, but like a single proprietorship, each partner is 100 percent responsible for debt acquired by the business. Nearly all partnerships are small businesses. They're most common in law, medicine, and real estate.

Corporations are owned by stockholders, who have shares of stock in these companies. The approval of a majority of the stockholders may be required for certain decisions that affect business operations. But it's the managers who run the everyday activities of a corporation. Profits are either distributed among the stockholders or reinvested in the corporation. And unlike single proprietorships and partnerships, the owners of a corporation aren't necessarily held responsible for the corporation's debt. Most corporations are larger than businesses owned by individuals or partners. Corporations dominate such industries as banking, insurance, and oil.

Narrator: Now get ready to answer the questions.

TRACK 2.30

Narrator: Listen to a lecture in a geology class.

Male Professor (MP): As Earth runs out of fossil fuels, which we use to make oil and gasoline, scientists race to find other sources of energy. And currently, one of the best candidates for relatively inexpensive and accessible energy is called "geothermal energy." The prefix "geo-" comes from the Greek work for "Earth." Thermal energy is the heat energy that comes from Earth's core. And there's a lot of heat inside of Earth. In fact, Earth's core—you know, the center of the Earth—is over 7,500 degrees Fahrenheit. This is actually hot enough to—(*To female student*) Yes, Selena. What's your question?

Female Student (FS): Where does all this heat come from? I mean, how does it get to be 7,500 degrees Fahrenheit at the center of the Earth?

MP: Well, some of the heat is left over from the Earth's formation billions of years ago. The rest of the energy comes from the decay of radioactive elements. And so, like I was saying, the heat at Earth's core melts rock into a thick liquid called "magma." And because magma is less dense than the rock surrounding it, some magma rises to the Earth's mantle and crust—the outer layers of the Earth, near the surface. Once in the mantle and crust, the magma sometimes gets close to underground reserves of water, and the intense heat from the magma causes the underground water to heat up. This heated water sometimes rises to Earth's surface, where it forms hot springs and geysers.

People have used the heated water in hot springs for bathing and heating for thousands of years. But recently, researchers have found a very modern use for the geothermal energy produced by heated subsurface water: generating electricity. Many countries generate some of their electricity by harvesting thermal energy from underground water and steam. So let's look at how, exactly, they do this…

Narrator: Now get ready to answer the questions.

TRACK 2.31

Narrator: Why does the professor say this?
MP: People have used the heated water in hot springs for bathing and heating for thousands of years.

TRACK 2.32

Narrator: What can be inferred from this?
MP: And so, like I was saying, the heat at Earth's core melts rock into a thick liquid called "magma." And because magma is less dense than the rock surrounding it, some magma rises to the Earth's mantle and crust—the outer layers of the Earth, near the surface.

TRACK 2.33

Narrator: Listen to a lecture in a political science class.
Female Professor (FP): Protectionism describes government activities that try to protect and promote the growth of domestic industries and business by controlling foreign imports. In other words, protectionism is where the government favors the success of domestic businesses over foreign ones.

Government protectionism occurs in a number of ways. The most common method of protectionism is taxing imported goods. This tax, called a "tariff," increases the price of imported goods, giving domestic industries a price advantage. Of course, the downside is that tariffs increase the price of imported products for consumers. Another protectionist strategy is to limit the amount of goods that can be imported into the country. This method means that the protected domestic industry will have less competition. Another way that governments enforce protectionism is by offering subsidies to domestic industries. Now a subsidy is (*slowly*) money that a government gives to a business when that business can't compete on its own. Basically, the government supports the business until it can make money. So to review, governments protect domestic businesses mainly through tariffs, limits on imports, and subsidies.

Ultimately, protectionist policies conflict with ideas of free trade, where a business must compete with other businesses to be successful, because protectionism means that a government will favor local businesses and industries, even if doing so means higher prices for consumers. As a result, many economists agree that supporting domestic industries by using protectionist policies doesn't help promote economic growth.

But now I want to hear what you guys think: Based on what we've learned so far this semester, can you guys point out any benefits or additional flaws to protectionist policies?

Narrator: Now get ready to answer the questions.

TRACK 2.34

Narrator: Listen to part of the lecture. Then answer the question.
FP: The most common method of protectionism is taxing imported goods. This tax, called a "tariff," increases the price of imported goods, giving domestic industries a price advantage. Of course, the downside is that tariffs increase the price of imported products for consumers.
Narrator: What can be inferred from this?
FP: Of course, the downside is that tariffs increase the price of imported products for consumers.

TRACK 2.35

Narrator: Why does the professor say this?
FP: As a result, many economists agree that supporting domestic industries by using protectionist policies doesn't promote economic growth.

TRACK 2.36

Narrator: Listen to a lecture in an ancient history class.

Male Professor (MP): So when counting, most of us will claim that it's easiest to keep track of numbers in groups of 5s and 10s. Why do you guys think this is?

Female Student (FS): Because we have five fingers on each hand and ten fingers in total.

MP: Yes, exactly. But throughout history, not all cultures have used the base 10 system, which is also called the decimal system. Today, I want to talk about a different counting system, which was developed by the Sumerians over 5,000 years ago. It's called the sexagesimal numeral system, which uses 60 as its base number. Now can anyone tell us how the sexagesimal system is in use today? Where do we use base 60?

Male Student (MS): Well, to measure time; like, there are 60 seconds in a minute and 60 minutes in an hour.

MP: Absolutely. And we see the sexagesimal system in use when we measure angles. For instance, there are 360 degrees in a circle—a result of 60 times six—and there are 180 degrees in a triangle—a result of 60 times three.

As was pointed out earlier, the base 10 system obviously originated as a result of our 10 fingers. But the origins of the sexagesimal system are a little less clear. So the last thing I want to teach you guys today is how to count in base 60 using just 10 fingers, much like ancient people may have.

So using your right hand, you can count up to 12 by using your thumb to point to each of the three knucklebones on your four free fingers. You can use your left hand to keep track of how many sets of 12 you've counted: every time your right hand counts to 12, put up one finger on your left hand. So when all five fingers on your left hand are raised, you've counted to 60. Go ahead and try this out yourself right now.

Narrator: Now get ready to answer the questions.

TRACK 2.37

Narrator: Listen to part of the lecture. Then answer the question.

MP: As was pointed out earlier, the origins of the based 10 system are pretty obviously based on our 10 fingers. But the origins of the sexagesimal system are a little less clear. So the last thing I want to teach you guys today is how to count in base 60 using just 10 fingers, much like ancient people may have.

Narrator: Why does the professor say this?

MP: So the last thing I want to teach you guys today is how to count in base 60 using just 10 fingers, much like ancient people may have.

TRACK 2.38

Narrator: Listen to a lecture in a biology class.

Male Professor (MP): Today we'll look at mutualism, which is a type of relationship between animal species. So the root word of mutualism is "mutual," and a mutual relationship is one where both parties feel or act in the same way. So, in nature, mutualism is where both species benefit, or gain something, from an interaction or a relationship.

So let's clear up this concept by looking at mutualism between some ant species and aphids. And, in case you haven't heard of them before, aphids are very small insects that feed off the sugar produced by plants.

Now we humans often think of ourselves as special because we have domesticated other species, like cats, dogs, cows, and so on. But some species of ants have been "herding" and "domesticating" aphids for millions of years. Some ant colonies will gather large groups of aphids together. These aphids feed on the sugary nectar of a plant, and excrete a substance called "honeydew," a waste product that's high in sugar. The ants then use this honeydew for food. In return for the aphids' honeydew, the ants protect the aphids from parasites and predators. Once the aphids have consumed all the nutrients from one plant, the ants will carry the aphids to a new one. Now this phenomenon is not—(*To female student*) You have a question, Allison?

Female Student (FS): Yeah. Sorry to interrupt, but I was wondering: don't the aphids ever wander off or try to run away or anything?

MP: Well, the ants' protection does come at a price. Researchers have discovered that the ants leave a chemical trail that basically subdues the aphids and makes them unlikely to try to escape or wander away. And, under certain environmental conditions, aphids will grow wings. So to ensure that the aphids don't fly off, the ants will sometimes remove these wings. So even though the relationship between ants and aphids is an example of mutualism, the ants are definitely the ones in charge.

Narrator: Now get ready to answer the questions.

TRACK 2.39

Narrator: Why does the professor say this?

MP: Now we humans often think of ourselves as special because we have domesticated other species, like cats, dogs, cows, and so on. But some species of ants have been "herding" and "domesticating" aphids for millions of years.

CHAPTER 3

TRACK 3.01

Narrator: Listen to a lecture in an anthropology class.

Female Professor (FP): As you've probably noticed from our discussions, many aspects of a culture develop for practical reasons. Today our focus is on the practical solutions that eventually led to the sophisticated culture of ancient Egypt. From about 5000 BCE—long before the first pharaohs or pyramids—people lived in farming villages along the Nile River. Let's look at what was available to them for daily life.

First and foremost was the Nile River. The river flooded every winter and then receded every spring. Farmers were able to grow crops on the floodplain during spring and summer, and build permanent homes just above the flood line. To either side of the river are vast deserts.

So, for making homes, early Egyptians had river mud, and plenty of it. They learned to make bricks from river mud mixed with straw, and they used the bricks to build rectangular homes with flat roofs. The mud bricks kept the rooms of these houses cool during hot days. At night, the structure supported people living on the flat rooftops. There is almost no rain in Egypt, so cooking and sleeping on the roof in the cool air made a lot of sense.

Second, people could use the plants that grew along marshy banks of the Nile River. Some of the most important types of plants were reeds. People picked the reeds, dried them, and used them in weaving. These reeds were woven into sandals, sleeping mats, and baskets. They could also be woven into window coverings to keep out flies and dust. And, by about 3100 BCE, Egyptians began making paper from the papyrus reeds.

In addition, the rich soil along the river was perfect for growing flax, a grass-like plant that could be made into cool linen fabric for clothes. Of course, linen was also used later to wrap mummies. Egyptians also had access to rocks and minerals from the desert. For example, there are lakes to the west of Cairo that dry up every summer, leaving behind special salts. Early Egyptians found that the salts could be used as cleansers and preservatives; eventually, the salts were processed and used to make the distinctive eye makeup that most of us recognize immediately as Egyptian. Modern science has shown that the black eye makeup had properties that prevented and treated eye infections.

Narrator: Now get ready to answer the questions.

TRACK 3.02

Narrator: Why does the professor say this?

FP: Modern science has shown that the black eye makeup had properties that prevented and treated eye infections.

TRACK 3.03

Narrator: Listen to a conversation between a student and a professor.

Male Student (MS): Hey, professor. I know your office hours are almost over, but do you have time for me to ask you a few questions?

Female Professor (FP): Certainly. What can I help you with?

MS: Well, it's about the paper you assigned. This is the first literature class I've taken in college, so I don't have much experience writing analysis papers—you know, where you have to closely analyze one feature of a book.

FP: So you're having trouble deciding on a topic?

MS: Actually, no. I know what I want to write about. In fact, I've even written most of the paper already.

FP: Oh, well that's good. What topic have you decided on?

MS: Well, when we read *The Great Gatsby* in class, I noticed that it shares a lot of features with the Greek tragedies. So I'm exploring the idea of Gatsby as the tragic hero—you know, the way he's presented reminds me of characters like Oedipus or Pentheus—and Nick is kind of like the chorus; he tells the audience what's going on, basically.

FP: I see. That sounds quite interesting. But it sounds like you've got this analysis thing down pretty well. So what is it, exactly, that you're having trouble with?

MS: It's just that, I don't know how to start the paper. How do you write an introduction when all your main ideas get developed in your body paragraphs?

FP: Well, there's really no one right way to write an introduction. But maybe I can give you a few pointers. So your paper will mention a lot of features of Greek tragedies, right?

MS: Yes, absolutely.

FP: And where in the paper do you introduce all these features?

MS: Well, I guess I just kind of bring up different features, like the characteristics of the hero and the chorus in Greek tragedy, as they become relevant to the topic.

FP: Which might confuse someone unfamiliar with Greek theatre.

MS: Huh. I guess that's true. So maybe I should just introduce all the features of Greek tragedy in the introduction. Then I can focus my body paragraphs on *The Great Gatsby*.

FP: My thoughts exactly.

MS: Thanks for your help! I guess I just needed a fresh perspective, and you've definitely given me that.

FP: My pleasure. Good luck on that introduction.

Narrator: Now get ready to answer the questions.

TRACK 3.04

Narrator: Listen to part of the conversation. Then answer the question.

MS: Well, it's about the paper you assigned. This is the first literature class I've taken in college, so I don't have much experience writing critical analysis papers—you know, where you have to closely analyze one feature of a book.

FP: So you're having trouble deciding on a topic?

Narrator: Why does the professor say this?

FP: So you're having trouble deciding on a topic?

TRACK 3.05

Narrator: What is suggested about Oedipus and Pentheus from this?

MS: Well, when we read *The Great Gatsby* in class, I noticed that it shares a lot of features with the Greek tragedies. So I'm exploring the idea of Gatsby as the tragic hero—you know, the way he's presented reminds me of characters like Oedipus or Pentheus—and Nick is kind of like the chorus; he tells the audience what's going on, basically.

TRACK 3.06

Narrator: Listen to a lecture in a psychology class.

Male Professor (MP): We have been talking about how 19 million Americans suffer from clinical depression and anxiety at any given time. Of course, temporary depression and anxiety are a normal part of everyone's life. We all worry, and we all get the "blues," right? But under certain circumstances, any of us could develop feelings of sadness that don't seem to go away, and in that situation, it might be time to see a doctor. Symptoms of clinical depression include getting angry easily, not enjoying activities that used to be enjoyable, having difficulty sleeping or sleeping too much, disliking oneself, and feeling hopeless.

Clinical depression is a disease that affects brain chemistry and the nervous system. It is treatable in most cases, but treatment is not simple. Let's say that two people, "X" and "Y," both tip over the threshold from normal bad feelings into clinical depression. Now, X and Y may have the same symptoms, but their symptoms may have completely different causes. Moods and emotions are affected by the very, very complicated relationships between an individual's genes, brain chemistry, overall health, and level of stress.

Normally, the brain is able to balance moods, so that our moods can go up and down within a range that allows us to function in daily life. So treating depression and anxiety is about helping patients' brains to do their jobs better by keeping emotions balanced. Researchers know that sometimes the brain cells of depressed people don't transmit or receive messages as they should. For one reason or another, there may not be enough exchange of a necessary chemical between neurons in the brain. As a result, neurons don't send or stop signals like they're supposed to. That's why it doesn't work to tell a clinically depressed person to "cheer up."

Researchers have identified many specific brain chemicals that seem to play a role in mood control. Let's take one example, the hormone called oxytocin. Oxytocin is thought to contribute to feelings of peacefulness, trust, and security. Some research suggests that the sense of a gentle touch to our skin somehow causes our brains to release oxytocin.

This may be the biochemical explanation for why depression and anxiety symptoms can be relieved in some people by therapeutic massage: the massage may lead to the production of more oxytocin. But oxytocin has many effects, and we still have little understanding of its exact mechanisms.

Narrator: Now get ready to answer the questions.

TRACK 3.07

Narrator: Why does the professor say this?

MP: Moods and emotions are affected by the very, very complicated relationships between an individual's genes, brain chemistry, overall health, and level of stress.

TRACK 3.08

Narrator: Now listen to a lecture in a philosophy class.

Female Professor (FP): Now I'd like to discuss a question that is thousands of years old but still has no definite answer. And that question is, "What is intelligence?" So if you go online and search for this question, you'll get dozens, maybe even hundreds of definitions for "intelligence." And although many definitions of intelligence are similar, psychologists, biologists, and philosophers can't always agree on one. With that in mind, I want to know what you guys think. What are some characteristics of intelligence?

Male Student (MS): Well, a lot of times an animal's intelligence is based on how well it adjusts to changes in its environment.

FP: Yes, very good. The ability to adapt to one's environment is often regarded as an indication of intelligence in both animals and humans. As an example, imagine two men are caught in a snowstorm. In order to adapt to the freezing temperatures, one man might create a small shelter out of blocks of snow to stay warm, while the other man might not know how to adapt and do nothing. Obviously, the man who adapted

to his environment is more likely to survive, and he's more likely to be considered the "intelligent" one of the two.
What are some other characteristics of intelligence?

Female Student 1 (FS1): Don't a lot of psychologists say that "intelligence" is the ability to think creatively and process abstract thoughts?

FP: Yes, that's a good point. And, in my opinion, this description is pretty much limited to human intelligence. After all, we can't speak to dolphins or ants, so we really can't measure their creativity accurately or tell if they're thinking abstractly.
(*To female student 2*) You have something to add?

Female Student 2 (FS2): Anna said that intelligence is the ability to "process abstract thoughts." What does that mean exactly? What are "abstract thoughts"?

FP: Well, essentially, "abstract thoughts" are ideas or concepts that cannot necessarily be seen or measured. So abstract thoughts might include metaphors, making a connection between two seemingly unrelated concepts, or ideals like honor and bravery, which can be described but not touched or seen.

And ultimately, we could try to define intelligence all day and not have definitive answers. And many people, myself included, believe that defining the word "intelligence" is impossible. Ideas of intelligence change when discussing the intelligence of humans versus the intelligence of animals. In fact, definitions of intelligence even change from culture to culture. So maybe coming up with characteristics that describe the term "intelligence" is a more productive pastime than trying to come up with one universal definition for the term.

Narrator: Now get ready to answer the questions.

TRACK 3.09

Narrator: What does the professor suggest when she says this?

FP: After all, we can't speak to dolphins or ants, so we really can't measure their creativity accurately or tell if they're thinking abstractly.

TRACK 3.10

Narrator: Listen to a conversation between a student and a university employee.

Female Student (FS): Hello. I saw on the university's announcement board that next week there will be a job fair in the campus' main plaza. I'm thinking of going, but I've never been to a job fair before. So I was wondering if you could give me some info about it.

Male University Employee (ME): Certainly. So at the job fair, a bunch of local businesses and organizations set up booths that have information about their company, job openings, stuff like that. Students go to the job fair to interact with representatives from businesses that they find interesting, and some companies will even let you apply for their positions on the spot.

FS: Oh, okay. That sounds like it could be really helpful. Well, I'm majoring in psychology. Do you know if there will be any jobs related to psychology there? Or is the job fair only for, like, business and accounting majors.

ME: Well, I'm not sure exactly what businesses and organizations will be there, but if you are interested, you can go on the school's website. Under the section titled "Upcoming Events," you can find all the information about the job fair.

FS: Awesome, I'll be sure to check that out. And, well, I hate to keep bothering you, but what should I bring to the job fair? I mean, should I dress nicely, or would that be weird? And should I bring my resume with me?

ME: Well, you should definitely dress nicely. I mean, you want to make a good first impression on all these businesses, and dressing well is a surefire way to impress anyone. And you should definitely bring a few copies of your resume. After all, that'll be the first thing any business or organization asks for if you decide to apply for a position with them.

FS: I guess those are all good points. Wow, sounds like I've got a bit of preparing to do for this job fair. But it sounds like it will be a great opportunity for me to explore all my career options.

ME: Yes, I strongly encourage you to attend.

FS: Well, thanks for all your help.

Narrator: Now get ready to answer the questions.

TRACK 3.11

Narrator: Listen to part of the conversation. Then answer the question.

FS: Awesome, I'll be sure to check that out. And, well, I hate to keep bothering you, but what should I bring to

the job fair? I mean, should I dress nicely, or would that be weird? And should I bring my resume with me?
Narrator: Why does the student probably say this?
FS: And, well, I hate to keep bothering you…

TRACK 3.12

Narrator: Listen to a lecture in an English literature class.
Male Professor (MP): You've probably heard of the British mystery writer Agatha Christie. Agatha Christie published hundreds of novels, short stories, and plays in the mid-20th century. More than 2 billion copies of her books have been sold. Yet, people often disagree about the quality of her work. So today, I want to explore two questions: Why do some people say the quality of Christie's writing is quite low, and why do others admire it?

First, people who are critical of Agatha Christie say that her stories are too much the same. They always follow a formula. Her settings are usually a train, a hotel, or a mansion in the countryside where rich or upper-middle-class people are staying and can't leave. Characters are stereotypes rather than seeming like "real" people. The formula calls for a murdered body to be found. Next, over several days, an amateur detective questions everyone, and everyone acts suspiciously. A second murder usually takes place, and it becomes even more urgent to find out who the murderer is. Then the detective solves the case and confronts the murderer, who usually confesses. Critics say it's too predictable, and too focused on rich people and luxurious settings.

Well, naturally, Agatha Christie's supporters disagree. They say that within the basic plot formula, Christie still found hundreds of ways to surprise readers. In fact, supporters say, Christie was brilliant at creating stories with interesting plots that seemed to speed up and become more suspenseful toward the end. Her characters were not deeply developed because, if the reader knew their motives and inner thoughts, it would give away the ending.

Supporters also say that while it's true that most of Agatha Christie's stories focus on fairly rich people, it's also true that the murderer usually turns out to be one of them. Christie doesn't seem dazzled by rich people. When it comes to finding a suspect, lords and ladies are just as likely to be guilty as poor villagers or servants. Christie also had a practical reason for setting her stories in rich country homes. The characters stay in a calm place with no real work to do, so the reader can focus on what they say to the detective. It's a way of keeping up a fast pace in solving the crime.

Narrator: Now get ready to answer the questions.

TRACK 3.13

Narrator: What does the professor suggest when he says this?
MP: Well, naturally, Agatha Christie's supporters disagree. They say that within the basic plot formula, Christie still found hundreds of ways to surprise readers.

TRACK 3.14

Narrator: Listen to a lecture in an education class.
Female Professor (FP): When you're evaluating the learning of a young child, one way to do so is to compare the child's artwork over time. For children who have access to art materials, artwork can reveal a great deal about their cognitive development; artwork can demonstrate their increasingly focused thinking abilities and ever-more detailed knowledge. So now let's look at some general stages of drawing.

First, when children are first able to manipulate markers and crayons, say from around one-and-a-half to three years old, they are in the "scribbling" stage. Most children begin by making large, circular movements, just enjoying the sensation of movement and color. Next in the scribbling stage they move on to making actual circles, and they may point to a circle and say what it represents, such as a dog or their mom.

By age three or four, children may enter the "pre-schematic" stage, where they begin adding lines to the circles. It is amazing what can be accomplished with lines and circles. A very typical picture in this stage is a face with two legs sticking out of it, and possibly two arms, as well. During the free and imaginative pre-schematic stage, the figures that children draw might be anywhere on the page, any color, and any size in relation to each other.

By around 5 or 6, children may be entering the *schematic* stage. During this stage, children seem to plan a scene and set it in a landscape. Their figures are more recognizable and detailed; people have bodies, hands, feet, fingers, noses, and so on. Figures start to become organized in space, such as standing on the ground. There tend to be more groups of people, along with buildings, trees, and animals. As they progress in this stage, children may add two baselines to indicate space, as in a "here" and an "over there." They may become incredibly creative. Their pictures may look like comic strips, showing sequences of actions. Often, children in this stage will draw as though they have X-ray vision—so they might draw a picture of a person, but include features such as bones, teeth, and organs such as the heart.

Around the age of eight or nine, children become more self-aware, and unfortunately, self-critical. Their concern is that whatever they draw should look exactly like the real object. Their art may reveal less about their development, as they may draw only images from popular culture, such as sports cars, animated characters, and so on.

Narrator: Now get ready to answer the questions.

TRACK 3.15

Narrator: Listen to a conversation between a student and a professor.

Male Student (MS): Excuse me, Professor Dryfus. Can I ask you a couple of questions?

Female Professor (FP): Yes, of course. How can I help you?

MS: Well, I'm kind of confused about what we need to include in our final project. I know it's a really big assignment, so I want to make sure I know exactly what I'm doing.

FP: I'm glad you came to me with your questions. The project is worth 25 percent of your grade, after all. So the project consists of three major parts: a written component, a translation component, and a presentation. So which of these are you confused about?

MS: Well, I know what to do for the written component. You want a seven- to ten-page paper on some topic in ancient Greek history that interests us, right?

FP: Yes, exactly. And this should be a research paper, so make sure you have at least four primary sources and several secondary sources as well.

MS: Okay, got it. And for the translation part, you want us to turn in our translation of some ancient Greek text, right?

FP: Yes, and that can be from any ancient Greek text you want. Just make sure you translate at least 40 lines. And when you turn your translation in, be sure to include the original text as well. That way I can make sure your translation is accurate.

MS: Okay, sounds good. And what about the presentation? Is the presentation topic the same as our research paper topic?

FP: It can be, if you want to do that. But if you use the same topic for your research paper and your presentation, make sure you don't just use all the same information for both.

MS: I see. So you want the thesis—you know, the main idea—of our research paper to be different than the main idea of our presentation.

FP: Yes, exactly. I want to see that you can conduct research on a variety of topics. And make sure there's some visual element to your presentation. So include a PowerPoint, a poster, or something like that to make your presentation visually interesting.

MS: Great. I think I understand exactly what I need to do now.

FP: I'm glad to hear that. And if you get confused, don't forget that I put all assignment and project information on my website.

MS: Awesome. Thanks for your help!

Narrator: Now get ready to answer the questions.

TRACK 3.16

Narrator: Why does the professor say this?

FP: I'm glad you came to me with your questions. The project is worth 25 percent of your grade, after all.

TRACK 3.17

Narrator: Listen to a lecture in a biology class.

Male Professor (MP): Alright. So now we're going to start our unit on microbiology, which is the study of very small organisms. And when I say small, I mean *really* small. The first microorganisms we'll discuss are viruses, which are thousands of times smaller than even a human cell.

So our first question today is, "Why are viruses so small?" Well, there are a couple reasons for this, but the simple answer is that they get away with being so small because they're such simple little organisms. Most viruses are made up of just three parts. The main part of the virus is its DNA or RNA, depending on the virus. The DNA or RNA of the virus holds its genetic instructions. Basically, it contains a code that tells the virus how to make copies of itself, so how to reproduce. These strands of DNA or RNA are surrounded by a protective protein coating, which is the second part of a virus. And some viruses have an outer coating of fat that protects it while it waits for a host.

Now the first virus was discovered—(*To female student*) Sorry, I didn't see your hand. What's your question?

Female Student (FS): When you say "host," what exactly do you mean?

MP: Ah, yes. Before I get into the history, let me answer that. So a virus' structure is so simple that it actually can't reproduce unless it "hijacks" the cell of another organism—we call the organism that a virus invades the "host organism."

The reason that a virus needs a host organism to reproduce is because, in order for any organism to reproduce, it needs certain proteins called "enzymes." These enzymes read the "code" stored in DNA or RNA and tell the cell what it needs to do to reproduce based on what this "code" says. So think of the virus as the architect, the one who makes the blueprints, and the enzymes as the construction workers, the ones who actually do the building.

But viruses lack these enzymes: they have the DNA or RNA code, but no way to put the code into action. So a virus invades a host organism and inserts itself into a host's cell. Once inside a cell, the virus releases its genetic instructions—that is, its DNA or RNA—and uses the host cell's enzymes to reproduce. In other words, the virus uses the host cell to make copies of itself. Then the copies break out of the cell, often destroying it, so they can go and "hijack" other cells to use for reproduction.

Narrator: Now get ready to answer the questions.

TRACK 3.18

Narrator: What does the professor suggest when he says this?

MP: In other words, the virus uses the host cell to make copies of itself. Then the copies break out of the cell, often destroying it, so they can go and "hijack" other cells to use for reproduction.

TRACK 3.19

Narrator: Listen to a lecture in a modern dance class.

Female Professor (FP): Now I'm sure that many of you will recognize the name George Balanchine. He was a dance choreographer who basically created ballet as we know it these days. George Balanchine helped start a famous ballet school in New York City, and then he opened the New York City Ballet in 1948. He choreographed and created ballets for the New York City Ballet, which revolutionized the ballet world. Under Balanchine's influence, ballet became less about sets, costumes, and story-telling, and more about the physical beauty of dance itself.

By the time he started the New York City Ballet, George Balanchine was in his forties. He had been exposed to many different influences already in his life. In his early years, he had undergone the rigor of training in Russia in both ballet and piano. He had danced and choreographed for many different ballet companies, and had also worked on Broadway shows and Hollywood movies. He even designed an elephant dance for a circus.

But Balanchine was most famous for his vision of what made women beautiful as dancers. Before Balanchine, ballerinas were expected to be dainty, small, and good at acting. But Balanchine wanted his female dancers to have long legs and necks. He wanted them to attack the moves with energetic athleticism and extreme flexibility.

Balanchine created many abstract ballets that do not tell a story. The dancers appear on an empty stage wearing simple costumes, and their goal is to explore the music. The dance itself is meant to be exciting. Balanchine choreographed dances with high jumps, quick movement, and deep lunges. Balanchine was also the first choreographer to require all female dancers to wear toe shoes and dance on their toes. As a result, his dances are difficult and painful to perform. He added unusual hand positions and other jazz touches. Overall, Balanchine's dancers had to be artistic, musical, and athletic.

George Balanchine died in 1983, yet his style continues to dominate the ballet world, and most of his 400 ballets are still performed. However, today there is some criticism of Balanchine. For one, he created very few interesting roles for men. He is also criticized for his demands that women dancers remain extremely thin. Ballet companies are also turning away from abstract ballets, as they believe that audiences want to see ballets with stories, sets, and costumes.

Narrator: Now get ready to answer the questions.

TRACK 3.20

Narrator: Why does the professor say this about George Balanchine?

FP: He had been exposed to many different influences already in his life. In his early years, he had undergone the rigor of training in Russia in both ballet and piano. He had danced and choreographed for many different ballet companies, and had also worked on Broadway shows and Hollywood movies.

TRACK 3.21

Narrator: Listen to a conversation between a student and a professor.

Female Student (FS): Hey, Professor Boyd. Can I talk to you for a minute?

Male Professor (MP): Of course, Kate. What can I do for you?

FS: Well, the end of the semester is coming up in a few weeks, and I was wondering if you are going to offer any extra credit opportunities.

MP: It's funny you should mention extra credit; I was going to talk about that first thing next week. But if I remember correctly, you've done quite well in my class. Why would you need any extra credit?

FS: Well, I did pretty horribly on the quiz a couple of weeks ago, so I think I have a "B" in the class now. But I really enjoy your class, so I want to get an "A."

MP: (*Laughs*) I admire your determination. I can tell you're pretty set on pursuing that extra credit opportunity, so I'll explain it to you now, even though I'll talk about it next week in class, too.

FS: Thanks, professor.

MP: It's no problem. So for extra credit, I want you guys to expand upon one of your research papers. I've had you guys write three papers so far this semester, right?

FS: Yeah, and I think all of them were about five pages or so.

MP: Exactly. So I want you guys to add 500 to 1,000 words to the paper, and then prepare a presentation that corresponds with the information in your paper. Basically, I want to see that you can creatively prepare and present your research.

FS: Okay. That sounds like it could be fun. How much extra credit is this whole assignment going to be worth?

MP: Well, if your research paper revisions and presentation are exceptional, I'll increase your current grade by five percent. But even if the presentation isn't perfect, you can still get a two or three percent grade boost.

FS: Oh, awesome! That means an "A" isn't out of the question.

MP: Not at all. I look forward to seeing your presentation. Oh, and I almost forgot to mention: presentations will be on the last day of class. So you have a few weeks to prepare.

FS: Thank you for all the information, professor.

Narrator: Now get ready to answer the questions.

TRACK 3.22

Narrator: Listen to part of the conversation. Then answer the question.

MP: It's funny you should mention extra credit; I was going to talk about that first thing next week. But if I remember correctly, you've done quite well in my class. Why would you need any extra credit?

Narrator: Why does the professor say this?

MP: But if I remember correctly, you have a done quite well in my class.

TRACK 3.23

Narrator: Listen to part of the conversation. Then answer the question.

FS: Well, I did pretty horribly on the quiz a couple of weeks ago, so I think I have a "B" in the class now. But I really enjoy your class, so I want to get an "A."

MP: (*Laughs*) I admire your determination. I can tell you're pretty set on pursuing that extra credit opportunity, so I'll explain it to you now, even though I'll talk about it next week in class, too.

Narrator: Why does the professor say this?

MP: (*Laughs*) I admire your determination.

TRACK 3.24

Narrator: Listen to part of the conversation. Then answer the question.
MP: Well, if your research paper revisions and presentation are exceptional, I'll increase your current grade by five percent. But even if the presentation isn't perfect, you can still get a two or three percent grade boost.
FS: Oh, awesome! That means an "A" isn't out of the question.
Narrator: What is the student's attitude when she says this?
FS: Oh, awesome! That means an "A" isn't out of the question.

TRACK 3.25

Narrator: Listen to a lecture in a psychology class.
Female Professor (FP): We've been talking about how people develop their own identity, which we may call their "sense of self." You probably feel like you mostly know who you are and what you believe. But is your sense of self solid and unbreakable? Can you imagine someone convincing you to completely change your most important opinions and values? That your friends and family are evil, for example? How about that two plus two equals five? Most of you will probably say, "I would never believe that!"

However, history can provide many examples of people becoming "brainwashed." What do we exactly mean by brainwashed? Anyone want to try that definition?
Male Student (MS): Isn't that what religious cults do, kind of, like, wipe out your old thoughts and put their own in your brain instead?
FP: Yes, that's a good way of putting it. Not only religious cults, but also kidnappers, wartime prison guards, and political dictators have been accused of brainwashing people. Brainwashing involves getting a target person to become emotionally desperate and deeply unsure of himself. Next, the brainwasher offers a solution. "If you just believe that I am right," he implies, "you will be safe and loved."
MS: It's kind of hard to believe that it could work. I mean, what experience could be so bad that it could make you believe things that aren't true?

FP: It is extraordinary, I agree. But researchers have described common methods. First, the brainwasher usually keeps the person that will be brainwashed sleepy, hungry, and alone for a long while. That way, the victim is easily confused. The person may also be kept in a constant state of fear, which affects his or her ability to think. Isolation, hunger, terror, exhaustion—they'd make anyone weak.

The next step is to cause the weakened person to feel immense shame and guilt, all of it associated with his past life. Through constant verbal and physical abuse, he's made to feel that he's extremely bad, even if he's not sure why. The final step is that the brainwasher offers the person a chance to change, to "be good," so to speak. The person feels grateful and relieved. He feels that he has been very, very wrong, but now he has a chance to start fresh with new, good beliefs. Whew! Two plus two *is* five! So, that's basically how thought-control begins in many cases.
Narrator: Now get ready to answer the questions.

TRACK 3.26

Narrator: What can be inferred from this?
Female Professor: Not only religious cults, but also kidnappers, wartime prison guards, and political dictators have been accused of brainwashing people.

TRACK 3.27

Narrator: Listen to a lecture from a nutritional science class.
Male Professor (MP): In recent years, a lot of misconceptions have developed around gluten. So today, I want to take some time to give you guys some information on gluten. Gluten is a combination of two proteins that are found in wheat-based products—so foods like bread and cereal. Gluten helps hold these foods together, and it's responsible for giving bread that satisfying, chewy texture.

And nowadays, many people claim that gluten is bad for you—that it causes sleepiness, memory loss, digestive problems, among other things. But a lot of these claims have no real scientific basis. So now let's look at what scientists do know about gluten.

Well, about one percent of people actually can't digest gluten properly. They suffer from something called celiac disease. Those who suffer from celiac disease report symptoms such as nausea, bloating, and dizziness after consuming gluten.

But currently, much more than 1 percent of the U.S. population claims to be negatively affected by products that contain gluten. Most of these people self-diagnose themselves as gluten intolerant. But while celiac disease is a medically recognized disease, gluten intolerance has no apparent scientific basis. Yet those who claim to be gluten intolerant often remove food products containing gluten from their diet. But removing gluten products from one's diet can be problematic. You see, many food products that contain gluten also contain essential nutrients like B Vitamins, fiber, and calcium.

Now don't get me wrong: I'm not saying that people who claim to be gluten intolerant are lying about how they feel after eating certain food products. But gluten is probably not what's making these people feel poorly. In fact, it's much more likely that those who claim to be gluten intolerant are actually sensitive to a group of carbohydrates known collectively as FODMAPs. The letters of the acronym FODMAPs stand for the names of several different carbohydrates that all people have some trouble digesting. And the carbohydrates in FODMAPs are very common. Some food products that contain FODMAP carbohydrates include apples, avocados, wheat products, and tofu. So like I said, all people have a little trouble digesting these carbohydrates, but some people have more trouble than others. So if you feel that you might be gluten intolerant, first go to a doctor and get tested for celiac disease. If you don't have celiac disease, try reducing or eliminating your intake of the carbohydrates that comprise FODMAPs.

Narrator: Now get ready to answer the questions.

TRACK 3.28

Narrator: Why does the professor say this?
MP: And the carbohydrates in FODMAPs are very common. Some food products that contain FODMAP carbohydrates include apples, avocados, wheat products, and tofu.

TRACK 3.29

Narrator: Listen to a conversation between a student and an advisor.

Female Advisor (FA): So what can I help you with today?
Male Student (MS): Well, I'm currently in the second semester of my third year here, so I just wanted to make sure I'm on track to graduate at the end of my fourth year.
FA: Okay, that should be no problem. Let me just bring you up on the computer system here so I can take a look at your transcript. What's your name and student ID number?
MS: My name is Kevin Flores, and my ID number is 7142087.
FA: (*Typing information into computer*) Ah, here you are. So you're a biology major, right?
MS: That's right.
FA: (*Reviewing transcript*) So it looks like you're right on track to finish your major by next year. You just need to take three more upper-division biology classes and two biology labs.
MS: Okay, great. That's what I thought.
FA: Ah, but you still have three general education requirements to complete.
MS: Oh, no way! I thought I finished all of those last year. What do I still have to do?
FA: Well, you still have to take two art classes and one history class to finish your general education requirements.
MS: Oh, man. I think this is going to mess up my plans to graduate next year.
FA: Let me see if I can help you. (*Advisor types into computer*) Ah, yes. There's an art history class that will be offered next year that fulfills both an art and a history general education requirement. So you'll just have to take that class and one more art class to complete your general education requirements.
MS: Oh, that's really helpful. I never would've thought to check for classes that fulfill two general education requirements. So I'll still be able to graduate by the end of next year?
FA: Definitely. So for your first semester next year, you should take two upper-division biology classes, the art history class, and a biology lab. That way, during your final semester, you only have to take one art class, one biology class, and one biology lab.
MS: That's a great idea. I was looking forward to having an easy schedule for my last semester.
FA: Most students do. I'll print out a list of the classes you

need to take next year now.
MS: Okay. Thanks for all your help.
Narrator: Now get ready to answer the questions.

TRACK 3.30

Narrator: Listen to part of the conversation. Then answer the question.
FA: Ah, but you still have three general education requirements to complete.
MS: Oh, no way! I thought I finished all of those last year. What do I still have to do?
FA: Well, you still have to take two art and one history class to finish your general education requirements.
MS: Oh, man. I think this is going to mess up my plans to graduate next year.
Narrator: What does the student imply when he says this?
MS: Oh, man. I think this is going to mess up my plans to graduate next year.

TRACK 3.31

Narrator: What best describes the student's attitude toward the advisor when he says this?
MS: Oh, that's really helpful. I never would've thought to check for classes that fulfill two general education requirements. So I'll still be able to graduate by the end of next year?

TRACK 3.32

Narrator: Listen to a lecture from a literature class.
Female Professor (FP): Let's review yesterday's discussion on situational irony. Now many things can be considered "ironic." In fact, situational irony is used in films, television, literature, and it's something that happens in daily life, too. Can anyone remind the class what, exactly, situational irony is?
Male Student (MS): Well, situational irony describes a situation where you expect one thing to happen, but then the exact opposite of what you expected occurs.
FP: Exactly. Situational irony is a situation that subverts —that is, goes against—your expectations. And this type of irony is often used for comedic effect, but it can also be quite poignant and sad. And keep in mind, what exactly qualifies as irony is subjective; in other words, whether an event is "the exact opposite of expectations" or not depends on who you ask.

Now let's look at an example of situational irony. Say a woman hears about an upcoming trivia competition. The winner of this competition will receive a "mystery prize." The woman decides that she wants to win, so she goes to the bookstore and buys all the books on trivia she can find. She spends almost all her time reading the trivia books, and on the day of the competition, she feels confident that she'll win and take home the mystery prize. And all her preparation pays off. The woman wins the competition and receives her prize, which comes wrapped in colorful wrapping paper. Eager to see what she has won, she tears off the paper and finds an extensive collection of trivia books—in fact, they're all the same trivia books she bought to prepare for the competition!

So how does this example highlight the features of situational irony?
Female Student (FS): Well, after hearing about how much time and effort the woman puts into preparing for the trivia competition, I think the audience expects the woman to win and for the mystery prize to be something really cool or valuable. So it's unexpected —I mean, it's ironic—that she wins something that she already bought to help her win in the first place.
FP: Yes. That's a wonderful explanation. Basically, the story's ending subverts our expectations. And in case some of you are still confused, here are a few more examples of situational irony: A fire station burns down; a police station is robbed; a tow truck gets towed away…
Narrator: Now get ready to answer the questions.

TRACK 3.33

Narrator: Why does the professor say this?
FP: And in case some of you are still confused, here are a few more examples of situational irony: A fire station burns down; a police station is robbed; a tow truck gets towed away…

TRACK 3.34

Narrator: Listen to a lecture in a European history class.
Female Professor (FP): …and while many viewed the mechanical and technological developments of the Industrial Revolution favorably, there were also many who opposed these same developments. Probably the most famous of these opposing groups is the Luddites. The Luddites were a British group, mostly

composed of skilled textile craftspeople, who believed that many of the machines that produced textiles were going to replace skilled craftspeople with unskilled, low-wage machine workers.

So, in the early 19th century, Luddite groups destroyed a number of textile mills and textile-producing machines, sometimes even attacking textile mill owners. (*To male student*) Yes, go ahead.

Male Student (MS): So why was this group called the "Luddites"?

FP: Well, before any of these Luddite attacks began, in the late 1700s, a young textile worker named Ned Ludd reportedly smashed some mill equipment in a fit of rage. Twenty years after this incident, some disgruntled textile craftspeople adopted him as their, well, mascot, so to speak. The textile craftspeople started calling themselves "Luddites," and they created an imaginary leader, General Ludd, who supposedly orchestrated the Luddites attacks.

And their attacks really worried the British government. You see, these attacks occurred during Britain's war with Napoleonic France, and the British government didn't want to deal with uprisings at home and a war with France at the same time. Thus, they tried to suppress the Luddites as quickly as possible. On several occasions, the British army fought against the Luddites, killing some Luddite protesters. And many of the Luddites that were captured during these conflicts were executed or shipped off to the then-prison-colony of Australia.

And really, it was this extreme government retaliation that brought about the end of the Luddites. Although the Luddite movement only lasted about 5 years, the Luddite name is still associated with a hatred or mistrust of technology. But ultimately, the Luddites didn't hate machines; they only attacked and destroyed machines that bypassed or undercut what the Luddites thought were "traditional" labor practices. In other words, the Luddites accepted textile-manufacturing machinery that produced high-quality products, and that were operated by trained, skilled textile workers. The machines that the Luddites destroyed usually produced low-quality textiles, and they required little or no skill with textiles to operate.

So, during the 19th century and even today, the Luddites appealed to many people because they seemed to be protecting the old, "good" way of life. The Luddites seemed like they were making sure that convenience would not replace quality, that machines would not replace humans. So to many, the Luddites were not terrorists, but revolutionaries.

Narrator: Now get ready to answer the questions.

TRACK 3.35

Narrator: Listen to a conversation between a student and a professor.

Male Student (MS): Excuse me, professor. I really enjoyed your lecture on Greek tragedy today, but I have a question about one of the terms you mentioned.

Female Professor (FP): What did you find confusing?

MS: Well, you were talking about something called *catharsis* a lot, but I still don't really know what that is.

FP: Okay. Well, *catharsis* is the process of relieving strong emotions, like pity and fear, by viewing someone else's misfortune. So, for example, what's one movie that always makes you really sad?

MS: Well, it's kind of embarrassing, but the end of the movie *Titanic* always gets me.

FP: And why do you think the movie makes you feel so sad?

MS: I guess it's because you want the two main characters to be happy together, so it's not fair when the main guy—what's his name—Jack dies.

FP: Yeah, exactly. So when you watch a sad movie, you get to feel strong emotions through the characters, right?

MS: I'm sorry, but you lost me there.

FP: Well, in *Titanic*, we all know that Jack and Rose, the main characters, are not real people. But we still feel sad when Jack dies. We all know what it feels like to lose something or someone, so when we see it happen, even in a movie, it affects us.

MS: Okay. I guess that's true.

FP: So now let's link this idea to *catharsis*. *Catharsis* is the process of releasing strong, pent-up emotions—you know, grief, fear, pity—in order to find emotional relief. And a lot of people argue that the *catharsis* we feel when we watch sad movies is why sad movies are so satisfying sometimes. Feeling sad for a fictional character allows you to vent your emotions, and makes

you feel grateful for your own blessings in life.
MS: Oh, so I see how *catharsis* links to Greek tragedy now. When ancient Greeks went to see a tragedy, they would feel scared for the protagonist when he got in trouble, and they would feel pity or grief for the protagonist when he dies. Then, after the play, the audience feels better because they were able to get rid of these emotions by feeling them for a fictional character, and get perspective on their own lives.
FP: Now you've got it.
Narrator: Now get ready to answer the questions.

TRACK 3.36

Narrator: Listen to part of the conversation. Then answer the question.
FP: Yeah, exactly. So when you watch a sad movie, you get to feel strong emotions through the characters, right?
MS: I'm sorry, but you lost me there.
Narrator: What does the student mean when he says this?
MS: I'm sorry, but you lost me there.

TRACK 3.37

Narrator: Listen to a lecture in a physics class.
Male Professor (MP): Today, we begin our unit on nuclear physics. We will spend most of today discussing the nuclear reactions called fusion and fission, but before we do so I'd like to review some basic information about atoms. As we discussed last time, atoms can be thought of as the "building blocks" of, well, everything. But these atoms are so small that each of us is composed of about seven billion billion billion atoms—that's a seven followed by 27 zeroes!

So the atom has three basic components: the center of an atom is called the nucleus, which is made up of positively charged protons and neutrally charged neutrons, and then there are tiny, negatively charged particles called electrons that orbit around the nucleus. Atoms with different numbers of protons, neutrons, and electrons form different elements, such hydrogen, helium, carbon, and even gold.

So now that we've reviewed the basics, let's discuss fusion. Essentially, fusion occurs when two atomic nuclei combine to form a heavier chemical element. Now that may sound straightforward, but, as far as we know, fusion reactions can only occur when two nuclei collide at incredibly high speeds.

During the fusion of lighter elements, a huge amount of energy is released. But oddly enough, the fusion of any element heavier than iron actually consumes energy. We'll talk about why that is later on, once we've discussed the fundamental forces.

Okay, so far we know that fusion is the combination of two or more atoms into a heavier atom, and we know that this process usually creates lots of energy. So now let's talk about some familiar examples of fusion. Every active star in the known universe owes its existence to fusion. In fact, all stars maintain a balance between the forces of gravity, which pulls everything toward a star's center, and of atomic fusion, which creates energy that pushes outward.

For decades now, scientists have been trying to control the process of fusion because doing so would give us a source of almost unlimited energy. Scientists conduct most fusion experiments using deuterium and tritium, two forms of hydrogen. They do this because hydrogen is the lightest element, and it takes less energy to fuse light elements. When deuterium and tritium come together, they form the element called "helium," releasing immense amounts of energy in the process.

Before I continue and introduce fission, I want to stop and ask if anyone has questions about fusion. Yes, Bobby.
Narrator: Now get ready to answer the questions.

TRACK 3.38

Narrator: Listen to part of the lecture. Then answer the question.
MP: During the fusion of lighter elements, a huge amount of energy is released. But oddly enough, the fusion of any element heavier than iron actually consumes energy.
Narrator: Why does the professor say this?
MP: But oddly enough, the fusion of any element heavier than iron actually consumes energy.

TRACK 3.39

Narrator: Listen to a lecture in a biology class.
Male Professor (MP): Examples of animal communication are all around us. Most of the time, all you have to do is step outside to hear birds calling to one another and crickets chirping to each other. Although it surrounds us, however, animal

communication is not well understood. But some scientists hear these animal calls and wonder: "Are these animals talking to each other?" The study of this kind of animal communication is called "signaling theory."

Biologists who study signaling theory look at the signals that animals send to each other. And when I say "signal," I mean a trait or behavior that helps one animal send a message to another animal. Now, a signal benefits the animal giving the signal, known as the "signaler," by warning its own species and by influencing the behavior of the animal receiving the signal, known as the "receiver." This can be a little confusing, so let me give an example to clarify this concept.

Many flocks of birds will choose an "alert bird" to keep a lookout for any predators lurking nearby. That way, all the other birds are free to feed and care for their young without constantly checking for predators. When an alert bird sees a stalking predator, it calls out a signal to the other birds. However, the alert bird's call is also a signal to the predator. It is like the alert bird is saying "I see you, so stop trying to stalk my flock. You're wasting your time." So, the predator usually decides to give up the hunt.

So in this case, the alert bird is the "signaler," and the predator is the "receiver." Now this is what we call an "honest signal," because the signaler conveys accurate information to the receiver.

But there are also dishonest signals. A dishonest signal benefits the signaler by deceiving the receiver. For example, sometimes an alert bird pretends to be hurt and moves away from the flock, distracting the predator and keeping the flock safe. Of course, dishonest signals are risky for the signaler because too much dishonest signaling ruins the signaling system. After all, if the alert bird dishonestly calls out "predator" too many times, it may not be believed when there really is a predator.

Narrator: Now get ready to answer the questions.

TRACK 3.40

Narrator: What can be inferred about signaling among alert birds from this?

MP: Of course, dishonest signals are risky for the signaler because too much dishonest signaling ruins the signaling system. After all, if the alert bird dishonestly calls out "predator" too many times, it may not be believed when there really is a predator.

TRACK 3.41

Narrator: Listen to a conversation between a student and an advisor.

Female Advisor (FA): Good afternoon. What can I do to help you?

Male Student (MS): Well, I was hoping you could tell me how many classes I still need to take in order to finish my major.

FA: Yes, I believe I can help you with that. Can I see your student ID so I can bring up your file in our system?

MS: Sure. Here you go. (*Student hands his student ID to Advisor*)

FA: (*Types on the computer*) Okay, here you are. So, Sam, you're a European History major, right?

MS: That's right.

FA: And it looks like this semester, you're taking two classes that count toward your major, which means you have three more upper-division history classes before you finish the major.

MS: Uh, wait a minute. I think I'm actually taking three classes for the history major this quarter.

FA: Not according to the information I have here. In our computer system, it says you're taking History 154: Rebellion and Revolution, and History 110: Conquest in the West.

MS: And I'm taking the class called "Excavating Ancient Britain."

FA: Ah, that's the problem. That's an archaeology class, so it only counts toward the anthropology major.

MS: No way! But we spend most of the class learning about the *history* of ancient Britain. Isn't there some way to get history credit for the class instead of anthropology credit?

FA: Well, you could petition to have the class count toward your history major.

MS: Okay. And what do I have to do to petition?

FA: Explain the situation to the professor for your ancient Britain class, and ask her to sign this form. (*Advisor hands Student a form*) Her signing the form indicates that she's giving you permission to take the class for history credit. Then the head of the history department will review your request and approve or deny it. But really, as long as the professor for your ancient Britain class signs it, you're pretty much guaranteed to have your petition approved.

MS: Okay, that sounds easy enough. I'll go try to find my professor right now. Should I bring the form back here once it's been signed?

FA: Yes, and I will send it to the head of the history department.

MS: Sounds good. Thanks for your help.

Narrator: Now get ready to answer the questions.

TRACK 3.42

Narrator: Listen to part of the conversation. Then answer the question.

MS: No way! But we spend most of the class learning about the *history* of ancient Britain. Isn't there some way to get history credit for the class instead of anthropology credit?

Narrator: Why does the student say this?

MS: But we spend most of the class learning about the *history* of ancient Britain.

TRACK 3.43

Narrator: Listen to a lecture in an art history class.

Male Professor (MP): Now let's turn to the work of photographer Richard Avedon. Let's start at the beginning: Richard Avedon began his photography career in New York City just after World War II. For essentially 60 years until his death in 2004, he had a huge influence on the art of photography. Most of his work was published in magazines. I'll focus for a bit on the photographs that Avedon took relating to fashion, social issues, and celebrity portraits.

First, Richard Avedon worked at major fashion magazines for most of his career, creating fashion photos and fashion advertisements. His models were usually moving, and his images suggested stories. One iconic black-and-white photo from 1955 shows a beautiful but angry woman sitting in a café with her chin on her hand. She is wearing an enormous fashionable hat, yet she is still shorter than the panting Afghan hound sitting next to her.

Secondly, Richard Avedon went out into the world to make portraits of working-class people and to document social issues. For example, in 1963 Avedon got permission to go into a mental health hospital in the state of Louisiana and photograph the patients. In the black-and-white photos, many of the mental patients are looking directly at the camera with completely honest misery. The conditions they are living in appear shocking, and they don't seem to be getting any meaningful treatment. The photos helped build support for a social movement at the time that sought to improve mental health care.

Finally, Richard Avedon also became known for his portraits of famous people. He photographed many celebrities, usually using plain white backgrounds and strong, clear light. Many of his portraits of rock stars became famous. He was known for saying just the right thing to make a celebrity's expression show emotion. For example, he got an assignment to create a portrait of the Duke and Duchess of Windsor in 1957. He didn't want an ordinary portrait, however. So while he was snapping photos of the royal couple, he told them that his taxi had hit a dog that day, even though it wasn't true. The royal couple loved dogs, and their faces showed distress and concern at what he had said. The photo that resulted now hangs in Great Britain's National Portrait Gallery in London.

Narrator: Now get ready to answer the questions.

TRACK 3.44

Narrator: Listen to a lecture in a world history class.

Female Professor (FP): Today, I'd like to talk about farming and food during the latter half of the 20th century. Remember that we talked about the nations that experienced hunger and famine during the 1950s and 1960s. Well, thanks to plant science, new strains of wheat and rice were developed during this time, and these new crops had a tremendous effect. Agricultural production in several developing countries boomed. Millions, perhaps even billions, of human lives were saved. The sudden increase in grain production starting in the late 1950s is referred to as the "Green Revolution."

It all started in 1944, when a plant geneticist named Norman Borlaug joined a project to help Mexican farmers grow more wheat. Norman Borlaug was very concerned about world hunger. In 1953, he began working with a variety of wheat that had a short, thick stem. Through his experiments, Borlaug found that the short-stemmed plants could hold more grain than their long-stemmed counterparts without falling over. Thus, using Borlaug's short-stemmed crop, farmers could use more fertilizer to grow more wheat, all while using the same amount of land as before.

Farmers in Mexico, Pakistan, and India began to plant Borlaug's short-stemmed wheat, adding fertilizer to stimulate growth. And the dramatic success of these efforts encouraged investment in farm machines, irrigations systems, and pesticides. The yield from wheat crops tripled in some places, allowing many more people to get enough food.

Another plant geneticist, M.S. Swaminathan, led the way for planting of high-yield wheat and rice varieties in India. China followed suit. In 1970, the Nobel Peace Prize went to Norman Borlaug for his ideas, and he was called a "peaceful revolutionary."

At the same time, it was clear that the Green Revolution was *creating* entirely new problems. For instance, the agricultural developments of the Green Revolution led to a decline in the number of small family farms, which had grown a diversity of crops in a sustainable way for thousands of years. In their place were large farms that used imported seeds, chemicals, and fuel, and grew only one variety of grain. Some have even claimed that people became malnourished because their diets became more limited.

Let's examine one example of a problem created by the Green Revolution. Many farmers in Southeast Asia once raised fish in their watery rice paddies. The fish ate insects and provided natural fertilization. When the rice was harvested, the farmers could eat the fish. Of course fish cannot live in rice paddies where pesticides and herbicides are used. So with the new methods, rice production went up, but another source of food disappeared.

Narrator: Now get ready to answer the questions.

TRACK 3.45

Narrator: What can be inferred from this?
FP: Remember that we talked about the nations that experienced hunger and famine during the 1950s and 1960s. Well, thanks to plant science, new strains of wheat and rice were developed during this time, and these new crops had a tremendous effect.

TRACK 3.46

Narrator: Listen to a conversation between a student and an advisor.
Female Student (FS): Thanks for seeing me on such short notice.
Male Advisor (MA): It's no problem. So what can I help you with?
FS: (*Sounding anxious*) Well, it's the beginning of my second year at the university, and I still have no idea what I want to major in.
MA: Ah, I see. Well, because this is a problem that many students have, we advisors have a lot of ways to help you guys out. So let me start by asking you a few questions.
FS: Okay.
MA: For starters, do you currently have a few majors that you're interested in?
FS: Well, kind of. I can definitely tell you what majors I'm not interested in.
MA: (*Laughs*) Okay. Well, that's a lot better than nothing. So what majors are you not interested in?
FS: Nothing with lots of math or chemistry. I mean, don't get me wrong: I like science; I just can't handle four years of doing derivatives or conversions.
MA: Well, that's okay. I'm sure we can figure out something for you. The first thing I want to do is narrow down your options. So here's what I recommend: take one of the university-provided aptitude tests.
FS: Okay. What's that?
MA: Well, it's a two-hour test that determines where your academic strengths lie.
FS: So like an SAT?
MA: Kind of. Except the aptitude test will give you more specific information about your strengths and weaknesses. So instead of telling you you're good at math, like the SAT would, an aptitude test might say your strengths are in accounting—so one type of math—but not in theoretical physics—another type of math.
FS: I see. That sounds like it could be really helpful.
MA: Many students in your situation say that they were able to choose a major because of the aptitude test.
FS: Well, then sign me up! When can I take the test?
MA: Let me see. (*Types into computer*) It looks like there's one coming up in two weeks, on a Wednesday at 8:00 p.m.

FS: That should work perfectly. I'm done with class by 5:00 p.m. on Wednesdays. Can I sign up now?
MA: Certainly. I'll go get the paperwork.
FS: Awesome. Thanks for all your advice.
Narrator: Now get ready to answer the questions.

TRACK 3.47

Narrator: Listen to part of the conversation. Then answer the question.
Female Student: (*Sounding anxious*) Well, it's the beginning of my second year at the university, and I still have no idea what I want to major in.
Male Advisor: Ah, I see. Well, because this is a problem that many students have, we advisors have a lot of ways to help you guys out. So let me start by asking you a few questions.
Narrator: Why does the advisor say this?
Male Advisor: Ah, I see. Well, because this is a problem that many students have, we advisors have a lot of ways to help you guys out. So let me start by asking you a few questions.

TRACK 3.48

Narrator: Listen to a lecture in a neuroscience class.
Female Professor (FP): I think science is unappealing to many people because it almost never provides simple answers. For example, understanding the answer to the seemingly simple question "Why is the sky blue?" requires an understanding of electromagnetic radiation, electron scattering, and the processes that allow for human vision. But sometimes, it seems like scientists are able to come up with short, simple, and amazing scientific truths. Unfortunately, these "truths" are often oversimplified to the point of being completely incorrect. I think the biggest myth that still gets presented as scientific fact is that we only use 10 percent of our brains. So I want to take some time today to dispel this pesky myth, and to encourage you guys to investigate claims that seem scientific, but that may not hold up well to scrutiny.

As far as I know, this myth first appeared about a century ago. And this myth implies that, if we only use 10 percent of our brains, there's another 90 percent waiting to be used. In other words, it means that humans don't use their brains to their fullest potential. And it's easy to see why this myth has proven to be so popular: it encourages people to believe that they might have incredible mental potential waiting to be "unlocked." Some even claim that brain scans prove this myth to be true. After all, in brain scans, only small portions of the brain are lit up at any given time, which seems to mean that a lot of the brain isn't in use.

So now let's disprove this enduring myth. We use all of our brains, pretty much all the time. After all, why would humans evolve to have this big, heavy, energy-consuming brain if we weren't going to use all of it? Each part of our brain has one or more functions, so catching a ball increases the electrical and chemical activity in different parts of the brain than taking a multiple-choice test does. And that's why our whole brain doesn't light up during a brain scan: the brain scan only shows what parts of a brain are *most* active during specific tasks. In fact, we use pretty much all of our brain all the time. Some parts will just be more active than others, depending on what a person is doing. Even during sleep, every part of the brain shows signs of some sort of activity.

Now these are only some of the arguments that dispel the "We only use 10 percent of our brain" myth. Can you guys think of any other facts that might disprove this myth?
Narrator: Now get ready to answer the questions.

TRACK 3.49

Narrator: Why does the professor say this?
FP: For example, understanding the answer to the seemingly simple question "Why is the sky blue?" requires an understanding of electromagnetic radiation, electron scattering, and the processes that allow for human vision.

TRACK 3.50

Narrator: Listen to a lecture from a nutritional science class.
Male Professor (MP): Today's topic might be a bit of a downer, but understanding the process of starvation is crucial to understanding many other topics in nutritional sciences. And what I really want to focus on today is what happens to the body during starvation. So let's start by clarifying this term.

"Starvation" is a process, but a person is considered to be "starving" if they've lost about 30 percent of their body mass.

When they consume a sufficient amount of food, people get their energy from a carbohydrate called glucose. Our body converts a lot of what we eat into glucose, which then provides the energy to power our brains and muscles, and to produce red blood cells. But after about a day of not eating, our glucose supply runs low. At this point, the body targets fat reserves and converts these fatty acids into a substance called ketone. However, for reasons we'll look at later, ketone compounds are too big to get to the brain, so the brain must use up the last of the glucose stored in your body. This process of using ketone and glucose for energy continues for up to about three days, at which point the brain runs out of glucose entirely and needs a new supply of energy.

So after three days of not eating, the body enters the next stage of starvation. At this point, the body starts to break down muscle, which it can convert to glucose for energy. Basically, your body starts consuming itself to survive. This process is called "autophagy." And, well, autophagy continues until the person dies from starvation. And this whole process, from running out of food to death, takes anywhere from a couple weeks to a couple months, depending on the individual. (*To female student*) Yes, you have a question?

Female Student (FS): When people die of starvation, what's actually killing them?

MP: Ah, that's a morbid, but good, question. Well, lack of vitamins and minerals during starvation damages the immune system, so many who are starving die of infections. Others die from organ failure because the organs can't function if they have no way to get energy.

And keep in mind: the process of starvation is not particularly well understood. After all, scientists have a lot of trouble studying a process that kills the person being observed. Thus, there have been very few scientific studies that document the process of starvation.

Narrator: Now get ready to answer the questions.

TRACK 3.51

Narrator: Why does the professor say this?

MP: When they consume a sufficient amount of food, people get their energy from a carbohydrate called glucose. Our body converts a lot of what we eat into glucose, which then provides the energy to power our brains and muscles, and to produce red blood cells.

TRACK 3.52

Narrator: Listen to a conversation between a student and a professor.

Male Student (MS): Sorry to bother you, professor. Can I ask you a couple of questions?

Female Professor (FP): Of course, Adrian. What can I do for you?

MS: Well, I've been working on the research paper you assigned—you know, the one where we have to analyze people's reactions to some past natural disaster. And for my topic, I'm looking at how people reacted to the volcanic eruption on Krakatoa island in the 1800s.

FP: That's an excellent topic. You should be able to find plenty of literature on that subject.

MS: Well, kind of. I've been trying to get all my sources together so I can start writing the paper, but so far I can only find good secondary sources—you know, reports from people who weren't eyewitnesses to the event.

FP: I see. I suppose that's a bit of a problem, isn't it. Second-hand accounts are useful, but you definitely need some primary sources for this report.

MS: I was wondering if you knew of any eyewitness accounts to the Krakatoa eruption that I could use as primary sources.

FP: (*Thoughtfully*) Good primary sources. Well, I think I know of at least one off the top of my head. I'm pretty sure the library has at least one copy of *The Eruption of Krakatoa and Subsequent Phenomena* by the Royal Society of Great Britain. It's even got some sketches that depict the color of the sky after the eruption.

MS: That sounds like exactly what I'm looking for! Thanks for the suggestion.

FP: It's no problem at all. I understand that primary sources can sometimes be hard to find.

MS: Oh, and I actually have one more quick question. How many primary sources do you want us to use?

FP: I want you to have at least two cited in your research paper. And make sure that you analyze your primary sources, too.

MS: What do you mean?

FP: Well, don't just quote an eyewitness account of the Krakatoa eruption without commenting on—for example—why the person made a certain statement. Or you can analyze primary sources by comparing and contrasting conflicting information in two different eyewitness accounts.

MS: Okay. I see what you mean. I'll be sure to analyze my primary sources.

Narrator: Now get ready to answer the questions.

TRACK 3.53

Narrator: Listen to part of the conversation. Then answer the questions.

MS: That sounds like exactly what I'm looking for! Thanks for the suggestion.

FP: It's no problem at all. I understand that primary sources can sometimes be hard to find.

Narrator: Why does the professor say this?

FP: I understand that primary sources can sometimes be hard to find.

TRACK 3.54

Narrator: Listen to a lecture in a marine biology class.

Male Professor (MP): So now let's continue with our unit on the deep sea. As I've said before, most of the deep sea is unexplored, and therefore a complete mystery. But researchers have made some amazing discoveries during their few trips into the ocean's depths.

What I consider to be one of the most remarkable discoveries is that of deep-sea hydrothermal vents. So a "hydrothermal vent" is the scientific term for places at the bottom of the ocean where the earth's crust splits, which allows water trapped under the crust to seep out. The water that emerges from these vents is incredibly hot and filled with minerals because of its closeness to mineral-rich subsurface magma. So as this water comes out of the vents, the minerals in the hot water are cooled by surrounding seawater. The cooled minerals in the water slowly harden and stack into chimney-like tubes. Some of these tubes, or hydrothermal vents, can grow to be over 150 feet tall.

These hydrothermal vents are thousands of feet underwater, where there's no sunlight, and jets of incredibly hot, chemically toxic water pour out of them. So understandably, the first people to explore these vents didn't expect to find any signs of life nearby. Yet amazingly, the vents provide homes for entire ecosystems. Species of crabs, shrimp, clams, and 7-foot tall tube worms all live on or around these vents, surviving off the hydrogen sulfide that comes pouring out of the vents.

Now hydrogen sulfide is a chemical compound that's toxic to pretty much all animals. But the animals living around the hydrothermal vents have developed a way to make this toxic compound into a source of food. Within the digestive systems of these vent-dwelling species, there lives a special type of bacteria. Now this bacterium extracts energy from hydrogen sulfide, and uses this energy to convert carbon dioxide into sugar. This sugar then feeds both the bacteria and the creature that the bacteria lives inside of. The used hydrogen sulfide then gets removed from the body as a harmless waste product.

In summary, the discovery of the abundant forms of life around hydrothermal vents was so exciting because it forced scientists to reassess where and how animals can survive. Even with no light, extreme temperatures, and a chemically toxic environment, many species have founds ways to make a living. The more we know about the deep sea, the more we realize that life is unimaginably diverse and adaptable.

Narrator: Now get ready to answer the questions.

TRACK 3.55

Narrator: Why does the professor say this?

MP: The cooled minerals in the water slowly harden and stack into chimney-like tubes. Some of these tubes, or hydrothermal vents, can grow to be over 150 feet tall.

TRACK 3.56

Narrator: What can be inferred from this?

MP: Even with no light, extreme temperatures, and a chemically toxic environment, many species have found ways to make a living. The more we know about the deep sea, the more we realize that life is unimaginably diverse and adaptable.

TRACK 3.57

Narrator: Listen to a lecture in an art history class.

Female Professor (FP): Let's look at some slides of the work of the Southern California artist James Turrell. Now naturally, since vision requires light, visual artists have long aimed to reproduce the effects of light on their subjects. But James Turrell's passion is light itself.

Turrell began his career in 1966 by renting an empty hotel in Santa Monica. He painted the rooms of the hotel all white and used a light projector to create optical illusions. For example, by shining the light into a corner, he found that he could create an image of a three-dimensional cube. He also experimented with natural light by painting over the windows and scratching careful lines in the paint. Light, absence of light, and colored light became his medium.

Over nearly five decades of experimentation, Turrell became one of the world's most famous artists, with exhibits and retrospectives in many major museums. Many of his works are experienced in darkened or specially lit rooms. He is also known for what he calls "sky spaces," which are special windows or openings in ceilings.

In general, Turrell's works control light in such a way that our eyes become confused; we become unsure of our actual perceptions. What are we actually seeing? Is that a real wall, or just light? Is that a real opening into a passageway, or is it something solid that sticks out?

In Turrell's "Breathing Light," viewers enter a very large room that is filled with light of one color that is so bright that the viewers lose a sense of the floor and the walls. Viewers have no sense of space, and may not even be quite sure whether they're still experiencing gravity. Some viewers have described the experience as being inside light.

However, Turrell's real masterpiece is called the Rodan Crater. For decades, Turrell has been digging into an ancient volcanic mountain in northern Arizona. Within the bowl of the mountain, he's creating 20 underground rooms with openings to the sky. Tunnels and staircases add to the many effects he has created. Inspired by ancient builders in many areas of the world, Turrell believes that viewing the sky in certain ways can be a powerful experience. His goal is to show the "thingness of light," as he puts it, and to show that the sky and light are not separated from us except in our own perceptions.

Narrator: Now get ready to answer the questions.

TRACK 3.58

Narrator: Why does the professor say this?

FP: Now naturally, since vision requires light, visual artists have long aimed to reproduce the effects of light on their subjects.

TRACK 3.59

Narrator: What does the professor mean when she says this?

FP: In general, Turrell's works control light in such a way that our eyes become confused; we become unsure of our actual perceptions.

TRACK 3.60

Narrator: Listen to a conversation between a student and an advisor.

Female Advisor (FA): Good morning. How can I help you?

Male Student (MS): Hi. I'm here today to register for classes, but the electronic registration system won't let me sign up for any of my writing or literature general education classes.

FA: Okay. Did you take any college-level literature or composition classes in high school?

MS: No, I didn't. Would taking those classes have helped me?

FA: Well, a little bit. Taking college-level writing classes in high school allows you to bypass the English placement exam that the university administers to incoming freshmen.

MS: Oh, so I have to take this English placement exam before I can sign up for any of my writing classes?

FA: That is correct. But luckily for you, we'll be administering one of those tests in about two hours.

MS: Okay. How long does the test take? I still have to do a lot more to finish registering for classes by the end of today.

FA: It should only take about an hour to complete.

MS: That's not too bad. But wait, what happens if I fail this entrance exam? Do I get kicked out of the university or something?

FA: Oh, no. Nothing like that. If you do poorly on the entrance exam, you'll just be placed in a lower-level writing and composition class.

MS: I see. I guess that's not so bad, then. Okay, so I guess I'll go take the exam in a couple of hours. Where should I go to take it?

FA: The test will be administered in the main auditorium. Do you know where that is?

MS: Yeah, that's where our tour group started today.

FA: Excellent. Is there anything else I can help you with?

MS: Not really. So I'll just take the placement exam, and then sign up for a composition or literature general education class after I'm finished?

FA: Not quite. We will place you in an appropriate composition or literature class based on your score on the exam.

MS: Oh, good. I guess I don't have to worry about registering for that, then. Thanks for all your help. I never would've known what to do otherwise.

FA: It's my pleasure. And good luck on the exam.

MS: Thanks!

Narrator: Now get ready to answer the questions.

TRACK 3.61

Narrator: Listen to part of the conversation. Then answer the question.

FA: Excellent. Is there anything else I can help you with?

MS: Not really. So I'll just take the entrance exam, and then sign up for a composition or literature general education class after I'm finished?

FA: Not quite. We will place you in an appropriate composition or literature class based on your score on the English entrance exam.

Narrator: Why does the student say this?

MS: So I'll just take the entrance exam, and then sign up for a composition or literature general education class after I'm finished?

TRACK 3.62

Narrator: Listen to a lecture in a physics class.

Female Professor (FP): Let's now talk about what's maybe the most famous equation in physics. Does anyone want to guess what equation I'm talking about?

Male Student (MS): Is it $E = mc^2$?

FP: That's it. Now this equation explains that the mass and energy are really just different ways of measuring the same thing. But before I delve into this idea, I want to spend a few minutes breaking down this equation. For starters, what does the "E" in the equation stand for?

Female Student (FS): It stands for "energy," right?

FP: Yep. And when Einstein formulated this equation, he used electromagnetic radiation, which is just a fancy term for "light," as his energy. But really, the equation stays true for any form of energy, such as heat and magnetic energies. So if the energy part is "E", then what does "mc^2" mean?

MS: Well, the "m" variable means "mass," and "c" is the variable used to represent the speed of light.

FP: Exactly. So the mass part of the equation should make sense, considering that the whole equation is about the relationship between energy and mass. And the speed of light's place in the equation... well, that's a little harder to explain. So next class, we'll talk about the speed of light more when we mathematically derive this equation.

But now that we know what "$E = mc^2$" means, let's turn our attention to a place where mass is constantly being turned into energy: the sun. For the sake of this discussion, think of the sun as a huge ball of hydrogen and helium atoms being forced together by gravity. Now the more intense the gravity, the closer these atoms are pushed together, and when four hydrogen atoms are squeezed together under so much pressure, they fuse—which is a way of saying they combine—into a single helium atom. But the mass of the newly formed helium atom is slightly less than the combined mass of the four hydrogen atoms that formed it, which means that a small amount of the hydrogen atoms' masses were converted to energy when they fused. This process shows us that, under the right conditions, mass will convert into energy. And, as a final note, during fusion, a little bit of mass will convert into *a lot* of energy, which explains why the sun produces enough energy to keep our planet running.

Narrator: Now get ready to answer the questions.

TRACK 3.63

Narrator: What can be inferred about the professor from this?

FP: Let's now talk about what may be the most famous and influential equation in physics. Does anyone want to guess what equation I'm talking about?

TRACK 3.64

Narrator: Listen to part of the lecture. Then answer the question.
FP: And when Einstein formulated this equation, he used electromagnetic radiation, which is just a fancy term for "light," as his energy. But really, the equation stays true for any form of energy, such as heat and magnetic energies.
Narrator: Why does the professor say this?
FP: But really, the equation stays true for any form of energy, such as heat and magnetic energies.

TRACK 3.65

Narrator: Why does the professor say this?
FP: But now that we know what "$E = mc^2$" means, let's turn our attention to a place where mass is constantly being turned into energy: the sun.

CHAPTER 4

TRACK 4.01

Narrator: Listen to a lecture in a Latin American history class.
Male Professor (MP): In terms of political geography, "Latin America" describes the nations from Mexico to the southern tip of South America. Latin American history is full of long, brutal dictatorships and short, unsuccessful revolutions. There are exceptions, however. The Sandanista revolution in Nicaragua, for example, led to democratic reform in that country. Another, very different kind of revolution was led by the Zapatistas in southern Mexico in the 1990s.

The Zapatista Army of 3,000 men took over towns and cities in the Chiapas State of southern Mexico on January 1, 1994. Although the men were armed, their takeovers involved none of the brutality you might expect. The Zapatistas released prisoners from one jail, and set fire to one police building.

They were acting, they said, to draw attention to the damage Mexico's corrupt government and foreign corporations were doing to the indigenous people of the Lacandon rainforest in Chiapas.

The Mexican Army attacked the next day. The Zapatista Army disappeared into the jungle, but they attracted much attention from the media in Mexico and around the world. By January 12, the Zapatistas and the Mexican government had reached an agreement, including a cease fire and some autonomy for the region.

Female Student (FS): Didn't the Zapatistas want to start a communist state in Southern Mexico?
MP: No. The Zapatistas resembled the guerrilla armies that fought for communist ideas in El Salvador and Nicaragua, but they did not want a separate communist nation. They didn't even want a war! They wanted media attention, and they wanted to protect the communities, the land, and the resources of the Chiapas region from exploitation by the Mexican government, other governments, or corporations.
FS: But, weren't their ideas very similar to communist ideas?
MP: Yes, but only because the indigenous people of Chiapas were already living a communal lifestyle. The Zapatistas didn't try to control local governments or groups in Chiapas. One thing they did do, however, was to insist on protecting the rights of women.
FS: Like the Equal Rights Amendment in the U.S.?
MP: Yes, but the Zapatistas made their proposal into law. It was a document called "Women's Revolutionary Law." Among other rights, it guaranteed women to be free from discrimination and violence, to decide for themselves how many children they would have and care for, and the right to work, vote, and get an education.
Narrator: Now get ready to answer the questions.

TRACK 4.02

Narrator: Why does the professor say this?
MP: Although the men were armed, their takeovers involved none of the brutality you might expect. The Zapatistas released prisoners from one jail, and set fire to one police building.

TRACK 4.03

Narrator: Listen to a conversation between a student and an advisor.

Female Advisor (FA): How can I help you?

Male Student (MS): I'm going to start attending State University in a couple of weeks, and I was confused about something I saw on the housing application.

FA: Okay. And what's confusing you?

MS: Well, it says here that I should choose what college I want to live in, and it lists four different choices. But I thought the college is State University, so I don't really know what I'm supposed to choose for this part of the application.

FA: I see. Don't worry, this confuses quite a few students. State University's housing is divided up into four different groups, and these groups are called "colleges." So really, when you choose a college, you're choosing where you want to live on campus.

MS: Oh, I think I understand. Are there any differences between the colleges, then?

FA: Yes, there are a few differences. The biggest difference is that each college has a different academic focus. So what major are you thinking of pursuing?

MS: Well, I'm not positive that I'm going to stick with it, but right now I'm thinking of doing psychology.

FA: Great. Well, Redwood College, which is on the other side of campus from here, is where most psychology, sociology, and anthropology majors choose to live. So you might want to consider that college.

MS: Okay, I'll be sure to check out Redwood College. But why do people of the same major usually choose to live in the same college together?

FA: Well, most lecture halls and classrooms for psychology, sociology, and anthropology courses are located in or near Redwood College, so it makes getting to class easier for those students.

MS: Oh, that makes sense. What majors are associated with the other colleges?

FA: Let's see. Most literature, history, and linguistics students live in Oak College. Many theater, film, and art students live in Cypress College. And our largest college, Sequoia College, houses students studying the sciences, such as biology, chemistry, physics, and engineering.

MS: Wow, this college system actually seems to make a lot of sense. I can see why you guys have different colleges within the university. I guess I'll head over to Redwood College to check it out right now, then.

FA: Sounds good. And you can just come back here if you have any further questions.

Narrator: Now get ready to answer the questions.

TRACK 4.04

Narrator: Listen to part of the conversation. Then answer the question.

FA: Yes, there are a few differences. So the biggest difference is that each college has a different academic focus. So what major are you thinking of pursuing?

Narrator: Why does the advisor ask this?

FA: So what major are you thinking of pursuing?

TRACK 4.05

Narrator: Listen to a lecture in a biology class.

Male Professor (MP): Today I want to talk about humans' unlikely relationship with a fascinating sea creature called the horseshoe crab. And while humans' relationship with the horseshoe crab started within the last century, these creatures have much more distant origins. Horseshoe crabs, which are really more closely related to spiders than crabs, evolved in shallow, coastal waters about 450 million years ago.

But as fascinating as these creatures' ancient origins are, humans value the creatures for something else: their blood. The chalky, blue blood of every horseshoe crab contains a compound called Limulus Amebocyte Lysate, or just LAL for short. And what LAL does is it detects the presence of harmful bacteria and the toxins that bacteria release, which are called "endotoxins." The LAL coagulates around the endotoxin, neutralizing it by completely surrounding it. This is the horseshoe crab's alternative to an immune system like ours, which actively fights harmful invaders in order to eliminate them. And for us humans, this LAL has literally proven to be a lifesaver.

Every year, trawlers and fishermen on the United States' East coast collect about 250,000 horseshoe crabs and deliver them to the Associates of Cape Code, in Massachusetts. Once there, the horseshoe crabs have about 30 percent of their blood drained into bottles. And don't worry about the crabs too much, this is a non-lethal amount. Afterward, the crabs are released back into the ocean, where they can recover from their blood "donation."

And once we have horseshoe crabs' blood, we extract the LAL from it. LAL can be used to determine whether or not a batch of medicine is safe to use. For example, a drug company that has prepared batches of a flu shot must first add LAL to a sample from each batch. If the LAL does not clot, the company has proven that no endotoxins are present and the flu shots are safe. And that's why we need so much of the stuff.

Female Student (FS): But why did the horseshoe crab evolve to have this LAL in their blood to begin with?

MP: Well, they evolved back in the old days, when immune systems like ours didn't exist yet. But their aquatic environment contains much higher concentrations of bacteria than ours does, so horseshoe crabs needed some really effective way to neutralize harmful bacteria and viruses. So really, LAL is just a different way of accomplishing the same thing as any other form of immune system.

Narrator: Now get ready to answer the questions.

TRACK 4.06

Narrator: Why does the professor say this?

MP: Afterward, the crabs are released back into the ocean, where they can recover from their blood 'donation.'

TRACK 4.07

Narrator: Listen to a lecture in an American literature class.

Male Professor (MP): For today's class, the assigned reading was Maxine Hong Kingston's book *The Woman Warrior: Memoir of a Girlhood among Ghosts*. In this book, Kingston writes about her experiences growing up as the child of Chinese immigrants in Stockton, California. But she writes as though describing a confusing dream. She includes stories her mother told her, which may or may not be true, and Cantonese legends, which she freely changes. Why do you think she added so many stories about other people, when the book is supposedly a memoir about her own childhood?

Female Student (FS): Well, it's kind of mentioned in the title, right? I mean, the part about *Memoir of a Girlhood among Ghosts*, to think of growing up among ghosts, it already sounds like she's describing something that may or may not be real.

MP: Yes, interesting point. Her Chinese mother calls everyone in America who is not Chinese a ghost, right? So it is like most of the people around her aren't quite real. But, as the young Maxine is aware, most of the Americans around them do not really notice them, and maybe see them as the ghosts. Then, she makes a connection between her ancestry and her own life in the U.S. by telling many stories about people she never met who lived in China, and these are like ghosts in the book, too; also, in some of the stories, dead ancestors are like helpful ghosts.

FS: So, it kind of depends on your viewpoint, who is and who isn't a ghost, and what the ghost is like?

MP: Yes, I think that is indeed her purpose here. Kingston wants to explore the idea that remembering events in one's life isn't a simple task. The more you think about things, the more you begin to wonder whether your own perceptions at the time were correct. Another example is the stories that her mother tells her. As a child, she felt that the stories were discouraging, and were meant to scare her or make her tough. But, looking back, she wonders if the stories also inspired her. Maybe the stories did both. Then, of course, there is her own confusion about Chinese culture, since she doesn't live in China. On behalf of all immigrant children, she wonders, "What part of what I think of as my culture is really just my individual parents' way of thinking?"

So we can infer that Kingston isn't just writing about events that she remembers. She's writing about memory itself.

Narrator: Now get ready to answer the questions.

TRACK 4.08

Narrator: What does the professor suggest when he says this?

MP: Kingston wants to explore the idea that remembering events in one's life is not a simple task. The more you think about things, the more you begin to wonder whether your own perceptions at the time were correct.

TRACK 4.09

Narrator: Listen to a conversation between a student and an advisor.

Female Advisor (FA): Hi, Timothy. So you're here today because you're thinking of applying to graduate school soon, right?

Male Student (MS): That's right. And I just want to go over what I should do to start preparing for graduate school applications and stuff.

FA: Sounds good. So you're in your third year now, and your major is psychology. Is that correct?

MS: Yes, that's right. And I'm hoping to go to graduate school to get a PhD in neuroscience, so I've taken a lot of cognitive psychology classes.

FA: That's good to hear. So in addition to taking the right classes, most graduate schools want to see that you have some experience working in your field. Have you had any psychology-related internships or jobs before?

MS: No, not really. I guess I didn't realize that I would need to for graduate school.

FA: Well, that's okay. You've still got plenty of time to prepare for graduate school. Ask your professors about upcoming internships; they should be able to point you in the right direction.

MS: Thanks, I'll definitely do that.

FA: Great. So one step toward preparing for graduate school is getting some work experience. And another important step is taking the GRE. Have you taken the GRE—you know, the standardized test required by graduate schools?

MS: No, but I've started studying for it. Do you happen to know when the next opportunity to take that test is?

FA: Not off the top of my head. But if you go online, you can find all future test dates. And if you want some help preparing for the GRE, the university offers free tutoring. All the GRE tutors here are graduate students themselves, so they have recent testing experience.

MS: Oh, that's good to hear. I'll have to stop by the tutoring center after this.

FA: Alright. So far, we've talked about seeking internships and taking the GRE in preparation for graduate school. (*Deliberating*) Let's see, what else is there? Oh, while you're asking your professors about internship opportunities, you might want to ask some of them to write you letters of recommendation. Most graduate schools will request at least two or three letters of recommendation as part of their application process. Other than that, you should be all set for now.

MS: Great. I'll work on getting all that done, and I'll get back to you when I have more questions.

FA: Sounds good.

Narrator: Now get ready to answer the questions.

TRACK 4.10

Narrator: Listen to part of the conversation. Then answer the question.

FA: So you're in your third year now, and your major is psychology. Is that correct?

MS: Yes, that's right. And I'm hoping to go to graduate school to get a PhD in neuroscience, so I've taken a lot of cognitive psychology classes.

Narrator: Why does the student say this?

MS: …so I've taken a lot of cognitive psychology classes.

TRACK 4.11

Narrator: Listen to part of the conversation. Then answer the question.

FA: Have you had any psychology-related internships or jobs before?

MS: No, not really. I guess I didn't realize that I would need to for graduate school.

FA: Well, that's okay. You've still got plenty of time to prepare for graduate school. Ask your professors about upcoming internships; they should be able to point you in the right direction.

Narrator: What does the advisor mean when she says this?

FA: …they should be able to point you in the right direction.

TRACK 4.12

Narrator: Listen to a lecture in a cosmology class.

Female Professor (FP): So now I want to tell you guys about the fascinating discovery of the cosmic microwave background, or just "CMB" for short. This story begins with the formation of the universe, about 14 billion years ago. Now, as you probably know, the Big Bang is the earliest event we know of. During the Big Bang, all the energy in the universe suddenly started expanding outward from one tiny point. And, well, no one knows why or how this happened, so don't bother asking me (*laughs*).

Anyway, as you can imagine, the early universe was an incredibly hot, chaotic place since all the energy around today was packed into such a small space. As the universe expanded, this heat became distributed over a larger and larger area. So during the 20th century, some mathematicians and scientists came to the conclusion that some of this heat energy left over from the Big Bang should still be around. After all, energy can never just "disappear," it just takes different forms. But of course, theorizing that the universe is filled with 14-billion year-old heat traces and actually finding evidence of this are two completely different tasks.

Yet, as is so often the case with science, the evidence was discovered completely by accident. In 1965, two scientists at Bell Laboratories in New Jersey were setting up a new radio receiver. This receiver was designed to pick up energy signals from deep space, so it was really sensitive. Yet anywhere in the cosmos that they pointed this receiver, they picked up a bit of excess noise. After they determined that the problem wasn't their receiver, they realized what this puzzling "space noise" was—evidence of the residual heat from the Big Bang. Yet because the universe has expanded so much during the past 14-billion years, the heat signal was weak, so the radio receiver picked up the energy signals as microwaves. And the fact that these—(*To male student*) You have a question, Matt?

Male Student (MS): Sorry, but I'm a little confused. What do microwaves have to do with heat and energy?

FP: Well, microwaves are just a form of energy, like x-rays or visible light. But microwaves carry less energy than visible light or x-rays. So remember, giving off heat is just something's way of getting rid of energy, and microwaves are themselves a form of energy.

And that's a very brief history of the discovery of the cosmic microwave background. And with this story, I'm not sure what I find more amazing: the fact that the universe still contains traces of the Big Bang from billions of years ago, or the fact that scientists were able to find evidence of these traces.

Narrator: Now get ready to answer the questions.

TRACK 4.13

Narrator: Why does the professor say this?

FP: But of course, theorizing that the universe is filled with 14-billion year-old heat traces and actually finding evidence of this are two completely different tasks.

TRACK 4.14

Narrator: What does the professor suggest when she says this?

FP: Yet, as is so often the case with science, the evidence was discovered completely by accident.

APPENDIX

Answer Key

CHAPTER 1

MAIN IDEA QUESTION - PRACTICE 1

Notes

stu. needs help creating email acct.
→ *go to "Stu. Center" website*
→ *click "Stu. Email," then "Sign Up"*

1) B

At the beginning of the conversation, the student gives her reason for visiting the employee when she says, "I was wondering if you could help me set up my student email account."

MAIN IDEA QUESTION - PRACTICE 2

Notes

prof. says stu. not participating in class enough
→ *stu. gets nervous in class*
→ *prof. = encouraging, but also threatens to ↓ grade*

2) C

The professor explains why he asked to speak with the student when he says, "here we are, three weeks into class, and I haven't heard you make a single comment." He then spends the rest of the conversation *encouraging* the student *to participate in class discussions.*

MAIN IDEA QUESTION - PRACTICE 3

Notes

woman asks man where to do group project
→ *man does many group projects*
→ *man recommends library basement (big tables, no need to be quiet)*

3) B

The woman approaches the man because she does not "know where to work on group projects." Thus, she asks the man *about good locations to work on group projects.*

MAIN IDEA QUESTION - PRACTICE 4

Notes

stu. says classes too big, no 1-on-1 time w/ profs.
→ *stu. = freshman*
advisor says upper-div. classes smaller, more time with prof.

4) D

The student states that the reason for her visit is to say that her "classes are impersonal" (*class sizes are too large*) and her "professors are never available for questions or anything" (*professors are rarely available*).

DETAIL QUESTIONS - PRACTICE 1

Notes

stu. looking for library book by Hildegard of Bingen
→ *for Medieval Europe class (Jodie Dayton = prof.)*
→ *book filed under different title*

1) C

The student says her religious studies class is "taught by Professor Dayton." Then, the advisor claims, "Jodie Dayton is a great lecturer."

2) A

The librarian says that the student was unable to find the book because her professor gave her the English title of the book, but the library files it "under the original Latin title, *Scivias*."

DETAIL QUESTIONS - PRACTICE 2

Notes

man wants to volunteer for on-campus garden
→ *man has landscaping experience (dad owns landscape business)*
woman tells man to come to garden at 9 am, Sat.

3) D

The man says that he wants to volunteer at the garden because, when he worked as a landscaper, he enjoyed doing garden-related work such as "getting to arrange and plant flowers and bushes."

4) A

The woman says, "me and the other volunteers meet at the garden every Saturday at 9 am."

DETAIL QUESTIONS - PRACTICE 3

Notes

man compliments woman's a cappella performance

→ woman in "Vocal Chords," recommends that man join
→ man wants to practice, tryouts in 2 weeks
man will talk to woman more later

5) D

At the beginning of the conversation, the man says to the woman, "I saw you perform with 'Vocal Chords' last night in the dining hall."

6) C

After the man says that he wants to practice his singing, the woman says, "you'd better practice quickly—we're having tryouts in two weeks."

DETAIL QUESTIONS - PRACTICE 4

Notes
stu. wants info. about study rooms
→ lib. says ppl. reserve them days in advance
→ stu. likes rooms (quiet, clean)
→ reserve study room on library website

7) C

The student claims that, while she was working in a study room, "someone came in and told me that he had reserved it [the study room] and that I needed to leave." Thus, we can conclude that *she had not reserved* a study room for herself.

8) A

The student says that she likes the study rooms because "they're never noisy (*quiet*), and they're always really clean (*tidy*)."

PURPOSE QUESTIONS - PRACTICE 1

Notes
man starting IM sports team
→ man says winning not important, asks woman to join his team
→ man will sign up for volleyball; woman's roommates play
man will sign up, woman will ask roommates, meet up again soon

1) D

The man says, "Nobody really cares who wins or anything," after the woman says that she is bad at sports. Thus, we can infer that he wants *to convince the woman to join his team* by telling her it will not be competitive.

2) B

Here, the woman is listing the positive qualities of volleyball, and we can assume that she is doing this *to explain why she will join* the man's team, even though she is not good at sports.

PURPOSE QUESTIONS - PRACTICE 2

Notes
stu. wants advice for improving grade
→ stu. has "C" in class, bad test scores
→ stu. misses a lot of class, test material presented in class
prof. says stu. grade will ↑ if stu. goes to class

3) B

According to the conversation, the student's test scores are bringing down his class grade. Since the professor says that the student misses class often, and that a lot of "test material is on information that's only mentioned in class," we can infer that the professor is rationalizing *the student's low test scores*.

4) C

The professor states that she does not take attendance. Thus, we can infer that her "test material is on information that's only mentioned in class" because she wants *to encourage students to attend class* so they know what information will be on upcoming tests.

PURPOSE QUESTIONS - PRACTICE 3

Notes
stu. getting tutor help in econ.
→ tutor = grad. stu. in accounting
→ stu. undeclared, doesn't want to study math/sci., maybe anthro.

5) D

Because the tutor says, "I've had to take a lot of economics classes, too," we can infer that he is assuring the student *that he is a qualified economics tutor*.

6) A

Studying "the development of different cultures" is a main topic in anthropology. Because she claims that she finds this topic interesting, we can infer that she is explaining *why she wants to study anthropology.*

PURPOSE QUESTIONS - PRACTICE 4

Notes

stu. wants to know about open-book test
→ stu. has never taken one before
prof. tells stu. to learn/bookmark major concepts
→ stu.: "why study at all," prof.: not enough time to look everything up

7) C

When the student says, "I've never takes one of those [open-book tests] before," she is explaining why she does not know how to prepare for the test. In other words, she is *explaining why she's asking the professor for advice.*

8) B

Here, the student is *questioning the purpose of preparing for open-book tests*, as she believes that studying is unnecessary because she will "have all the information right in front of" her.

INFERENCE QUESTIONS - PRACTICE 1

Notes

prof. says stu. missing too much class
→ stu. late almost every day, has other class that ends 10 mins. before
→ other class prof. doesn't let him leave
prof. excuses stu. tardiness (diligent stu., good excuse)

1) C, D

The professor probably excuses the student's tardiness because, according to the professor, he "seems like a smart, diligent student," and because the reason the student gives for his "tardiness is somewhat understandable."

2) B

The professor reveals that she is *concerned* for the student when she says, "I'm a little worried about your attendance in this class."

INFERENCE QUESTIONS - PRACTICE 2

Notes

stu. has very busy sched., wants extension on essay
→ prof. says student is hardworking, gives stu. 1-week extension

3) B

The phrase "you've bitten off more than you can chew," refers to accepting more work than one has time for. Thus, *the student has taken on more work than he can handle.*

4) D

When the student is explaining the reason for his visit, he seems to hesitate to ask for an extension on his paper. Therefore, we can infer that the student *is nervous about asking the professor for an extension.*

INFERENCE QUESTIONS - PRACTICE 3

Notes

stu. wants to be on-campus tour guide
advisor gives 3-step process:
    1) fill out simple form
    2) interview
    3) write a short paper
stu. will return w/ complete appl.

5) A

Because the student wants to be a tour guide, which is a position that requires extensive social interaction, we can infer that *she is outgoing and enjoys interacting with others.*

6) B

At the end of the conversation, the student says, "I'll come back later with this application filled out," so we can assume that she will *fill out the application* after the conversation.

INFERENCE QUESTIONS - PRACTICE 4

Notes

stu. lab partner missing, won't respond to text/call; infer: first time he's missed a lab
instructor tells stu. to do lab tomorrow w/ partner, or do lab now w/ different group
→ stu. will do lab now

7) B

Because the student does not know what to do when her lab partner is missing, we can assume that she has never dealt with this situation before. therefore, we can infer that *her lab partner has never been missing from lab before today.*

8) A

The instructor says that the "lab is pretty difficult and requires a lot of work." From this, we can infer that the lab is meant to be completed with a partner, so *the student cannot complete the lab assignment by herself.*

Exercise 1

Notes

stu. wants on-campus parking permit
sold out
off-campus parking: 2 mi. from dorms, shuttle transport
off-campus cheaper than on-campus parking
→ stu. buys off-campus permit

1) B

   Main Idea Question

   At the beginning of the conversation, the student asks the employee, "Is this where I go to buy an on-campus parking permit?"

2) A

   Detail Question

   The employee says, "usually, students buy their parking permits… toward the end of summer…"

3) D

   Purpose Question

   When the student says, "I have to move it [his car] every few days so I don't get a parking ticket," he is indicating the reason that parking in residential neighborhoods is inconvenient. In other words, he is *explaining why he needs a parking permit.*

4) C

   Inference Question

   Because the employee says that on-campus parking permits usually sell out before the school year begins, we can infer that *there are many more students than there are available parking spaces* on campus.

5) B

   Detail Question

   At the end of the conversation, the student decides to *purchase an off-campus parking permit* to avoid having to park in residential neighborhoods.

Exercise 2

Notes

woman talks to man about Andrew, project partner who isn't doing his share of work
→ Andrew's gf broke up w/ him, explains lack of motivation
→ man will talk to Andrew about doing his share

1) D

   Main Idea Question

   The woman approaches the man because he is roommates with Andrew, her partner on a group project. The woman is unable to contact Andrew, so she talks to the man *to find out if he can help her find* Andrew.

2) C

   Detail Question

   When the woman asks the man, "You're still roommates with Andrew, right?" he responds by saying, "I sure am." Thus, the man and Andrew *are roommates.*

3) A

   Purpose Question

   Here, the man explains that *Andrew has not been attending class* because he is upset that his girlfriend broke up with him.

4) B

   Inference Question

   The phrase "to pull one's weight" means that a person is doing their share of a task or a project. If Andrew has "not been pulling his weight on the project," we can infer that he *has not completed his portion of the group project.*

5) B

   Inference Question

   Toward the end of the conversation, the man offers to talk to Andrew and encourage him to finish his share of the project. From this, we can infer that the man *is sympathetic toward the woman's desire to finish the group project.*

Exercise 3

Notes

stu. wants to rent sports equip.—tennis
never rented before
stu. must give ID for equip., rent for 3 hours
→ late fee if more than 3 hours

1) B

Main Idea Question

At the beginning of the conversation, the student reveals his reason for visiting when he says to the employee, "I was hoping to check out a couple of tennis rackets and tennis balls (*athletic equipment*)."

2) A

Purpose Question

Because the employee spends time explaining the rental system after asking the student this question, we can infer that the question served to *determine if the student is familiar with the... rental system*.

3) D

Detail Question

When explaining the rental system, the employee says, "give me your student ID, and I'll give you whatever equipment you need."

4) B

Detail Question

The student says that he will be back within three hours after the employee reveals, "I have to charge you five dollar per piece of equipment that is turned in late."

5) C

Inference Question

At the end of the conversation, the employee says to the student, "So I have your ID, let me go get your equipment."

Exercise 4

Notes

man looking for Lecture Hall 203 (net to uni.)
→ *man has psych. 1 there*
→ *woman took psych 1 there, knows location (walk north, left at courtyard)*
man's prof. = Duarte
woman had, too; says he's good prof. (nice, smart)

1) C

Main Idea Question

The man reveals his reason for talking to the woman when he says, "do you know where Lecture Hall 203 is?" From this question, we can assume that he is talking to the woman *to ask for directions to a location on campus*.

2) B

Purpose Question

When the man first asks for directions to the lecture hall, the woman says that she does not know where it is. But when he says that he is taking Psychology 1 there, she remembers the lecture hall's location because it is where she took Psychology 1, too. Thus, she says this *to explain how she knows the lecture hall's location*.

3) D

Detail Question

After the man says that he "must have walked right by" the lecture hall, the woman responds, "the lecture halls here really aren't that well labeled."

4) A

Detail Question

The woman says that Professor Duarte is "really nice (*kind*), and he definitely knows his stuff (*knowledgeable*)."

5) B

Inference Question

At the beginning of the conversation, the man says, "I don't really know my way around campus yet." From this, we can infer that he has not been at the university for very long. Thus, *he is a relatively new student at the university*.

Exercise 5

Notes

stu. wants to borrow textbook for Sociology 143
lib. explain textbook lending policies:
→ *only check out 3 hours/day*
→ *stay in library*
lib. says will get textbook for stu.

1) D

Main Idea Question

The student clarifies her reason for talking to the librarian when she says, "Can you see if you have the textbook for Sociology 143." From this, we can gather that the student wants *to find out if the library has a copy of a certain textbook*.

2) B

Purpose Question

The woman says, "I really need to catch up on the reading," in response to the librarian's question about checking out the textbook. Thus, the student's response serves *to explain why she needs to use the textbook*.

3) B

Detail Question

When explaining the library's textbook lending policy, the librarian says, "we can only let you use the book for a three-hour period, once per day."

4) A

Inference Question

Because the librarian has to explain the rules for checking out a textbook to the student, we can infer that the student *has not checked out a textbook from the library before*.

5) C

Inference Question

At the end of the conversation, the librarian says, "I'll go get that sociology textbook for you right now."

Exercise 6

Notes

stu. wants to learn about/sign up for uni. health care, employee explains
→ *sign application, pay fee, get health care*
→ *uni. health center convenient, performs simple procedures (no complex surgeries)*
→ *costs $310/year*
stu. decides to sign up (thinks price is good)

1) C

Main Idea Question

At the beginning of the lecture, the student asks, "Is this where I come to sign up for the university's health care program?" And at the end of the lecture, the student decides to purchase health care. Thus, the student's reason for visiting is *to sign up for the university's health care program*.

2) A, D

Detail Question

According to the employee, the student has to "fill out this application… and pay a one-time fee" to receive health care.

3) B

Purpose Question

Here, the employee is comparing the distance of the nearest urgent care center to the nearness of the university health center. Thus, the employee is *emphasizing the university health center's convenient location*.

4) D

Detail Question

According to the employee, the university health center does not "have the proper medical equipment for more complicated procedures."

5) C

Inference Question

The student seems both surprised and pleased when she learns how much a year of health care costs. Thus, we can infer that the fee is *lower than the student expected*.

CHAPTER 2

MAIN IDEA QUESTION - PRACTICE 1

Notes

mech. drawings show how things work
topic = blueprints (mech. drawing copy)
→ *guide construction workers/managers*
→ *traced drawing on blue background*

1) B

The main topic of the lecture is blueprints, which are "copies of mechanical drawings." In other words, the main topic is a *copying technique for architects*.

MAIN IDEA QUESTION - PRACTICE 2

Notes

UK med. system = Nation Health Service (NHS)
→ *citizens get free care, paid through taxes*
→ *people visit GPs/specialists*
→ *keeps costs ↓ by emph. primary care*

2) D

The professor mainly talks about the National Health Service, which is *the healthcare system of the United Kingdom*.

MAIN IDEA QUESTION - PRACTICE 3

Notes

desert formation
→ *hot air rises at equator, travels north & south*
→ *hot air descends, becomes dry, prevents rainfall*

3) C

The professor reveals the main topic of his lecture when he says, "To find out how these deserts formed…."

MAIN IDEA QUESTION - PRACTICE 4

Notes

folk music = music for ordinary people
→ *flamenco = Spanish folk music*
→ *intense: uses guitars, dance, singing*
→ *fast tempo, plucking guitars*

4) B

The professor starts the lecture by discussing *folk music*. Then, he introduces the main topic, flamenco music, which *probably originated in Spain*.

DETAIL QUESTIONS - PRACTICE 1

Notes

topic = butterfly effect (small event → large event)
→ *important to chaos theory*
→ *thought of by meteorologist (studies weather)*
→ *explains why weather is hard to predict*

1) A

According to the lecture, the butterfly effect theorizes that "a small and seemingly insignificant event can lead to a large event."

2) D

The professor says, "a meteorologist, which is the name for someone who studies weather patterns," came up with an example that lead to the creation of the term "butterfly effect."

DETAIL QUESTIONS - PRACTICE 2

Notes

socialism = econ. system
→ *supports public property, social harmony (Rob Owen)*
→ *Louis Blanc = trade unions, help working class, influenced nations*

3) D

According to the lecture, "socialists believed that public ownership would solve issues such as poverty and social unrest," so socialists hoped to secure the *public ownership of property*.

4) B

According to the professor, Owen claimed that "the sharing of property created social harmony and progress." In other words, he believed that *sharing property leads to a better society*.

DETAIL QUESTIONS - PRACTICE 3

Notes

Kuiper belt = outer solar system debris/rocks
→ *debris/rocks called KBOs (mostly ices)*
→ *at least 70,000 big KBOs (Pluto biggest)*
→ *named for astronomer, confirmed in 1992*

5) A

The professor says, "Astronomers think that this debris [from the Kuiper belt] is left over from the formation of the solar system itself."

6) B

According to the professor, "the biggest KBO is Pluto," so Pluto *is a Kuiper belt object*.

DETAIL QUESTIONS - PRACTICE 4

Notes

topic = animal domestication, neoteny
neoteny = adults have qualities of young (in salamanders)
→ *neoteny in humans = small nose, big eyes, small size (true of most mammals)*
→ *most dogs neotenic, probs. b/c of domestication*

7) B

According to the professor, all young salamanders have gills. Then, "some salamanders keep their gills even as adults." Thus, we can conclude that *retaining gills into adulthood* is a neotenic trait of salamanders.

8) A, D

A student lists several human neotenic traits, such as "a small nose, big eyes," and he says, "babies are smaller than adults" (*small size*).

PURPOSE QUESTIONS - PRACTICE 1

Notes

wheel origin = 6,000 years ago
→ invented many places in Europe/Middle East
→ used in chariot (horse-pulled battle cart)
no wheel in ancient Americas (no animals for pulling)

1) B

The professor says, "One of the most common uses for the wheel… was for the chariot." From this, we can infer that professor mentions the chariot *to give an example of an early use for the wheel.*

2) C

The professor says, "very few ancient North and South American civilizations ever invented anything that functions like a wheel." Thus, the professor mentions the Americas *to give an example of cultures that did not use wheels.*

PURPOSE QUESTIONS - PRACTICE 2

Notes

Mary Grandin (autistic, doctor) improved livestock slaughter
→ she related to livestock sensitivity to light, sound
→ created walled path to reduce livestock sensitivity

3) C

The professor says that Grandin's autism caused anxiety and sensitivity to loud noises, and that "Grandin felt that she could relate to their [livestock's] feeling of stress and anxiety from overstimulation."

4) A

According to the professor, Grandin's curved path "ensures that the livestock can't see the slaughterhouse in front of them, and it eliminates excessive light and noise." In other words, the curved path is an example of one way that Grandin *made the killing of livestock more humane.*

PURPOSE QUESTIONS - PRACTICE 3

Notes

obsessive compulsive disorder (OCD)
→ person is obsessed with fearful thoughts (dirtiness, harming others)
→ OCD person realizes condition, but cannot stop

5) D

By describing how "a person can… have OCD," the professor is essentially explaining *how OCD is diagnosed.*

6) C

The professor says that a compulsion is a "highly repetitive behavior, aimed at easing a fear" Washing one's hands constantly is a repetitive behavior, so we can infer that the professor says this *to give an example of a compulsion.*

PURPOSE QUESTIONS - PRACTICE 4

Notes

rabies; we've had cure since 1800s
→ if rabies reaches brain, fatal
vector = pt. where virus moves from animal to human
→ bats most common vector; marsupial (opossum) can't carry, blood too cold

7) C

The professor reveals a main reason for his lecture when he says, "Because this virus is so dangerous, it's important for public health officials to educate people" about rabies.

8) B

According to the professor, "the Carolina opossum… cannot carry the [rabies] virus," so the opossum is mentioned *to give an example of an animal that cannot transmit rabies.*

INFERENCE QUESTIONS - PRACTICE 1

Notes

Voyager 1 = space probe
→ took photos of Jupiter & Saturn
→ in 2012, first craft to leave solar system
→ now 18 light-hours from Sun

1) C

Because the professor says, "*Voyager 1* became the first and only spacecraft to leave our solar system," we can infer that *it has traveled further than any other man-made object.*

2) D

At the end of the lecture, the professor says, "now let's discuss how *Voyager 1* sends and receives data," so the class will talk about *how Voyager 1 communicates with Earth.*

INFERENCE QUESTIONS - PRACTICE 2

Notes
protein = macronutrient (body requires)
→ *lots of protein in body (cells, skin, hair, nails)*
→ *made of chains of amino acids; body needs 20 amino acids (9 come from diet); meat/dairy has most amino acids*

3) A

Because protein is made "from long chains of... amino acids," we can infer that proteins must be *much larger than amino acids.*

4) D

While fruits and vegetables have some, but not all, necessary amino acids, "meat and dairy products contain all the amino acids the human body needs." Thus, we can infer that meat and dairy *are among the best sources of amino acids.*

INFERENCE QUESTIONS - PRACTICE 3

Notes
life began 3.5 bil. years ago, Earth formed 4.5 bil. years ago
→ *Earth too harsh for life first bil. years*
→ *earliest life = microbe towers (stromatolites)*

5) B

Because the first life probably formed about 1 billion years after Earth formed, and because the professor says, "life began as soon as Earth's conditions could accommodate it," the Earth's conditions probably *were too extreme to accommodate life.*

6) A

The professor emphasizes the phrase "at least" when talking about when the first life appeared on Earth, so we can infer that it is possible *that life began more than 3.5 billion years ago.*

INFERENCE QUESTIONS - PRACTICE 4

Notes
types of stages
→ *proscenium stage = view from front, curtains, uses scenery*
→ *open stage = view from three sides, scenery at back of stage*
→ *theater-in-the-round = view from all sides, exit/entrance through auditorium*

7)

	Theater-in-the-round	Proscenium Stage	Open stage
Spectators sit around three sides of a raised platform that extends into an auditorium			✓
Spectators sit on all four sides of the stage	✓		
Spectators can only see the front of the stage		✓	

In a theater-in-the-round, "viewers sit on four sides of the stage." A proscenium stage "can only be viewed from the front." And an open stage has "seat around three sides of a raised platform."

Exercise 1

Notes
rumination = 'to chew again,' to obsess on an event
→ *reflection = good, think about something; different from rumination*
→ *stop rumination by occupying mind elsewhere*

1) B

Main Idea Question

The main topic of the lecture is rumination, the process of "thinking about the same injustice or embarrassment over and over." In other words, rumination is a *process in which a person remembers an event over and over.*

2) D

Detail Question

According to the professor, rumination also describes a process in which animals "chew it [food] up completely more than once," so rumination describes *the process of rechewing food.*

3) A

Purpose Question

The professor's examples are all situations that might lead to rumination, so we can infer that examples are listed *to point out possible causes and effects of rumination.*

4) C

Detail Question

According to the professor, reflection involves gaining "insight into something by considering it for a bit," while rumination "means to almost uncontrollably think about upsetting feeling and their causes."

5) D

Detail Question

The professor says that "people should distract themselves" *with physical or mental activities* in order to avoid rumination.

6) B

Inference Question

The professor's examples of events that cause rumination involve a friend saying something mean, or you doing something regrettable. From this, we can infer that rumination *is triggered by an upsetting encounter or event.*

Exercise 2

Notes

3 types of business ownership
  1) single proprietorship: 1 owner, owner responsible for company's debt, pop. in construction, food service
  2) partnership: 2+ owners, each person responsible for company's debt, pop. in law, medicine, real estate
  3) corporation: owned by stockholders, run by managers, profits go to holders/back into company, owners not responsible for debt, pop. in banking, insurance, oil

1) D

Main Idea Question

The professor explains the main topic when she says, "I want to focus today's lecture on three main types of business ownership in the United States."

2) A

Detail Question

The professor says, "Partnerships can usually handle more business than a single proprietor."

3) A, C

Detail Question

According to the professor, "Corporation are owned by stockholders," but managers "run the everyday activities of a corporation."

4) D

Inference Question

Because the owners of both single proprietorships and partnerships are "completely responsible for any debt that the business accumulates," we can infer that *founding and maintaining these types of businesses are financially risky.*

5)

	Corporation	Single Proprietorship	Partnership
Banking and insurance	✓		
Law and real estate			✓
Construction and food service		✓	

Inference Question

According to the lecture, "Corporations dominate such industries as banking, insurance, and oil;" "Single proprietorships are the most common… in farming, construction, and food service;" and partnerships "are most common in law, medicine, and real estate."

Exercise 3

Notes

geothermal energy = energy from Earth's heat
heat from Earth formation, radioactive decay
→ magma just below crust, water near magma
→ heated water come to surface (once used for heating/bathing; now used to generate electricity)

1) C

Main Idea Question

The main topic of the lecture is geothermal energy, which is the process of harvesting "the energy that comes from Earth's internal heat." Thus, the topic of the lecture is *a method of deriving energy from the Earth's heat.*

2) A

Detail Question

The professor says, "Many countries generate some of their electricity by harvesting thermal energy from underground water and steam," so geothermal energy comes from *hot, underground water*.

3) C

Detail Question

According to the professor, the Earth maintains it internal temperature because "some of the heat is left over from the Earth's formation billions of years ago. The rest of the energy comes from the decay of radioactive elements."

4) A

Purpose Question

This statement explains that people *in the past made use of geothermal energy* by using "the heated water in hot springs for bathing and heating."

5) D

Inference Question

Here, the professor explains that "magma rises to the Earth's crust and mantle" because "magma is less dense than the rock from which it formed." From this, we can infer that the Earth's rocky core is *denser than* the magma and rock *in the mantle and crust*.

6) B

Inference Question

At the end of the lecture, the professor explains that many places generate electricity from geothermal energy. Then he says, "let's look at how... they do this." Thus, we can infer that the professor will discuss *how geothermal energy is converted into electricity*.

Exercise 4

Notes

protectionism = gov. favors domestic industries over int'l ones
→ protectionist = taxing imports, ↓ competition for domestic industries; limit # of imports; offer gov. $ to domestic markets
→ protectionism goes against free trade; many agree protectionism not good for econ.

1) C

Main Idea Question

The main topic of the lecture is protectionism, which is when "the government favors the success of domestic businesses." In other words, protectionism describes *ways that the governments help domestic businesses succeed*.

2) B

Inference Question

According to the professor, "raising taxes on imports often increases the prices of products." Because consumers do not want to pay more for goods, we can infer that *consumers often oppose tax raises on imported goods*.

3) A, D

Detail Question

Protectionist policies mentioned by the professor include "taxing imported goods" and limiting "the amount of goods that can be imported into the country."

4) A

Detail Question

The professor describes a subsidy as "money that a government gives to a business."

5) B

Purpose Question

Here, the professor is explaining why economists do not support protectionist policies by *presenting a downside to a government's use of protectionism*.

6) A

Detail Question

The professor explains that protectionism gives domestic businesses an advantage, thus decreasing competition, while "free" trade forces businesses to compete.

Exercise 5

Notes

counting systems: modern = decimal system (5s &10s), Sumerian = sexagesimal (count by 60s)
→ sexagesimal still used in time, angles
→ sexagesimal counting based on knuckles
prof. tells class to try counting using sexagesimal system

1) D

Main Idea Question

Throughout the lecture, the professor discusses the sexagesimal counting system, which was developed over 5,000 years ago. Thus, the purpose of the lecture is *to introduce an ancient counting system*.

2) B

Detail Question

The professor says, "most of us will claim that it's easiest to keep track of numbers in groups of 5s and

10s," which he later calls *the decimal system*.

3) C

Detail Question

According to the professor, the sexagesimal numeral system was developed by the Sumerians over 5,000 years ago."

4) B, D

Detail Question

A student notes that the sexagesimal numeral system is used "to measure time," and the professor says that the sexagesimal system is used "when we measure angles."

5) A

Purpose Question

The professor wants to show students how to count "much like ancient people may have," so he wants to show the class *how* ancient people counted, and thus *how the sexagesimal counting system may have originated.*

6) A

Inference Question

A student claims that we use the decimal system "because we have five fingers on each hand and 10 fingers in total," and the professor says that the sexagesimal system involves counting "in base 60 using just 10 fingers." Thus, we can infer that *many counting systems keep track of numbers using hands and fingers.*

Exercise 6

Notes

mutualism = both species benefit from interacting
mutualism in ants & aphids
→ *ants herd aphids*
→ *ants get honeydew (food), aphids get protection*
→ *ants give off chem. that subdues aphids, sometimes bite off wings*

1) B

Main Idea Question

The professor mainly discusses mutualism—where two or more animals "benefit… from an interaction or relationship"—between aphids and ants.

2) D

Detail Question

According to the professor, "aphids feed on the sugary nectar of a plant."

3) A

Purpose Question

Here, the professor introduces the concept of domestication by talking about humans' domestication of animals, but then he transitions to *the concept of domestication among insect species.*

4) C

Detail Question

The professor explains that aphids excrete honeydew, and "ants then use this honeydew for food," so we can assume that ants domesticate aphids *to harvest a fluid that the aphids produce.*

5) A

Detail Question

The professor says, "ants leave a chemical trail that basically subdues the aphids and makes them unlikely to try to escape or wander away."

6) C

Inference Question

The professor starts the lecture by *introducing a concept* (mutualism), and then he *elaborate on it using the example* of the mutualism among aphids and ants.

CHAPTER 3

ACTUAL PRACTICE 1 - PRACTICE SET 1

Notes

development of Egypt culture
→ *Nile River flooding good for farming, river mud for houses (hot so sleep on roof)*
→ *use reeds for weaving, paper; grew flax for fabric, mummy wraps*
→ *minerals from desert (salt) for eye makeup (prevented/ treated eye infections)*

1) B

Main Idea Question

The professor says that the lecture's "focus is on the practical solutions that eventually led to" Egyptian culture. In other words, the professor shows *how Egyptians used the resources of the Nile.*

2) A
Purpose Question
By saying that "to either side of the [Nile] river are vast deserts," the professor is highlighting the importance of the Nile by explaining *why most resources had to come from the Nile*.

3) D
Detail Question
The professor states that Egyptians grew "a grass-like plant that could be made into cool linen fabric for clothes," and that they made "paper from the papyrus reeds."

4) C
Detail Question
The Egyptians used salts (minerals) from the desert "to make the distinctive eye makeup that most of us recognize immediately as Egyptian."

5) A
Purpose Question
Here, the professor reveals that the cultural practice of applying makeup to improve one's appearance may have developed because early eye makeups "prevented and treated eye infections." Thus, the professor shows *that aspects of culture... may develop for practical reasons*.

6) D
Inference Question
The professor spends much of the lecture discussing products and activities in ancient Egypt that required the Nile River, so we can infer that *ancient Egypt would not have thrived without the Nile*.

ACTUAL PRACTICE 1 - PRACTICE SET 2

Notes
stu. wants advice for analysis paper (has not written one before)
writing about connection bet. Great Gatsby and Greek tragedy
→ *Gatsby = tragic hero (like Oedipus, Pentheus), Nick = chorus*
stu. not sure how to start paper
→ *prof. suggests that stu. write about Greek tragedy in intro., discuss Gatsby in body*

1) B
Main Idea Question
At the beginning of the conversation, the student says that he has questions "about the paper you [the professor] assigned." Later in the conversation, the student says, "I don't know how to start the paper." Thus, the student wants *help writing an introduction to his paper*.

2) D
Purpose Question
The professor asks this question after the student says that he has never written a analysis paper before, so we can infer that the professor is *anticipating what the student's problem is*.

3) A
Detail Question
When talking about *The Great Gatsby*, the student says, "I noticed that it shares a lot of features with the Greek tragedies."

4) D
Inference Question
Here, the student compares *The Great Gatsby* to Greek tragedies, so it is logical that he is also comparing Gatsby, a character from *The Great Gatsby*, to characters from Greek tragedies.

5) C
Inference Question
Throughout the conversation, the professor provides helpful information and positive feedback for the student. Thus, we can infer that the professor is being *supportive*.

ACTUAL PRACTICE 1 - PRACTICE SET 3

Notes
clinical depression affects 19-mil. Americans
→ *symptoms = anger, no fun, sleep problems, self-resentment*
→ *caused by genes, brain chem., health, stress levels*
→ *treatment = balancing emotions*
→ *depressed people = not enough oxytocin (creates peace, trust) released by touch*

1) B
Main Idea Question
The lecture lists *the symptoms of* depression and describes the complicated *causes of it*.

2) B

Detail Question

According to the professor, "19 million Americans suffer from clinical depression and anxiety at any given time."

3) B

Detail Question

The professor says that some symptoms of depression include "having difficulty sleeping or sleeping too much… and feelings of hopelessness."

4) A

Purpose Question

Here, we can infer that the professor is *explaining why depression is often so difficult to treat*, because the he says that depression arises from "very, very complicated relationships" between biology and environment.

5) C

Purpose Question

When talking about brain chemistry, the professor mentions that "the brain cells of depressed people don't transmit or receive messages as they should," so we can assume that the professor talks about brain chemistry *to explain some possible biological causes of clinical depression.*

6) C

Inference Question

Because depressed people often feel a lack of "comfort and security," we can infer that *many people with depression do not produce enough oxytocin.*

ACTUAL PRACTICE 2 - PRACTICE SET 1

Notes

main question: What is intelligence?
→ *ability to adapt to env't (ex. men in snowstorm)*
→ *ability to process abstract thoughts (think about things that can't be seen/measured)*
definition impossible, description more useful

1) A

Main Idea Question

The professor reveals that the main purpose of the lecture is to answer the question: "What is intelligence?" So the class *discusses some definitions of intelligence.*

2) B

Purpose Question

After mentioning that "intelligence" has many definitions, the professor says, "psychologists, biologists, and philosophers cannot always agree on one" definition. Thus, he is *emphasizing that different professions assign different characteristics to intelligence.*

3) C

Detail Question

After the professor mentions "adapting to one's environment," he says that, in a snowstorm, a "man might create a small shelter out of blocks of snow to stay warm."

4) D

Inference Question

The professor says, "we can't speak to dolphins or ants" to measure their abstract thoughts, so he mentions *communication barriers that prevent humans from determining animals' levels of intelligence.*

5) B

Detail Question

The professor describes abstract thoughts as "ideas or concepts that cannot necessarily be seen or measured (*perceived with the senses*)."

6) D

Inference Question

At the end of the lecture, the professor says that "coming up with characteristics that describe" intelligence is better than coming "up with one universal definition" for it. Here, he points out when *describing a term is more useful than defining it.*

ACTUAL PRACTICE 2 - PRACTICE SET 2

Notes

stu. wants to learn about job fair
employee says local businesses give info./job openings in campus plaza
→ *stu. wants psych job (should look for info. on school website)*
→ *stu. should dress nicely, bring resume*
stu. looking forward to job fair

1) C

Main Idea Question

At the beginning of the lecture, the student asks the

employee, "I was wondering if you could give me some information about" the upcoming job fair.

2) D

Detail Question

After the employee tells the student what a job fair is, the student says, "I'm majoring in psychology."

3) A

Inference Question

When someone says, "I hate to keep bothering you," he or she usually means to acknowledge taking up the other person's time, such as by *asking too many questions*.

4) B, D

Detail Question

The employee tells the student, "you should definitely dress nicely… [and] you should definitely bring a few copies of your resume" to the job fair.

5) A

Inference Question

The student says that she thinks that the job fair "will be a great opportunity," so we can infer that job fairs *benefit students*. And because job fairs allow local businesses to recruit college-educated students, we can infer that job fairs *benefit local businesses*.

ACTUAL PRACTICE 2 - PRACTICE SET 3

Notes

Agatha Christie = 1900s mystery writer; some like, some hate (main topic)

critics say her stories are too similar

→ *same settings, chars. undeveloped, stories similar, only focus on rich*

supporters say diversity in formula

→ *good plot momentum, chars. hide motives*

→ *criticizes rich (rich no better than poor)*

1) C

Main Idea Question

The professor reveals the main topic when he says, "Why do some people say the quality of Christie's writing is quite low, and why do others admire it." Thus, he is exploring *the debate surrounding… Christie's writing*.

2) D

Purpose Question

Because much of the lecture explores the reasons for Christie's popularity, we can infer that the professor mentions how many of her books have been sold *to show that her books are very popular*.

3) D

Detail Question

According to the professor, some claim that Christie's "stories are too much the same," so they have *predictable plots*, and that they take place "where rich or upper-middle-class people are staying," so they focus on *the lives of the rich*.

4) B

Inference Question

Because Christie "found hundreds of ways to surprise readers" even though she used a similar plot each time, we can infer that she *changed plot details to make each story original*.

5) D

Inference Question

To be "dazzled" by something means to be impressed. Therefore, if Christie was not dazzled by the rich, it means that she *thought that rich people were much the same as other people*; she was not impressed by wealth.

6) C

Detail Question

According to the professor, Christie sets her novels in country homes so that "the characters stay in a calm place with no real work to do." In other words, a country home is somewhere *characters could believably stay until the mystery was solved*.

ACTUAL PRACTICE 3 - PRACTICE SET 1

Notes

child artwork relates to mental development

→ *scribbling stage: until 3 years old, making circles*

→ *pre-schematic stage: 3-4 years old, making circles and lines, simple people*

→ *schematic stage: 5-6 years old, detail, special awareness, x-ray vision art*

→ *8-9 years old, realistic, pop culture*

1) D

Main Idea Question

The professor primarily talks about *artistic development* in children. She also claims, "artwork can reveal a great deal about [children's] cognitive development."

2) C

Detail Question

According to the professor, a typical pre-schematic drawing "is a face with two legs sticking out of it," which is very similar to *a figure with a circular face, legs, and possibly arms.*

3) A

Detail Question

The professor says that, during the schematic stage, "children seem to plan a scene and set it in a landscape."

4) C

Purpose Question

The professor says that children in the schematic stage may "include features such as bones, teeth, and organs" in their art. Thus, x-ray vision is mentioned *to explain that children in* the schematic stage *may draw the inside of things.*

5) C

Inference Question

At the beginning of the lecture, the professor says, "For children who have access to art materials, artwork can reveal a great deal about their cognitive development." From this, we can infer that *children's access to art supplies will help teachers measure their cognitive development.*

6) C

Inference Question

The lecture mainly explores the relationship between children's art and their cognitive development. Thus, we can infer that describing stages of artistic development *shows a typical pattern of growth in thinkers.*

ACTUAL PRACTICE 3 - PRACTICE SET 2

Notes

stu. reviewing requirements for final project
project worth 25% of grade, 3 parts (written, translation, presentation)
→ *written = 7-10 pg. on Greek his.*
→ *translation = Greek text, include original*
→ *presentation = different topic than written, visual component*
project info. on prof. website

1) B

Main Idea Question

The student reveals his reason for visiting when he says, "I'm kind of confused about what we need to include in our final project."

2) D

Purpose Question

Because 25 percent is a large portion of the student's grade, we can infer that the professor mentions this *to emphasize the importance of the final project.*

3) B, C

Detail Question

The professor says, "the project consists of three major parts: a written component (*research paper*), a translation component, and a presentation."

4) B

Detail Question

The professor tells the student, "be sure to include the original text as well. That way I can make sure your translation is accurate."

5) A

Inference Question

The professor says to write a "paper on some topic in ancient Greek history," and to translate "any ancient Greek text you want." From this, we can infer that she probably teaches *The Cultures of Ancient Greece.*

ACTUAL PRACTICE 3 - PRACTICE SET 3

Notes

viruses = thousands of time smaller than cell
→ *main part = DNA/RNA, instructions on how to reproduce*
→ *DNA surrounded by protein, protection*
→ *some have fat coat that protects, too*
host = organism a virus uses to reproduce
→ *virus invades host cell, uses cell enzymes to reproduce, destroy host cell*

1) A

Main Idea Question

The main topic of the lecture is viruses, which are *small, simple organisms that need other (host) organisms to reproduce.*

2) C

Detail Question

The professor says, "The main part of the virus is its DNA or RNA, depending on the virus."

3) D

Detail Question

According to the professor, an organism needs enzymes to reproduce, "but viruses lack these enzymes." Thus, "a virus invades a host organism" so it can use that organism's enzymes to reproduce.

4) A

Detail Question

The professor tells the class to "think of the virus as an architect, the one who makes the blueprints," and the professor compares blueprints to *the DNA or RNA code*.

5) A

Detail Question

The professor tells the class to "think of... the enzymes as the construction workers, the ones who actually do the building" of *the new virus*.

6) B

Inference Question

Because viruses often destroy their host's cells, we can infer that *viruses often harm their host organism*.

ACTUAL PRACTICE 4 - PRACTICE SET 1

Notes

George Balanchine = ballet choreographer, dancer
→ *opened New York City Ballet (1948)*
→ *trained in Russia*
→ *wanted dancers to be strong, athletic*
→ *created abstract dances; used toe shoes, jazz moves criticized for demands on woman dancers, lack of male parts*

1) C

Main Idea Question

The professor talks about George Balanchine, who she says, "revolutionized the ballet world." Thus, the main topic is *a choreographer who revolutionized ballet*.

2) C, D

Detail Question

According to the professor, "Balanchine wanted his female dancers to have long legs… He wanted them to attack the moves with energetic athleticism."

3) D

Inference Question

Because choreographers before Balanchine wanted dancers who were "good at acting," we can infer that ballets before Balanchine were story-driven. Balanchine, however, "created many abstract ballets that do not tell a story."

4) A

Purpose Question

Throughout the lecture, the professor highlights the ways that Balanchine broke away from traditional ballet. But she mentions that Balanchine "had undergone the rigor of training in Russia in both ballet and piano" *to show that Balanchine also understood traditional ballet*.

5) B

Purpose Question

The professor says that Balanchine's dances are still performed, but that "Ballet companies are also turning away from abstract ballets." Thus, the criticisms are included to show that Balanchine is still influential, but also that *views of ballet have changed in recent decades*.

6) A

Inference Question

Because Balanchine's "style continues to dominate the ballet world," we can infer that ballet *is influenced by the past*, but because some "ballet companies are also turning away from abstract ballets," like the ones Balanchine created, we can infer that ballet *still changes over time*.

ACTUAL PRACTICE 4 - PRACTICE SET 2

Notes

stu. wants to know about extra credit (wants an "A" in class)
→ *add 500-1,000 words to research paper, create corresponding presentation*
→ *worth up to 5% grade increase*
→ *presentations on last day of class (few weeks away)*

1) D

Main Idea Question

At the beginning of the conversation, the student

reveals her reason for visiting when she asks, "I was wondering if you are going to offer any extra credit opportunities."

2) B

Purpose Question

If the student has "done quite well in" the professor's class, she probably doesn't need to improve her grade with extra credit. Thus, we can infer that the professor is *questioning the student's desire for extra credit.*

3) A

Inference Question

The professor says, "I admire your determination" in response to the students saying that she "wants to get an 'A'" in his class. Thus, we can infer that the professor *appreciates the student's desire for a good grade.*

4) B

Detail Question

The professor says, "presentations will be on the last day of class."

5) C

Inference Question

We can infer that the student is *optimistic*, because she is happy that she might be able to get an "A" in the professor's class.

ACTUAL PRACTICE 4 - PRACTICE SET 3

Notes

Is identity unchanging? (topic = brainwashing)
religious and political groups have brainwashed
brainwash = making person afraid, then changing their mind

　1) person isolated, afraid, tired
　2) person feels shame at old life
　3) make person change to become "good"

1) D

Main Idea Question

The professor describes the process of brainwashing, which includes *the steps involved in changing a person's beliefs.*

2) A

Inference Question

Because religious cults brainwash people, we can infer that people are brainwashed for *religious reasons*; and because kidnapper and dictators have brainwashed people, we can infer that people are brainwashed for *social* and *political* reasons.

3) C

Detail Question

The professor says, "First, the brainwasher usually keeps the person that will be brainwashed sleepy, hungry, and alone for a long while."

4) B

Detail Question

According to the professor, "the final step [of brainwashing] is that the brainwasher offers the person a chance to change, to 'be good'," which involves making the person *feel safe and loved.*

5) A

Inference Question

According to the professor, people who are being brainwashed are made to feel guilty about their past, and brainwashers offer them new, "good" beliefs. Thus, a brainwashed person wants *to feel cared for and accepted.*

6) C

Inference Question

Because people who are brainwashed adopt new beliefs about themselves and their surroundings, we can infer that *personality and identity... can be changed.*

ACTUAL PRACTICE 5 - PRACTICE SET 1

Notes

gluten = proteins in wheat products
1% of ppl. have celiac (allergic to gluten)
many have "gluten intolerance" (no celiac, but they remove gluten from diet)
→ no gluten can lead to vitamin deficiencies
gluten intolerance maybe = FODMAP intolerance
→ FODMAP = hard-to-digest carbs. (in apples, avocados)

1) B

Main Idea Question

The professor introduces gluten, and then he addresses claims made about gluten that "have no real scientific basis." Thus, the lecture is about *common misconceptions about gluten intake.*

2) C

Detail Question

The professor says, "about 1 percent of people actually can't digest gluten properly."

3) A

Detail Question

The professor explains, "FODMAPs stand for the names of several different carbohydrates that all people have some trouble digesting."

4) A

Purpose Question

We can infer that the professor says, "the carbohydrates in FODMAPs are very common," *to explain why so many people* often complain of digestive problems *that they mistakenly attribute to gluten intolerance.*

5) D

Detail Question

According to the professor, "it's much more likely that those who claim to be gluten intolerant are actually sensitive to a group of carbohydrates collectively known as FODMAPs."

6) C

Inference Question

The professor claims that "removing gluten products from one's diet can be problematic" because doing so may remove *important vitamins and nutrients from their diets*, such as "B Vitamins, fiber, and calcium."

ACTUAL PRACTICE 5 - PRACTICE SET 2

Notes

stu. wants to make sure graduation plans OK
→ stu. is bio. major, needs to take 3 upper-div. classes, 2 labs, 3 GE requirements
→ stu. thought GEs were done
→ advisor recommends class that fills 2 GE requirements
stu. can graduate on time, easy final semester

1) C

Main Idea Question

The student reveals the purpose of the conversation when he says, "I just wanted to make sure I'm on track to graduate at the end of my fourth year."

2) D

Detail Question

The advisor asks for the student's name and ID number so she can look the student up "on the computer system" and "take a look at [the student's] transcript."

3) A

Inference Question

The student says that he thought he had finished all of his general education requirements, so we can infer that he now *has to take more classes than he had thought.*

4) B

Detail Question

The advisor says, "There's an art history class that… fulfills both an art and a history general education requirement."

5) D

Inference Question

We can infer that the student is *appreciative* of the advisor's help because he says, "Oh, that's really helpful."

ACTUAL PRACTICE 5 - PRACTICE SET 3

Notes

situational irony = expect one thing, the opposite happens explained with ex.
→ woman buys books to prep. for trivia contest and win prize
→ woman wins trivia contest, wins books she bought to prepare
→ not what you expect
prof. gives more ex. at end of lecture

1) C

Main Idea Question

The main topic of the lecture is situational irony, which are situations "where you expect one thing to happen, but then the exact opposite of what you expected occurs."

2) A

Inference Question

The professor says that "situational irony is used in films, television, literature, and it's something that happens in daily life, too," so we can infer that it *occurs very often in media and in our daily lives.*

3) D

Detail Question

According to the professor, the woman "buys all the books on trivia she can find," and "she spends almost all her time reading the trivia books."

4) B

Detail Question

After the woman wins the trivia competition, she opens her prize and "finds an extensive collection of trivia books."

5) B

Purpose Question

Here, the professor lists "more examples of situational irony," which are *situations with unexpected results*.

6) C

Inference Question

The professor says, "Situational irony... subverts your expectations," and that it "is often used for comedic effect." From this, we can infer that a lot of comedy *subverts our expectation to make us laugh*.

ACTUAL PRACTICE 6 - PRACTICE SET 1

Notes

Luddites = skilled craftspeople in Britain who rejected some of Industrial Rev.
→ *destroyed textile mills that replaced skilled craftspeople*
→ *fictional leader = General Ludd*
Britain at war with France, didn't want to deal w/ Luddites
→ *used military against Luddites, sent some to prison (Australia)*
now, viewed as resisting tech., really they wanted old ways to be integrated into tech.

1) A

Main Idea Question

The lecture is about the Luddites, who *rejected certain aspects of industrial manufacturing*, such as the replacement of "skilled craftspeople with unskilled, low-wage machine workers."

2) D

Detail Question

Because "the machines that the Luddites destroyed usually produced low-quality textiles," we can conclude that they wanted to *ensure that factories would have to keep skilled textile craftspeople*.

3) D

Detail Question

According to the professor, the Luddite "attacks occurred during Britain's war with Napoleonic France...."

4) C

Purpose Question

The professor says that the British government "tried to suppress the Luddites as quickly as possible," so some of them were "shipped off to the then-prison-colony of Australia." In other words, Luddites were sent to Australia *to keep them from demonstrating in England*.

5) B

Inference Question

The professor says that today, Luddites stand for those who ensure "that machines would not replace humans," so we can infer that "Luddites" are *associated with a mistrust of technology*.

6) C

Inference Question

According to the professor, Luddites are appealing because "they seemed to be protecting the old, 'good' way of life" by ensuring that "machines would not replace humans." From this, we can infer that *some people fear changes in technology*.

ACTUAL PRACTICE 6 - PRACTICE SET 2

Notes

stu. doesn't understand "catharsis"
prof. says its releasing emotions by watching something
→ *stu. sad at Titanic, prof. says we feel strong emotions for chars. that aren't real*
→ *catharsis is feeling pity for char. to find relief from the emotion*
stu. relates to Greek tragedy

1) D

Main Idea Question

At the beginning of the conversation, the student gives his reason for visiting when he says, "I have a question about one of the terms you mentioned." From this, we can conclude that the student wants the professor *to clarify a confusing concept*.

2) B

Purpose Question

The professor uses the film *Titanic* to explain why the

student gets sad when watching certain movies, so she uses the sad film *to help illustrate the concept of* catharsis.

3) D

Inference Question

When someone uses the phrase "you lost me" in regards to a conversation, it means that the person is *confused about* what is being said.

4) C

Detail Question

According to the professor, people often seek *catharsis* "in order to find emotional relief" *by releasing strong feelings of pity and fear*.

5) A

Inference Question

In the conversation, the professor and the student discuss how watching the film *Titanic* or viewing an ancient Greek tragedy can lead to *catharsis*. Because *Titanic* and ancient Greek tragedies are separated by thousands of years, we can infer that *catharsis spans generations and cultures*.

ACTUAL PRACTICE 6 - PRACTICE SET 3

Notes

topics = fission, fusion, atoms
parts of an atom:
→ *nucleus: made of protons (+ charge),*
   neutrons (neutral charge)
→ *electrons (- charge), orbit nucleus*
fusion = atoms combine, form bigger atom, occurs when two atoms collide
→ *releases energy*
→ *occurs in stars*
→ *sci. experiment w/ fusion (could provide energy), use hydrogen in fusion exp.*
talk about fission next

1) D

Main Idea Question

Although the professor begins the lecture by describing the structure of an atom, he spends the majority of the lecture describing fusion, where *two atoms merge together to create a heavier element*.

2) B, C

Detail Question

The professor says that the nucleus "is made up of positively charged protons and neutrally charged neutrons."

3) A

Purpose Question

Because the professor begins the statement by saying, "oddly enough," we can infer that he is pointing out an unusual or *peculiar feature of atomic fusion*.

4) B

Detail Question

According to the professor, "Every active star in the known universe owes its existence to fusion," so fusion must commonly occur *within active stars*.

5) C

Detail Question

The professor says that controlling fusion "would give us a source of almost unlimited energy," so scientists hope to *harvest the energy created during fusion*.

6) D

Inference Question

At the end of the lecture, the professor asks if any students have questions before he "introduces fission." Thus, we can infer that the class will talk about *the process of fission* next.

ACTUAL PRACTICE 7 - PRACTICE SET 1

Notes

animal communication = signaling theory
→ *signal = trait/behavior animals use to communicate*
→ *signaler = animal that gives signal*
→ *receiver = animal to receives signal*
bird flocks have alert bird (signaler)
→ *alert bird signals when predator near; other birds know danger, predator knows he's seen; ex. of honest signal*
→ *dishonest signal = benefits signaler, tricks receiver; when signaler says there's danger when there isn't*
→ *must be a balance bet. honest & dishonest signals*

1) D

Main Idea Question

The professor discusses signaling theory, which is the study of different *forms of animal communication*.

2) B

Detail Question

The professor says, "Many flocks of birds will choose an 'alert bird' to keep a lookout for any predators lurking nearby."

3) C

Detail Question

According to the professor, dishonest signals work by "distracting the predator and keeping the flock safe."

4) B

Detail Question

The two types of signals that the professor discusses are *honest signals*, which "convey accurate information to the receiver," and *dishonest signals*, which work by "deceiving the receiver."

5) A

Inference Question

The professor says that, if an alert bird gives too many dishonest signals, "it may not be believed when there really is a predator." From this, we can infer that *honest signals are more common than dishonest signals* because otherwise the signaling system would be ineffective.

6) C

Inference Question

By understanding honest and dishonest signaling, we can infer that bird calls act as a sophisticated form of communication. So based on the lecture information, *animals communication is more complicated than it may seem.*

ACTUAL PRACTICE 7 - PRACTICE SET 2

Notes

stu. wants to know how many classes left in major
stu. studying Euro. history
→ *stu. in 2 his. classes now, has 3 left*
→ *stu. argues that he is in 3 his. classes now; advisor says one is arch. class, not his.*
→ *stu. arch. class = "Excavating Ancient Britain"*
stu. will petition to get history credit for arch. class (get form signed by prof., bring back to advisor)

1) D

Main Idea Question

The student states his reason for visiting when he says to the advisor, "I was hoping you could tell me how many classes I still need to take in order to finish my major."

2) B

Detail Question

After the student says, "I'm taking the class called 'Excavating Ancient Britain'," the advisor says, "That's an archaeology class."

3) B

Purpose Question

Here, the student is arguing that the archaeology class he is *taking should count toward his* history *major* because the class "spends most of the time learning about the *history* of ancient Britain" rather than learning about archaeology.

4) A

Inference Question

When the student exclaims, "No way!" we can infer that he feels *confused and somewhat upset* because he just found out that he is taking an archaeology class unnecessarily.

5) C

Inference Question

After the professor tells the student that he needs to get his archaeology professor's signature in order to petition the class, the student says, "I'll go try to find my professor right now."

ACTUAL PRACTICE 7 - PRACTICE SET 3

Notes

Richard Avedon = photographer (fashion, social issues, celeb. portraits)
→ *began as fashion photographer; black & white, movement, stories*
→ *social photos; 1963 mental hospital photo-shoot, subjects looked sad, brought awareness to mental health care*
→ *celeb. portraits; white background, relied on face for emotion (ex. Windsor royalty dog story)*

1) D

Main Idea Question

The professor mainly discusses the photography of Richard Avedon, who was famous for photography "relating to fashion, social issues, and celebrity portraits."

2) B, D

Detail Question

According to the professor, in Avedon's fashion photography, "his models were usually moving, and his images suggested stories."

3) D

Detail Question

When discussing Avedon's photo shoot in a mental hospital, the professor says, "many of the mental patients are looking directly at the camera with completely honest misery," so they *appear to be miserable*.

4) B

Purpose Question

In the story about the portrait of the Duke and Duchess, Avedon "didn't want an ordinary
portrait," so he lied to shock the royal couple. We can infer that the professor included this story to show Avedon's commitment to taking unique photos, and *to give an example of how far he
would go to get a good picture*.

5) C

Inference Question

According to the professor, Avedon's 60-year career included fashion photography, celebrity portraits, and photography that inspired social change, so we can infer that he *was interested in photographing a wide variety of subjects*.

6) A

Inference Question

The professor says that Avedon's photos from the mental health hospital "helped build support for a social movement at the time," we can infer that *some photography can inspire social change*.

ACTUAL PRACTICE 8 - PRACTICE SET 1

Notes

Green Revolution = agriculture developments in 1950s and 1960s

1944, Borlaug bred wheat with short stem, more efficient
→ *many countries grow Borlaug's wheat with fertilizer for more production*

Swaminathan did the same for rice, helped India and China

Green Rev. problems:
→ *increased production hurt small farms*
→ *diets became less diverse*
→ *SE Asia, pesticides mean no fish in rice patties*

1) B

Main Idea Question

Throughout the lecture, the professor discusses the *pros and cons* of the Green Revolution, a movement involving *important 20th-century agricultural innovations*.

2) C

Inference Question

Here, the professor claims, "new strains of wheat and rice were developed" when many nations were faced with famine. We can infer that these new strains of crops were developed to help reduce
famine, so *crises can lead to important innovations*.

3) A

Detail Question

According to the professor, "thanks to plant science, new strains of wheat and rice were developed" causing "agricultural production in several developing countries to boom."

4) D

Detail Question

One problem created by the Green Revolution, which used science to increase grain production, was that small farms were replaced by "large farms that used imported seeds, chemicals, and fuel."

5) A

Purpose Question

After the professor mentions that "the Green Revolution was *creating*" problems, she says that it "led to a decline in the number of small family farms," and it led to the development of large farms that only "grew one variety of grain," so *new plants and technology damaged family farms and crop diversity*.

6) C

Inference Question

Although the innovations of the Green Revolution were supposed to solve problems related to global famine, they ended up causing some new problems. From this, we can infer that *scientific innovation often has unforeseen*, and sometimes undesirable, *consequences*.

ACTUAL PRACTICE 8 - PRACTICE SET 2

Notes

stu. can decide on major (2nd year stu.)

→ stu. doesn't want to study math/chem.
advisor recommends aptitude test
→ will test stu. academic strength, tell stu. what she's best at
→ next test in two weeks (Wed. at 8 p.m.)
advisor get aptitude test paperwork for stu.

1) C

Main Idea Question

The student explains why she is visiting the advisor when she says, "I still have no idea what I want to major in." From this, we can infer that the student wants *help with deciding on an area of study*.

2) D

Purpose Question

The advisor says several things *to calm and reassure the student*, such as assuring her that deciding on a major "is a problem that many students have," and by offering to help the student out.

3) A

Detail Question

The advisor tells the student that the aptitude test will help "determine where your academic strengths lie."

4) B

Inference Question

Because the student sound nervous when she says, "I still have no idea what I want to major in," we can infer that *she is anxious to declare a major*.

5) D

Inference Question

At the end of the conversation, the advisor leaves to get the student the paperwork that will allow her to take the aptitude test. Thus, we can infer that the student will *sign up for the aptitude test* once she has the paperwork.

ACTUAL PRACTICE 8 - PRACTICE SET 3

Notes

prof. wants to disprove 10% of brain myth
myth implies that humans have lots of untapped potential
prof. says we use all brain most of the time.
→ *why else develop big brain?*
→ *brain scans only show MOST active parts of brain, not all active parts*
prof. asks stu. for other pieces of evidence

1) B

Main Idea Question

The professor explains the main idea of the lecture when she says, "I want to take some time today to dispel this pesky myth" on brain usage; thus, she wants *to dismiss a commonly held scientific belief*.

2) C

Detail Question

The professor says that she is discussing the brain myth "to encourage [the class] to investigate claims that seem scientific, but that may not hold up well to scrutiny."

3) D

Purpose Question

The professor asks, "Why is the sky blue?" to give an example of a *seemingly simple question that has a complex answer* that requires an understanding of many scientific phenomena.

4) B

Detail Question

The professor claims that the brain usage myth is so popular because "it encourages people to believe that they might have incredible mental potential waiting to be 'unlocked' (*undiscovered mental capabilities*)."

5) A

Inference Question

The professor spends the first part of the lecture *explaining* the brain usage myth, and then she spends the majority of the lecture *discrediting*, or disproving, that same myth.

6) A

Inference Question

Because the professor says, "these are only some of the arguments that dispel" the brain usage myth, we can infer that *there are other facts that refute the brain usage myth*.

ACTUAL PRACTICE 9 - PRACTICE SET 1

Notes

the body during starvation (person starving if lost 30% of mass)
normally, people converts food to glucose
→ *glucose runs low after a day, body gets energy from ketone instead (brain still needs glucose)*
→ *after 3 days, body breaks down muscle (autophagy), this continues until death (weeks to months)*

→ *death from infection/organ failure*
not well studies b/c results in death

1) C

Main Idea Question

At the beginning of the lecture, the professor states, "what I really want to focus on today is what happens to the body during starvation."

2) A

Detail Question

According to the professor, "a person is considered to be 'starving' if they've lost about 30 percent of their body mass."

3) C

Purpose Question

Because the professor begins by saying, "when they [people] consume a sufficient amount of food," we can infer that he is describing *how people process food under normal circumstances.*

4) B

Detail Question

After three days of not eating, the body begins *autophagy*, the process in which "the body starts to break down muscle."

5) A

Purpose Question

The professor explains that starvation leads to death by infection or organ failure to answer a student's question about *how extreme starvation affects the body.*

6) D

Inference Question

The professor divides the *biological process* of starvation into a series of *stages*, from normal food consumption to extreme starvation.

ACTUAL PRACTICE 9 - PRACTICE SET 2

Notes

stu. can't find primary sources for essay on natural disaster
→ *researching eruption of Krakatoa*
→ *prof. recommends book called Eruption of Krakatoa in library, includes illustrations*
prof. wants 2 primary sources & analysis

1) A

Main Idea Question

The student expresses his problem when he says, "so far I can only find good secondary sources," so he has *a lack of primary sources.*

2) C

Detail Question

The professor says, "I'm pretty sure the library has at least one copy of *The Eruption of Krakatoa and Subsequent Phenomena*."

3) B

Purpose Question

When the professor says, "I understand…" in response to the student's problem, we can infer that she does so *to show that she sympathizes with the student*'s problems finding primary sources.

4) B

Detail Question

After the student asks, "How many primary sources do you want us to use?" the professor responds, "I want you to have at least two…."

5) D

Inference Question

Because the professor is able to think of the name of a primary source of the eruption of Krakatoa, and where to find it, off the top of her head, we can infer that *she has researched the volcanic eruption of Krakatoa before.*

ACTUAL PRACTICE 9 - PRACTICE SET 3

Notes

hydrothermal vents = split in bottom of ocean where water comes out
→ *water close to magma; hot, mineral-filled*
→ *minerals in water cause chimneys to form*
→ *thousands of feet deep, no light*
many species found here
→ *species have bacteria in them that digests hydrogen sulfide (toxic)*
→ *shows how diverse/adaptable life is*

1) C

Main Idea Question

The professor discusses hydrothermal vents and the unique species that have evolved around them; in other words, the main topic of the lecture is *a unique deep-sea ecosystem.*

2) **D**

Detail Question

The professor says, "The water that emerges from these [hydrothermal] vents is… filled with minerals because of its closeness to mineral-rich subsurface magma."

3) **A**

Purpose Question

Here, the professor describes the vents as "chimney-like tubes" that "grow to be over 150 feet tall" in order to *describe the appearance of hydrothermal vents.*

4) **B**

Detail Question

According to the professor, the organisms near the vents survive "off the hydrogen sulfide that comes pouring out of the vents."

5) **B**

Inference Question

Because the bacteria near hydrothermal vents survive off of hydrogen sulfide, which is toxic to most organisms, we can infer that these bacteria *are mostly found in* hydrogen-sulfide rich *environments that are toxic to other organisms.*

6) **C**

Inference Question

Here, the professor describes the areas around hydrothermal vents as having "no light, extreme temperatures," and as being chemically toxic, making them *extreme environments* that *deep-sea creatures have evolved special adaptation to survive in.*

ACTUAL PRACTICE 10 - PRACTICE SET 1

Notes

Turrell = artist, works with light
→ *1966, lit up Santa Monica hotel*
→ *his art confuses viewers senses*
→ *'Breathing Light' = room filled w/ light*
→ *Rodan Crater = lit up rooms created in a volcano in AZ*

1) **A**

Main Idea Question

Because the purpose of the lecture is to talk about the work of artist James Turrell, who works with "light, absence of light, can colored light," we can infer that the lecture shows that *light itself can be an artistic medium.*

2) **D**

Purpose Question

Here, the professor is talking about how artists try "to reproduce the effects of light," in their artwork, so she is *introducing the relationship between light and the visual arts.*

3) **D**

Detail Question

The professor says, "Turrell began his career in 1966 by renting an empty hotel in Santa Monica," which he *painted and lit up.*

4) **B**

Inference Question

Here, the professor is describing the experience of viewing Turrell's work, which "confuses" our eyes and causes us to "become unsure of our actual perceptions." In other words, *viewing Turrell's work can be disorienting.*

5) **C**

Detail Question

According to the professor, "Turrell's real masterpiece is called the Rodan Crater," in which Turrell *excavated and lit up an ancient volcano.*

6) **A**

Inference Question

Because Turrell's artwork does not focus mainly on images, we can infer that his *primary goal is to* explore *our perception of light.*

ACTUAL PRACTICE 10 - PRACTICE SET 2

Notes

stu. can't register for GE writing class, has to take placement exam, stu. = freshman
→ *take test in 2 hours*
→ *decide writing class placement*
→ *test in main auditorium (stu. familiar w/ location)*
→ *stu. will be placed in appropriate writing class after test*

1) **B**

Main Idea Question

At the beginning of the conversation, the student says, "I'm here today to register for classes, but the electronic registration system won't let me," so we can conclude that the student wants *to find out how to register for a class.*

2) C

Purpose Question

The student asks this question, which summarizes what he will do, after he is asked if he needs any more help. Thus, the student says this *to confirm with the advisor that he knows what he should do.*

3) D

Detail Question

The advisor says, "The test will be administered in the main auditorium."

4) B

Detail Question

According to the advisor, the test "should only take about an hour to complete."

5) A

Inference Question

Because the student is having trouble registering for entry-level, general education classes, we can infer that *he has not registered for university classes before.*

ACTUAL PRACTICE 10 - PRACTICE SET 3

Notes

discuss $E = mc^2$

→ E = energy, m = mass, c = speed of light

mass converted to energy in every star

→ 4 hydrogen turns to 1 helium

→ fusion releases lots of gas

1) B

Main Idea Question

The professor discusses the equation $E = mc^2$, which describes *the relationship between matter and energy.*

2) A

Inference Question

Because the professor invites the students to guess what equation she will be talking about, we can infer that *she expects the class to be familiar with the equation.*

3) A

Purpose Question

Here, the professor implies that the equation $E = mc^2$ describes the relationship between mass and any form of energy, we can infer that she is *hinting at the equation's versatility.*

4) D

Detail Question

A student claims, "'c' is the variable used to represent the speed of light."

5) D

Purpose Question

The professor says, "let's turn our attention to a place where mass is constantly converted into energy." Thus, we can infer that the professor is *introducing a real-world application* of the equation.

6) C

Detail Question

According to the professor, the process of fusion in the sun "shows us that, under the right conditions, mass will convert into energy."

CHAPTER 4

LISTENING 1

Notes

Latin America = south of U.S., many revolutions/dictatorships

Zapatistas of Mexico (1990s)

→ army of 3,000, little violence, wanted to bring attention to gov. mistreatment of natives, successful

→ wanted media attention, native autonomy, indigenous beliefs = similar to communism

→ 'Woman's Revolutionary Law' = no discrimination/violence, women decide children, women can vote/seek education

1) D

Main Idea Question

The main topic of the lecture is the Zapatistas, who led *a successful revolution from Latin American history.*

2) D

Detail Question

The professor says, "Latin American history is full of long, brutal dictatorships and short, unsuccessful revolutions."

3) D

Purpose Question

The professor says that the Zapatistas' "takeovers involved none of the brutality you might expect" *to show that the Zapatistas did not want a violent war*.

4) C

Purpose Question

Although "the Zapatistas resembled the guerrilla armies that fought for communist ideas," the professor makes it clear that the Zapatistas were not communist in order *to show how the Zapatistas were different from other groups in Latin America*.

5) C

Detail Question

According to the professor, some of the rights guaranteed in the "Women's Revolutionary Law" are women's right "to decide for themselves how many children they would have and care for, and the right to… an education."

6) B

Inference Question

Because "Latin American history is full of long, brutal dictatorships," and because the Zapatistas had to lead an armed insurrection to bring attention to government issues, we can infer that *political control in Latin America has often been maintained through force*.

LISTENING 2

Notes

stu. incoming freshman, confused about college vs. univ. on application
advisor explains, college = housing (4 colleges)
→ each college has different academic focus
→ stu. considering psych.
→ Redwood = psych. / Oak = humanities / Cypress = art / Sequoia = science
stu. will go to Redwood College

1) C

Main Idea Question

Early in the conversation, the student asks the advisor, "Are there any differences between the colleges, then?" The advisor then spends the rest of the conversation discussing *the purpose of the different colleges at the university*.

2) C

Detail Question

Because the advisor explains that "each college has a different academic focus," and that "Redwood College… is where most psychology, sociology, and anthropology majors choose to live," most students choose colleges *based on the student's major*.

3) A

Purpose Question

The advisor says, "each college has a different academic focus," so we can infer that she asks what major the student is considering *to recommend a college for the student* based on the student's academic focus.

4) B

Detail Question

The advisor explains that *Redwood College* is where most psychology majors live, and she says to the student, "you might want to consider that college."

5) D

Inference Question

At the end of the conversation, the student says, "I guess I'll head over to Redwood College to check it out now then." Thus, we can infer that the student will *walk to Redwood College* after the conversation.

LISTENING 3

Notes

horseshoe crabs (species 450 mil. yrs. old)
their blood as LAL (neutralizes pathogens)
→ 250,000 crabs collected yearly, non-lethal blood harvest
→ FDA uses crabs' LAL to test drugs effectiveness
LAL in crabs developed as alternative to immune system (coastal water = lots of bacteria)

1) C

Main Idea Question

The professor discusses the importance of the LAL, a compound that makes *the blood of horseshoe crabs an important scientific resource*.

2) A

Detail Question

According to the professor, "all new drugs certified by the FDA must be tested using LAL to ensure that they work effectively."

3) D

Detail Question

Because the LAL in horseshoe crab blood effectively "detects the presence of harmful bacteria, viruses, and fungi," we can infer that the professor refers to the blood as "a lifesaver" *to emphasize that LAL is used to certify that all new drugs are safe and effective.*

4) B

Purpose Question

Because the crabs are able to "recover from their blood 'donations'," we can infer that the professor wants *to point out that the horseshoe crabs don't die from the procedure.*

5)

	This neutralizes pathogens	This fights and destroys pathogens	This forms a barrier around some poisons
Human Immune System		✓	
Horseshoe Crab Immune system	✓		✓

Inference Question

According to the professor, the compound LAL in horseshoe crab blood functions as an immune system by "neutralizing harmful invader" organisms by "completely surrounding" the toxins they release. Meanwhile, he says that the human immune system "actively fights harmful invaders in order to eliminate them."

LISTENING 4

Notes

Maxine Hong (The Woman Warrior) about growing up as Chinese immigrant in CA
→ *dream-like writing, stories, legends*
→ *many meanings of 'ghost': white ppl. = ghosts, immigrants = ghosts, Chinese ghosts of past*
→ *causes reader to question perceptions*
→ *writing about memory*

1) C

Main Idea Question

The main topic is a memoir by Maxine Kingston about "her experiences growing up as the child of Chinese immigrants." In other words, the topic is *a unique account of an immigrant's childhood in America.*

2) B, C

Detail Question

The professor says that Kingston "includes stories her mother told her… and Cantonese legends."

3) B, D

Detail Question

According to the professor, Kingston claims that "most of the Americans around them do not really notice them [Chinese immigrants], and maybe see them as the ghosts." She also tells "many stories about people she never met who lived in China, and these are like ghosts in the book, too."

4) B

Detail Question

The professor claims that Kingston "makes a connection between her ancestry and her own life in the U.S. by telling many stories about people she never met who lived in China."

5) D

Purpose Question

Because the professor argues that Kingston wants readers "to wonder whether your own perceptions at the time [in the past] were correct," we can infer that the professor believes that people reevaluate their past experiences, so *perceptions change as a person grows and develops.*

6) A

Inference Question

When she was young Kingston "felt that [her mother's] stories were discouraging," but later in life, she "wonders if the stories also inspired her." Thus, the stories' messages were ambiguous for her.

LISTENING 5

Notes

stu. wants help preparing for grad. School
→ *stu. major = psych, wants PhD in neurosci.*
→ *stu. should apply to psych.-related internship*
→ *stu. should take GRE (get help at tutoring center)*
→ *get prof. letters of recommendation*

1) D

Main Idea Question

The student explains the main topic of the conversation when he says, "I just want to go over what I should do to start preparing for graduate school applications and stuff."

2) A

Purpose Question

Because cognitive psychology classes include information on neuroscience, we can infer that the student says this *to explain how he has prepared for the neuroscience graduate programs* that he wants to pursue.

3) B

Inference Question

The phrase "to point someone in the right direction" means to give him or her advice or guidance. Thus, the advisor says this because *the student's professors should be able to suggest some available internships*.

4) D

Detail Question

The advisor says to the student, "if you want some help preparing for the GRE, the university offers free tutoring," so the student should visit the tutoring center *to receive help preparing for the GRE*.

5) C

Detail Question

Early in the conversation, the professor implies that the student is "taking the right classes" for graduate school right now, so we can conclude that she does not recommend *switching majors* to the student.

LISTENING 6

Notes

CMB discovery

CMB = leftover heat from the Big Bang, theorized in 20th c.

discovered in 1965 (Bell labs), found while testing radio receiver

→ receiver picked up microwaves throughout universe

→ microwaves = form of energy, heat = energy

1) C

Main Idea Question

The professor discusses the discovery of the cosmic microwave background, which is *leftover energy from the origin of the universe*.

2) D

Detail Question

According to the professor, the Big Bang, which is "the formation of the universe," occurred "about 14-billion years ago."

3) A

Detail Question

The professor says, "During the 20th century, some mathematicians and scientists came to the conclusion that some of this heat energy left over from the Big Bang should still be around."

4) D

Purpose Question

Here, the professor is implying that theorizing the existence of the CMB was simpler than proving its existence, so she is *emphasizing the difficulty of detecting the* CMB.

5) B

Inference Question

The professor implies that accidental scientific discoveries are very common, so we can infer that *many scientific discoveries are made unintentionally*.

6) B

Detail Question

The professor states that a *radio receiver* at Bell Laboratories picked up excessive "space noise" that turned out to be evidence of the CMB.

ANSWER KEY ♦ APPENDIX

APPENDIX

Simple Answers

CHAPTER 1

Main Idea Question:
Practice 1
  1) B
Practice 2
  2) C
Practice 3
  3) B
Practice 4
  4) D

Detail Questions:
Practice 1
  1) C
  2) A
Practice 2
  3) D
  4) A
Practice 3
  5) D
  6) C
Practice 4
  7) C
  8) A

Purpose Questions:
Practice 1
  1) D
  2) B
Practice 2
  3) B
  4) C
Practice 3
  5) D
  6) A
Practice 4
  7) C
  8) B

Inference Questions:
Practice 1
  1) C, D
  2) B
Practice 2
  3) B
  4) D

Practice 3
  5) A
  6) B

Practice 4
  7) B
  8) A

Exercise 1
  1) B
  2) A
  3) D
  4) C
  5) B

Exercise 2
  1) D
  2) C
  3) A
  4) B
  5) B

Exercise 3
  1) B
  2) A
  3) D
  4) B
  5) C

Exercise 4
  1) C
  2) B
  3) D
  4) A
  5) B

Exercise 5
  1) D
  2) B
  3) B
  4) A
  5) C

Exercise 6
  1) C
  2) A, D
  3) B
  4) D
  5) C

CHAPTER 2

Main Idea Question:
Practice 1
  1) B
Practice 2
  2) D
Practice 3
  3) C
Practice 4
  4) B

Detail Questions:
Practice 1
  1) A
  2) D
Practice 2
  3) D
  4) B
Practice 3
  5) A
  6) B
Practice 4
  7) B
  8) A, D

Purpose Questions:
Practice 1
  1) B
  2) C
Practice 2
  3) C
  4) A
Practice 3
  5) D
  6) C
Practice 4
  7) C
  8) B

Inference Questions:
Practice 1
  1) C
  2) D
Practice 2
  3) A
  4) D
Practice 3
  5) B
  6) A
Practice 4
  7)

	Theater-in-the-round	Proscenium Stage	Open stage
Spectators sit around three sides of a raised platform that extends into an auditorium	✓		
Spectators sit on all four sides of the stage			✓
Spectators can only see the front of the stage		✓	

Exercise 1
  1) B
  2) D
  3) A
  4) C
  5) D
  6) B

Exercise 2
  1) D
  2) A
  3) A, C
  4) D
  5)

	Corporation	Single Proprietorship	Partnership
Banking and insurance	✓		
Law and real estate			✓
Construction and food service		✓	

Exercise 3
1) C
2) A
3) C
4) A
5) D
6) B

Exercise 4
1) C
2) B
3) A, D
4) A
5) B
6) A

Exercise 5
1) D
2) B
3) C
4) B, D
5) A
6) A

Exercise 6
1) B
2) D
3) A
4) C
5) A
6) C

CHAPTER 3

• ACTUAL PRACTICE 1
Practice Set 1
1) B
2) A
3) D
4) C
5) A
6) D

Practice Set 2
1) B
2) D
3) A
4) D
5) C

Practice Set 3
1) B
2) B
3) B
4) A
5) C
6) C

• ACTUAL PRACTICE 2
Practice Set 1
1) A
2) B
3) C
4) D
5) B
6) D

Practice Set 2
1) C
2) D
3) A
4) B, D
5) A

Practice Set 3
1) C
2) D
3) D
4) B
5) D
6) C

• ACTUAL PRACTICE 3
Practice Set 1
1) D
2) C
3) A
4) C
5) C
6) C

Practice Set 2
1) B
2) D
3) B, C
4) B
5) A

Practice Set 3
1) A
2) C
3) D
4) A
5) A
6) B

• ACTUAL PRACTICE 4
Practice Set 1
1) C
2) C, D
3) D
4) A
5) B
6) A

Practice Set 2
1) D
2) B
3) A
4) B
5) C

Practice Set 3
1) D
2) A
3) C
4) B
5) A
6) C

• ACTUAL PRACTICE 5
Practice Set 1
1) B
2) C
3) A
4) A
5) D
6) C

Practice Set 2
1) C
2) D
3) A
4) B
5) D

Practice Set 3
1) C
2) A
3) D
4) B
5) B
6) C

• ACTUAL PRACTICE 6
Practice Set 1
1) A
2) D
3) D
4) C
5) B
6) C

Practice Set 2
1) D
2) B
3) D
4) C
5) A

Practice Set 3
1) D
2) B, C
3) A
4) B
5) C
6) D

• ACTUAL PRACTICE 7
Practice Set 1
1) D
2) B
3) C
4) B
5) A

6) C

Practice Set 2
1) D
2) B
3) B
4) A
5) C

Practice Set 3
1) D
2) B, D
3) D
4) B
5) C
6) A

• ACTUAL PRACTICE 8
Practice Set 1
1) B
2) C
3) A
4) D
5) A
6) C

Practice Set 2
1) C
2) D
3) A
4) B
5) D

Practice Set 3
1) B
2) C
3) D
4) B
5) A
6) A

• ACTUAL PRACTICE 9
Practice Set 1
1) C
2) A

3) C
4) B
5) A
6) D

Practice Set 2
1) A
2) C
3) B
4) B
5) D

Practice Set 3
1) C
2) D
3) A
4) B
5) B
6) C

• ACTUAL PRACTICE 10
Practice Set 1
1) A
2) D
3) D
4) B
5) C
6) A

Practice Set 2
1) B
2) C
3) D
4) B
5) A

Practice Set 3
1) B
2) A
3) A
4) D
5) D
6) C

CHAPTER 4

• ACTUAL TEST
Listening 1
1) D
2) D
3) D
4) C
5) C
6) B

Listening 2
1) C
2) C
3) A
4) B
5) D

Listening 3
1) C
2) A
3) D
4) B
5)

	This neutralizes pathogens	This fights and destroys pathogens	This requires a compound that colors blood blue
Human Immune System		✓	
Horseshoe Crab Immune system	✓		✓

Listening 4
1) C
2) B, C
3) B, D
4) B
5) A
6) D

Listening 5
1) D
2) A

3) B
4) D
5) C

Listening 6
1) C
2) D
3) A
4) D
5) B
6) B

www.ingramcontent.com/pod-product-compliance
Lightning Source LLC
Chambersburg PA
CBHW081847170426
43199CB00018B/2837